D1131702

The fruit of years of painstaking study, Pat Brereton's Hollywood Utopia is a landmark in the emerging field of ecological media criticism. The more urban human societies become, the more our media reflect upon the landscapes, the animals and the fragile unities of our planet. Of no media formation is this more true than of Hollywood, as Brereton argues in this meticulously researched and carefully organised work. Far from trashing the planet, Hollywood films have, Brereton claims, a tradition stretching back to the 1950s of care and concern for humanity estranged from its roots, and a world at risk of destruction. Through innovative analyses of *Jurassic Park, Easy Rider, Thelma and Louise, Star Trek, Terminator 2* and *Blade Runner* among countless older and newer films, Brereton traces a utopianism often overlooked in traditional film criticism. Not only films with explicitly Green agendas like *Emerald Forest* and *Medicine Man*, but in films noted for far different qualities exhibit the saving grace of nature. Films like *Dances With Wolves* or the towering spectacle of the tornado's heart in *Twister* provide grist for an original and far-reaching account of the place of nature in contemporary popular cinema. Dissent and disorder emerge in science fiction films of the 1950s and blockbusters of the early 21st century. The book traces complex negotiations with the meanings of nature and humananity's place in it through costume dramas and high-tech special effects bonanzas, always with an eye to the telling contradiction and the emergence of a generalised and liberal but nonetheless impressive and perhaps heartfelt need to restore the bonds that have been sundered between humans and their environment. To these analyses Brereton adds a powerful and persuasive thesis concerning the spatial concerns of contemporary Hollywood, a thesis that leads him through a broad overview of the literature of green cultural studies and postmodernism. Throughout, Brereton manages an easy, graceful prose to immense purpose. Its clarity, its reach, its honesty and its originality should ensure this book a place on the shelves of any media scholar and many Green activists, The ultimate optimism of its case is a challenge to other critics to write for makers and audiences who want more from cinema, both the cinema we have and the cinema we may yet make in the new century.

(Sean Cubitt, University of Waikato, New Zealand)

Hollywood Utopia
Ecology in Contemporary American Cinema

Pat Brereton

First Published in the UK in 2005 by

Intellect Books, PO Box 862, Bristol BS99 1DE, UK

First Published in the USA in 2005 by

Intellect Books, ISBS, 920 NE 58th Ave. Suite 300, Portland, Oregon 97213-3786, USA

Copyright ©2005 Intellect Ltd

All rights reserved. No part of this publication may be reproduced, stored in a retrieval system, or transmitted, in any form or by any means, electronic, mechanical, photocopying, recording, or otherwise, without written permission.

A catalogue record for this book is available from the British Library

ISBN 1-84150117-4
Cover Design: Gabriel Solomons
Copy Editor: Wendi Momen

Printed and bound in Great Britain by 4edge, UK

Contents

ACKNOWLEDGEMENTS

I would like to thank media staff at my previous university in Luton as well as in DCU for their assistance and encouragement. Other readers who helped in various ways include Nick Heffernan, Peter Brooker, Christine Geraghty and Steve Neale. Finally I wish to thank Angela and my family for their support over the many years it took to complete this project.

SELECT FILMOGRAPHY

Andromeda Strain (1970) Robert Wise
Alien Resurrection (1997) Jean-Pierre Jeunet

Blade Runner (1982) Ridley Scott

Blade Runner: The Director's Cut (1991) Ridley Scott

Contact (1997) Robert Zemeckis

Dances with Wolves (1990) Kevin Costner

Dances with Wolves - Special Edition (1991) Kevin Costner

Dark City (1998) Alex Proyas

Easy Rider (1969) Denis Hopper

Emerald Forest (1985) John Boorman

Endangered Species (1982) Alan Rudolph

Fifth Element, The (1997) Luc Besson

Grand Canyon (1991) Lawrence Kasdan

Incredible Shrinking Man (The) (1957) Jack Arnold

Invasion of the Body Snatchers (1956) Don Siegel

Jaws (1975) Steven Spielberg

Jurassic Park (1993) Steven Spielberg

Last of the Mohicans (1992) Michael Mann

Logan's Run (1976) Michael Anderson

Lost World, The: Jurassic Park (1997) Steven Spielberg

Medicine Man, The (1992) John McTiernan

Men in Black (1997) Barry Sonnenfeld

Safe (1995) Todd Haynes

Searchers, The (1956) John Ford

Soylent Green (1973) Richard Fleischer

Star Trek: First Contact (1996) Jonathan Frakes

Straight Story, The (1999) David Lynch

Terminator (1984) James Cameron

Terminator 2: Judgement Day (1991) James Cameron

Thelma and Louise (1991) Ridley Scott

Them(1954) Gordon Douglas

Titanic (1997) James Cameron

Twister (1996) Jan De Bont

Waterworld (1995) Kevin Reynolds

Yearling, The (1946) Clarence Brown

1 HOLLYWOOD UTOPIA: ECOLOGY AND CONTEMPORARY AMERICAN CINEMA

Prologue

Ecology has become a new, all-inclusive, yet often contradictory meta-narrative[1], which this book will show to have been clearly present within Hollywood film since the 1950s. This study focuses particularly on feel-good films whose therapeutic character often leads to their being dismissed as ideologically regressive. By concentrating on narrative closure and especially the way space is used to foreground and dramatise the sublime pleasure of nature, Hollywood cinema can be seen to have within it a 'certain tendency'[2] that dramatises core ecological values and ideas.

The study is committed to a strategy of building bridges and creating cross-connections between film and other disciplines. In particular, the investigation draws on Geography (space/place, tourism and so on), Philosophy (aesthetics, ethics and ontological debates), Anthropology, Feminism and Cultural Studies, while maintaining close contact with the traditional literary and historical disciplines.

In the light of this cross-disciplinary approach, the first section of this introductory chapter sets the scene for an ecological investigation, drawing on a wide range of ideas and historical contexts, while the second section has a narrower focus, clarifying a methodology for film analysis to be used throughout the study. Within many blockbuster films, the evocation of nature and sublime spectacle[3] helps to dramatise contemporary ecological issues and debates. Filmic time and space is dramatised, often above and beyond strict narrative requirements, and serves, whether accidentally or not, to reconnect audiences with their inclusive eco-system.

As Bryan Norton puts it, environmentalism needs to educate the public 'to see problems from a synoptic, contextual perspective' (Norton 1991: xi). In this respect, Hollywood films can be seen as exemplifying, and often actually promoting, this loosely educational and ethical agenda, particularly through the use of ecological/mythic expression, evidenced in a range of narrative closures.

Introduction

The primary justification for this study is the dearth of analysis of the utopian ecological themes which pervade mainstream Hollywood cinema. There continues to be a preoccupation with narratology in Film studies, which often avoids the formal exploration of space. Coupled with this is the predominately negative ideological critique of Hollywood film, with many cultural histories predicating their analysis on Fredric Jameson's view that 'mass culture' harmonises social conflicts, contemporary fears and utopian hopes and (more contentiously) attempts to effect ideological containment and reassurance. Relatively little academic effort is given over to understanding and appreciating rather than dismissing the utopian spatial aesthetic that permeates Hollywood film. This phenomenon will be examined most particularly through a close reading of closure in a range of Hollywood films from the 1950s to the present day, which can privilege a 'progressive' conception of nature and ecology generally.

In his dictionary of 'green' terms, John Button defines ecology and the growth of eco-politics as

> a set of beliefs and a concomitant lifestyle that stress the importance of respect for the earth and all its inhabitants, using only what resources are necessary and appropriate, acknowledging the rights of all forms of life and recognising that all that exists is part of one interconnected whole

(Button 1988: 190).

The very idea of being 'green' only came into popular consciousness in the late 1970s, though since the 1950s 'green' has been used as a qualifier for environmental projects like the 'green front', a tree planting campaign popularised in America. The minimum criteria includes a reverence for the earth and all its creatures but also, some radical greens would argue, a concomitant strategy encompassing a willingness to share the world's wealth among all its peoples. Prosperity can be achieved through 'sustainable alternatives' together with an emphasis on self-reliance and decentralised communities, as opposed to the rat-race of economic growth (see Porritt 1984).

While the 'ideological' analytical strategy, focusing on power inequalities across class, gender and race boundaries, continues to preoccupy critical analysis of Hollywood cinema, there is little if any critical engagement with the more all-encompassing phenomenon of ecology. Yet, if so-called ecological readings are to remain critical and avoid degenerating into endorsing 'naive' polemics, they must explicitly foreground a variety of interpretations and perspectives, which question any universal utopian project.

To anchor this approach, notions of visual excess specifically drawn from feminist studies of melodrama illustrating a breakdown in 'conventional' patriarchal readings of film will be applied. By interrogating the over-determination of visual excess in films by Douglas Sirk from the 1950s, for instance, with their accentuated use of deep colours, together with heightened styles of acting, critics like Christine Gledhill (Gledhill 1991) explored how such films helped to sustain a mise-en-scène which stays with the audience long after the 'tagged-on' conformist closures. This critical position articulates how excessive and overdetermined stylistic devices serve to rupture and critique normative ideological readings, while also helping to produce a more 'progressive' representation of feminist values. This radical notion of visual excess will be reapplied, through an analysis of the narrative resolutions of a range of Hollywood blockbuster films, to expose their latent predisposition to excessively dramatise an ecological agenda.

Apparently unmediated and excessive representations of nature and landscape are consciously foregrounded in many Hollywood films discussed in this book. In particular, the film-time and space given over to this explicit form of unmediated evocations of eco-nature help to dramatise and encourage raw nature to speak directly to audiences, together with their protagonists, who finally find sanctuary from particular environmental problems. This expression of therapeutic sanctuary is often valorised over and above the strict narrative requirements of the text through, for instance, framing, narrative point-of-view and shot length. Rather than merely serving as a romantic backdrop or a narrative deus-ex-machina, these evocations of eco-nature become self-consciously foregrounded and consequently help to promote an ecological meta-narrative, connecting humans with their environment.

Together with the visual aesthetic, the protagonists in the films discussed will also be shown to embody various forms of ecological agency. This can be highlighted through the evolution within mainstream Hollywood cinema of what can be typified as a white, liberal-humanist, middle-class, ecological agenda across a range of genres whose filmic agency in turn serves to reflect mainstream attitudes, values and beliefs embedded in the ecology movement generally. This positive trajectory is at odds, however, with the influential criticism of Christopher Lasch, who notices a similar 'hunger for a therapeutic sensibility' but dismisses the impulse owing to its complicity with the normlessness of 'narcissistic American culture' (Lasch 1978: 7).

Titanic

A recent blockbuster success story like *Titanic* (1998) is helpful in signalling many of the often abstract preoccupations raised in this study. While *Titanic* appears, at the outset at least, to have very little to do with ecology per se, it can nevertheless be read using these lenses. Especially when interpreted in terms of myth, together with its engagement with textual excess and spectacle, the film provides a provocative forum for articulating an ecological agenda.

The most common question critics address in relation to *Titanic* is why such an 'old-fashioned' film has become so commercially successful. Gilbert Adair explains its fascination in terms of myth:

> In the north Atlantic on 14th April 1912 at 11.40 pm, an immovable object met an irresistible force, a state of the art Goliath was felled by a State-of-the-Nature David, and our love affair with the Titanic was born

> *(Adair 1997: 223).*

But why specifically do audiences want to experience (and re-experience) the visceral sensation of a ship going down in all its awesome horror and observe its passengers drown or freeze to death, especially while the heroine recounts her personal epic and fulfils her destiny with her dead lover by sending the most expensive diamond back to the bottom of the sea. A straightforward ideological reading would critique the film's apparent romantic renunciation of materialism in favour of 'love',[4] which consequently problematises its feel-good, utopian expression.

However, adapting Adair's idea, one could also argue that mythical harmony, which can be translated into the language of deep ecology, has also been restored by the narrative. Audiences and protagonists experience how the past cannot always be successfully salvaged for financial profit, in spite of advanced technology. Conspicuous consumption is effectively critiqued when the most authentically evidenced valuables are destroyed and slowly disappear as the ship succumbs to the pull of the sea. Many of the films to be discussed similarly explore how primal elemental forces of nature finally provide a renewed form of balance within the narrative and become potent metaphors for a renewed expression of eco-praxis.

Extended moments of almost Gothic visual excess, often expressed through long static takes of a sublime nature that help resolve the narrative, also serve as an effective cautionary tale for audiences ruled by materialist values. Thomas Berry, for example, reads *Titanic* as a 'parable' of humanity's 'over-confidence' when, even in dire situations, 'we often do not have the energy required to alter our way of acting on the scale that is required' (Berry 1988: 210).

Speed, movement and action remain synonymous with the myth of America itself. This is very much evidenced by the popular male lead, Leonardo DiCaprio, standing on the prow of the fantasy ship with his hands outstretched like a benevolent deity as the camera triumphantly tracks down its length. Audiences at the end of the century appeared to crave such spectacle, as the allegory of this terrible disaster of a sinking ship testifies.[5] Nature, in the form of solid frozen water and its equally potent liquid form, will inevitably claim its human victims. Metaphorically, the humans become sacrificial victims for the sins of capitalism, which tries to ignore the innate potency of nature.

While this film cannot easily be described as a conventional ecological text, nonetheless it does create a form of excess, which can be used to promote an ecological reading. This is embodied in the ship itself, which becomes the representational embodiment of nineteenth-century western industrial capitalism and is affirmed by many audiences' response to it as a primary focus of identification and attraction. As one reviewer concludes, at the end of the millennium, 'what grandeur and pathos the film possesses belongs to the mythic story of the shipwreck itself' (Arroyo 1998: 16).

Thus the (pre)modernist scientific certainties together with the hierarchical social controls, which include a fatal dismissal of the potency of nature, symbolically represented by the intractable icebergs, are finally called to account. From a textual point of view, this 'shallow' representational narrative device remains successful, if only on a mythic romantic level. As in the hero's intertextual link with his previous film role in *Romeo and Juliet*, love conquers all, even death. James Cameron, the director, who will be discussed in detail later regarding the development of cyborgs in *Terminator* (1984) and other films, has succeeded in creating what appear at first sight to be mythic agents who can embody audiences' fantasies, needs and fears for a new millennium, by indulging and legitimising a renewed form of nostalgia for nature. This overblown text, which comfortably fits into the natural disaster sub-genre, is not necessarily designed to be strong on praxis through the resolution of problems, yet can be read as provocative, as its narrative implications prompt a renewed symbiosis between 'eco-sapiens' and their environment.

At the outset, the most overt critique embedded in the text centres on class. But most critics agree that it presents a simplistic evocation of class politics, with its working classes more easily enjoying themselves yet trapped in the bowels of the ship, in contrast to their stuffy counterparts 'upstairs'. Audiences are clearly positioned to identify with the *jouissance* of the lower orders, yet invited at the same time to wallow in the luxuriant pleasures and material benefits of the wealthy. Nevertheless, because ecological concepts are not as clear-cut as ideological power divisions like class, *Titanic* can at least question outmoded notions of rationality and affirm a more eco-centred consciousness.

By representing and establishing holistic if enigmatic ecological tropes, *Titanic* begins to extend a nascent thematic and aesthetic lexicon which often unconsciously expresses, even legitimises, core ecological precepts, especially ecologism which promotes the principle of sustainability. *Titanic* suggests humans have to be educated to consume less and to produce more self-sufficiently to satisfy their basic needs.

Nature and the Roots of Ecology

'Ecologism', argues Andrew Dobson, makes

> the Earth as physical object the very foundation-stone of its intellectual edifice, arguing that its finitude is the basic reason why infinite population and economic growth are impossible and why consequently, profound changes to our social and political behaviour need to take place

(cited in Talshir 1998: 13).

Dobson reconstructs ecologism as a comprehensive ideology in which the philosophical basis (limits to growth), the ethical perspective (ecocentrism), the social vision (a sustainable society) and the political strategy (radical transformation, not reformism) provide a coherent and cohesive ideology (ibid.: 15). Ecologism most certainly validates the non-sustainability of resources together with its central premise of human interconnectivity with the rest of the biotic community and even with the cosmos. The abiding strength of these 'holistic' approaches is that they regard the interrelationship of environmental variables as a primary concern which is 'explicitly anti-reductionist' (Sklair 1994: 126). This holistic utopian, even spiritual, perspective will be illustrated in detail in subsequent chapters, most notably through a comparative study of *The Incredible Shrinking Man* (1957) and *Contact* (1997).

But to begin this process of analysis, a working definition of ecological utopianism needs to be outlined by tracing its historical, cultural and theoretical antecedents. Particular emphasis will be placed on the divisions between 'deep' and 'light' (shallow) ecology which is also reflected in the tensions inherent in ideological critiques and the debates about utopianism to be explored later. Finally, before an evolving prototype for the textual analysis of film can be considered, a survey of philosophical/ political positions will also be used to illustrate critical positions emerging from ecology. In many ways, ecology has become the most dominant and inclusive discourse of the late twentieth century.

Most cultural critics generally begin with the premise that 'our representation of nature' usually reveals as much, if not more, about our inner fears and desires than about the environment.[6] Nevertheless the two attributes can be regarded as coterminous, since our inner fears and desires often reflect or at least constitute in large part the 'external' environment.

Utopian (and dystopian) fantasies remain pervasive across popular film culture, most explicitly within the science fiction genre, with the concept of nature often acquiring more universal and less contentiously nationalistic connotations (as displayed most notoriously within German Nazism). However, David Pepper's wish to combine 'red' and 'green' ideologies to create a new 'third way' is more often obscured and seldom reconciled within Hollywood cinema, as signalled in *Titanic*. But these fantasies, which often encompass a deep ecological framework, more easily pervade the explicit nature genres explored in Chapter 2, as well as westerns, road movies and science fiction films, discussed in subsequent chapters. This study cannot limit itself to unpacking an ideological framework, however, since the ecological predisposition evidenced through textual analysis often seeks to transcend the particularities of ideological spatio-temporal power conflicts and affirm a more universal ecological framework. The resultant trend of using the often contradictory therapeutic romantic power of nature to help audiences overcome the distresses of modern living is explored most specifically in the following chapter. These therapeutic narratives have possibly become more prolific as western society has acquired a greater appreciation of core ecological debates together with awareness of the issues involved. This in turn has stimulated the need and the search for new forms of human agency to engage with and promote ecological utopianism.

Philosophical Myths of Nature

Nature, like Utopianism, can nonetheless mean almost anything one wishes, a particular danger when the term is co-opted for direct political use.[7] Norton, while accepting these consequences, nevertheless states that the:

> rules governing our treatment of nature are guided neither by the authority of God nor by a priori, precultural moral norms such as rights of natural objects. Environmentalism has been forced to recognise that we must struggle to articulate limits on acceptable behaviour by learning more and more about how we affect, and are affected by our environmental context

(Norton 1991: 253).

His edict, cited above, that environmentalists must educate the public 'to see problems from a synoptic, contextual perspective' (ibid.: 250-3) must be applied to Hollywood films in this investigation also. These ecological manifestations will be historically mapped through various readings, beginning with 1950s science fiction films and concluding with recent commercially successful science fiction texts which explicitly focus on a range of global ecological fears.

As a new millennium approached, many critics pointed out that globally inclusive myths became even more necessary, whereas others suggested that 'the psychic and social structures in which we live, have become profoundly anti-ecological, unhealthy and destructive'. Consequently, there appears to be a need for 'new forms, (re)emphasising our essential interconnectedness rather than our separateness, evoking the feeling of belonging to each other' (Gablik 1991: 5).

'Man lives in a progressive, expressive, non-repetitive time; [whereas] ecology is the science of cyclical repetition' (Gunter in Glotfelty 1996: 54). Hollywood mythic texts serve to connect these contrasting time frameworks. The British philosopher Kate Soper (Soper 1995) reiterates how even Marx recognised the civilising impulse implicit in mythic expression and its 'escape' from encrusted modes of rationalisation. The central problem for modern-day human agency remains how to avoid putting too much stress on the environment from an apparently unreconcilable desire for fulfilled individual lives.

Soper concludes her polemic:

> Rather than becoming more awe-struck by nature, we need perhaps to become more stricken by the ways in which our dependency upon its resources involves us irre-deemably in certain forms of detachment from it. To get 'closer' to nature, in a sense [is] to experience more anxiety about all those ways in which we cannot finally identify with it, not it with us. But in that very process, of course, we could also be transforming our sense of human identity
>
> *(Soper 1995: 278).*

One of the ways of trying to understand this ethical relationship with nature has been through ecological frameworks and most notably through the application of the Gaia thesis.

Gaia and Eco-ethics

The Gaia thesis, like Aldo Leopold's seminal 'land ethic', affirms that the biosphere[8] together with its atmospheric environment forms a single entity or natural system. Gaia is regarded not only as an entity but a process which, like evolution, can be regarded as a goal directed one. Nature, therefore, is seen as neither 'omniscient nor omnipotent' (Goldsmith in Jencks 1992: 399-408) since life processes can go wrong, a scenario depicted in *Jurassic Park*, which will be discussed in detail in the following chapter.

If the world is recognised as one self-regulating system, then progress through competition logically becomes fundamentally anti-evolutionary and co-operation becomes 'the true evolutionary strategy' (Goldsmith in Jencks 1992: 399). Gaia, the Greek deity who brought forth the earth from chaos (or the void), symbolises, for both feminists and the environmental movement in particular, a potentially powerful force for progressive evolution. Gaia inspires a sense of the earth as a holistic living organism, which for many twentieth-century environmentalists evokes a new earth ethic.[9] Both feminist spirituality and scientific theory recast Gaia as a compelling signifier for a new understanding of, and reverence for, life on earth, while also becoming a forceful metaphor for the new postmodern age.

Yet problems remain with this conception, since it carries a cultural baggage that could undercut its inspirational power, in particular the understanding of Gaia primarily as a 'maternal mother' or even a 'super servant' who will keep the planet 'clean' for humans. If Gaia is in fact a 'self-regulating homeostatic system, then "she" can correct problems caused by humans or even find humans expendable' (Merchant 1995: xx-xxi) - which does not equate with the benevolent image of a nurturing mother or even a servant.

The ecological imperative seeks to reiterate a dominant global and holistic ethic for all sentient beings on the planet. Leopold was possibly the first person to articulate this green ethic by declaring: 'a thing is right when it tends to preserve the integrity, stability and beauty of the biotic community. It is wrong when it tends otherwise' (Leopold 1947: 224-5).

This apparently simple if evocative mantra of primary 'natural' ethics, becomes very appealing within a world which has become for many 'fractured and incoherent' (Bunce 1994: 49).[10] As Frederick Ferre reiterates, 'we need to learn in new modes of ethical holism, what organic interconnectedness means for human persons'(in Attfield and Belsey 1994: 237). Utopian Hollywood films which tend to endorse these assumptions serve this project extremely well.[11]

Paul Taylor effectively consolidates environmental ethics as including:

- An ultimate moral attitude of 'respect for nature';

- A belief system, which he calls 'the biocentric outlook';

- A set of rules of duty that express 'the attitude of respect' (Taylor in Gruen 1994: 43).

Taylor goes on to suggest that this produces several basic rules of conduct:

1) 'Rule of Non-maleficence' - prohibits harmful and destructive acts done by moral agents.

2) 'Rule of Non-interference' - to refrain from placing restrictions on the freedom of individual organisms and requiring a general 'hands-off' policy with regard to whole eco-systems and biotic communities, as well as individual organisms.

3) 'Rule of Fidelity' - applies only to human conduct in relation to individual animals that are in a wild state and are capable of being deceived or betrayed by moral agents.

4) 'Rule of Restitutive Justice' - the duty to restore the balance of justice between a moral agent and a moral subject when the subject has been wronged by the agent.

The first of these rules is implicit in most Hollywood narratives while the second is most clearly detected within the science fiction genre. In particular the rule of non-interference directly supports Roddenberry's 'Prime Directive' in the *Star Trek* franchise, to be discussed in Chapter 4. Issues like the rule of fidelity will be specifically addressed through an analysis of more overtly thematic 'light' eco-texts like John Boorman's *Emerald Forest* (1985), while the rule of restitutive justice is most explicitly discussed in relation to the Disney/Spielberg oeuvre. These ecological and ethical guidelines remain central to this study and naturally become more explicit in films when some ethical norm is called into question. These rules are applied most extensively in later discussions of science fiction where extra-terrestrial ecological systems serve to highlight the uniqueness of the earth's symbiotic life forces over and above human dominance.

In many cases, as the Gaia myth affirms, the earth can look after itself in spite of humanity's impotence and ignorance. This can, in turn, serve to question the necessity of an ethical system, since it suggests that human agency is finally unimportant within the greater macro-system. Within such a green evolutionary utopianism there are many further anomalies which must be exposed and hopefully re-evaluated. For instance, must ecologists solve the primary conflict inherent in most utopian structures, namely the rights of individuals as opposed to the 'ideal' communal system? Or put another way, must ecology privilege the (organic, self-regulating) 'system' at the expense of, or in opposition to, individual human agency? The risk of legitimising a potentially totalitarian system, which reduces individual expression to systematic homogeneity, remains ever present.

Another thorny anomaly linked to the above is the problem of how, if there is no pre-defined hierarchical order, with 'man' at the apex, one can determine 'human' value(s) outside of the multitude of conflicting biological 'needs' of various flora and fauna within the earth's eco system. Inherent contradictions such as those indicated here remain ever present in the texts considered and can become magnified by attempts to foreground an all-encompassing meta-narrative for human behaviour, or even representing and privileging an ecological utopian ideal. More often, however, a dystopian environment is foregrounded, particularly in many of the science fiction narratives to be discussed in this book.

The central tenet of ecology as affirmed by many of the major ecological critics embodies 'harmony with nature' together with the recognition of 'finite resources'. Everything else in this view is therefore either peripheral to, or at best ancillary to, these all-inclusive affirmations. But there is often little agreement through the large rainbow of 'green supporters' on the specific means, especially the priorities and timescales, for achieving these ends. Simply looking for hope, through an artificial development of holistic systems, can be a recipe for disaster. Consequently there is an inherent danger of endorsing the trend of using the therapeutic romantic representation of nature to help audiences overcome the distresses of modern living, which has become prevalent in Hollywood and designed to appeal to audiences across class, race and ideology. In spite of such dangers and while it is critically easier to dismiss aspects that conform to this broad therapeutic premise, it remains crucial to clarify and tie down how films promote broadly utopian values. Meanings continually shift and slide within Hollywood cinema.

As a relatively modern phenomenon, however, ecology remains a totalising concept, which is inclusive rather than exclusive.[12] This naturally causes severe problems in trying to create and maintain strict guidelines and terms of reference. As Tim Unwin postulates, 'it would be difficult to find a set of issues which symbolise more vividly the torment of a way of life gone astray, which captures more exactly the transformative urge propelling political and economic works' than those raised by modern ecology (cited in Norton 1991: 188). Furthermore, as Andre Gorz warns in *Ecology as Politics*, environmentalism is continually being 'commandeered' by the dominant groups in western society for their own ends. The forces of capitalism are very capable of adapting an 'environmental conscience' to meet the needs of the dominant culture (Gorz 1987: 114B30). Such contradictions and ambiguities must be faced up to.

Utopianism versus Ideology

Utopianism can be broadly defined as the desire for a better way of living expressed in the description of a different kind of society that makes possible an alternative way of life. Utopianism has a long and distinguished pedigree and has informed thinkers from the Frankfurt School to Ernst Bloch and Fredric Jameson.[13] The

Frankfurt School critique of ideological domination which preoccupied much academic debate over the last few decades provided a primary focus for beginning to appreciate how ecology could be understood within this cultural context.[14]

Having laid aside the working class as the agents of changing history, the Frankfurt School had difficulty in finding an alternative locus of action. Herbert Marcuse, especially, put his faith in youthful rebellion powered by 'Eros', a theme that will be explored in the example of road movies like *Easy Rider* (1969). Youth culture could aspire to throwing off the shackles of ideological repression and begin to conceptualise new, more harmonious modes of living. Marcuse was possibly the most optimistic of the Frankfurt School thinkers with regard to the potency of this utopian impulse. He considered art as the socially sanctioned realm of fantasy and the bearer of utopia. In *The Aesthetic Dimension*, he asserted, 'Art cannot change the world, but it can contribute to changing the consciences and drives of men and women who change the world' (Marcuse 1979: 32). His optimism lay in the belief that the sheer power of truth revealed would transform consciousness and ultimately create a 'democratic public out of an inert mass' (cited in Seidman 1994: 187).

Unlike Marcuse, Theodor W. Adorno was consistently more pessimistic, regarding art as only offering glimpses of a utopia, which in any case was unobtainable (Bird *et al.* 1993: 262).[15] Many earlier utopian visions were, in fact, not designed to promote change at all and it is 'only with the advent of progress and the belief in some degree of human control over social organisation that the location of Utopia in the future (coupled) with human action became a possibility' (Levitas in Bird *et al.* 1993: 259).

Ernst Bloch's great work *The Principle of Hope* (translated into English in 1986) asserts that radical cultural criticism should seek out those utopian moments, those projections of a better world, which he claimed are found in a wide range of texts. Bloch provides a systematic examination of the ways that daydreams, popular culture, great literature, politics and social utopias, philosophy and religion -often dismissed out of hand by some Marxist critics -contain emancipatory moments which project visions of a better life that question the organisation and structure of life under capitalism (or state socialism).

For Bloch, ideology was 'Janus-faced', since it simultaneously contained errors, mystifications and techniques of manipulation and domination, while also containing a utopian residue or surplus that can be used for social critique and to advance political emancipation. Bloch believed that all ideological artefacts contain expressions of desire which socialist theory and politics should heed in order to provide programmes, which appeal to the deep-seated desires for a 'better life' within everyone. I would suggest that many Hollywood texts contain a surplus or excess of meaning that is not explained by so-called ideological criticism, which privileges notions of 'mystification or legitimation', and critical claims of 'systematicity even comprehensiveness' (Hurley 1999). Ideological readings nevertheless contain normative ideals against which the existing society can be criticised and from which models of an alternative society can be developed. Applying this general premise, but most importantly extrapolating upon 'excessive significations' in the Hollywood aesthetic, an ecological discourse can also be forged.

Bloch distinguishes two types of utopia: abstract and concrete, which in many ways repeat assumed differences between high and low culture, even deep and light ecology. At one extreme, images are purely escapist, compensatory wishful thinking, whereas at the other, they are 'transformative', with images driving forward action to a (real) transformed future. Emmanuel Levinas's overarching critique of all utopian art is that it is incapable of engaging with change in this post)modern world, because of the complexity of social structures and the lack of human agency. Nor is it capable of gravitating to Bloch's 'higher order' utopian dreams. Writers and visionaries (including film-makers) have 'retreated to the more limited role of estrangement, critique and escapism' (Levinas in Bird *et al.* 1993: 262). I would contend, however, that these so-called negative attributes of utopian art can also promote a potentially progressive, even pro-active, agency. Hollywood is never good at forthright polemics and in any case they can lead to extreme or even polarised positions; but popular commercial film can sow the seeds of utopian ideals and values which can simultaneously serve the ecological cause.

Jameson appears to reiterate the sentiments of Bloch and Levitas, and affirms:

> The works of mass culture cannot be ideological without at one and the same time being implicitly or explicitly utopian as well: they cannot manipulate unless they offer some genuine shred of content as a fantasy bribe to the public about to be manipulated

(Jameson 1979: 144).

Jameson often reiterates how 'left-wing' politics cannot always appreciate the immense utopian appeal of 'energies' like religion, nationalism or, for that matter, popular culture, and proposes that radical cultural criticism should analyse both the social hopes and fantasies of film and the ideological ways in which these fantasies are 'regressively' presented, conflicts are resolved and potentially disruptive hopes and anxieties are managed. However, critics like Paul Coates suggest that Jameson appears to reinforce the dismissal of audiences and popular cultural pleasures when he asserts that 'the shallow fantasies of mass culture can justly claim to provide their audiences with approximate conceptualizations of hopes of escape' (Coates 1994: 6).

Jameson, while at first appearing to believe in utopian ideals, moved towards a more pessimistic position which reaffirmed the commodification of late capitalism. In particular he suggested that this had moved into the last two available domains, 'the unconscious (pornography, psychotherapy, fantasy) and nature (wilderness, parks, zoos and anthropology)' (cited in Ellman 1992: 6). This apparent 'total' commodification of nature will be strongly contested in this study.

Less pessimistic critics assert, however, that the American brand of utopia evokes a more pragmatic present quest which rests on an 'ingrained belief in the value of equality' and the 'perfectibility of man' (Rooney 1985: 174). In this context the suggestion of Richard Dyer remains enticing:

> Faced with the cynicism of liberal culture and the widespread refusal of contemporary left culture to imagine the future, we would do well to look at the utopian impulse, however and whenever it occurs in popular culture

(Dyer et al. 1981: 16).

Dyer provocatively but also convincingly argues that the appeal of all forms of popular entertainment and culture generally lies in the way they offer 'utopian solutions to real needs' and 'social longings created by capitalist society, providing images of abundance, energy, and community to counter actual problems of scarcity, exhaustion and fragmentation' (Dyer in Harrison *et al.* 1984: 96).

Utopian Space

David Harvey asserts that all classic utopias propose a fixed spatial order that ensures social stability by destroying the possibility of history and containing all processes within a fixed spatial frame. Jameson also speaks of the evolution of (eco-)spatial utopias from the 1960s 'in which the transformation of social relations and political institutions is projected onto the vision of place and landscape, including the human body' (Jameson 1991: 160). This notion of continuous change as preferable to a finished utopia, which would inevitably only be utopic for some, has influenced much progressive utopian thinking and can be seen most clearly in the exploration of counter-cultural agency as evidenced within road movies.

Harvey goes so far as to argue that a utopianism 'of pure process' as he describes it, 'can liberate the human spirit into a dematerialized world', a virtual reality. He continues by enigmatically affirming that 'becoming without being is empty idealism while being without becoming is death' (Harvey 1996: 438). Such philosophical polarities seek to adapt counter-cultural, and even Eastern mystical notions as applied to a new postmodernist perspective, by forging connections between 'becoming' and 'being'. Harvey passionately concludes his inspiring 1996 treatise by asserting:

> If the current rhetoric about handing on a decent living environment to future generations is to have even one iota of meaning, we owe it to subsequent generations to invest now in a collective and very public search for some way to understand the possibilities of achieving a just and ecologically sensitive urbanization process under contemporary conditions. That discussion cannot trust in dead day dreams resurrected from the past. It has to construct its own language...

(Harvey 1996: 438).[16]

Even if such readings are constructed at the margins and are severely contested especially by ideological criticism, the blockbuster texts addressed in this book create a metaphorical forum, which can herald a provocative utopian debate. These debates became focused most particularly in the counter-cultural movement of the 1960s, which initiated the beginnings of a radical eco-politics.

1960s Counter-culture

The beginnings of an explicit appreciation of a nascent western ecological consciousness occurred within the 'individualist' framework of the counter-cultural 1960s. Environmentalism as a pressure group can be traced back, intellectually at least, to Rachel Carson's seminal *Silent Spring* (1962), which first suggested DDT could be a human as well as an environmental pollutant[17] Chapter 4 will demonstrate in particular the cultural resonance of these connections, which were sown by 1950s science fiction primarily through the articulation of radiation fears. Farrell emphasises the roots of such agency when he asserts: 'American radicalism had, to a great extent, been personified by activists with personalist perspectives.' They believed in a 'politics of personal responsibility, a politics of example' (Farrell 1997: 252, 254). In many ways this ethical form of individual agency continues up to the present day through positive representations of ecological activists as 'warriors' and selfless humanitarians in films such as *Grand Canyon.*

A systemic shift in social attitudes appeared in the 1960s, however, and although the hippie quest permitted a critique of small-town (Southern) provincialism, it was essentially aimed at an ideal of freedom that in American terms is highly 'traditional'. For some critics it almost went so far as to recall the Jeffersonian yeoman ideal of small rural capitalism, comparing bikes (and automobiles) to horses. Road movies, like westerns, traverse space as well as time, presenting continuous ideological shifts and contrasts between cultures, and are consequently closely connected with debates concerning nature and ecology. This form of hippie romanticism both articulates and feeds off the myth of the western: a man and his mount, acting as frontier-men, wanting to go where no other man has gone before, believing that life must be kept simple; if there is some problem, just move on.

It is nevertheless paradoxical that the road movie, which coincidentally exploited counter-cultural attitudes, also signalled the beginning of the contemporary western ecology movement. By beginning to push towards legislation to protect the environment and promote the rediscovery of 'natural' agriculture and foods, the counter-culture became a culture of alternative values based in nature - which were sometimes articulated through drugs like LSD (Kearney 1988: 322). Nevertheless the universal appreciation of ecological growth and awareness and its corollary, the planet's destruction, became fully articulated within the conventional constraints of this 'philosophical' genre.

 However, in contrast to what can be typified as the counter-culture's noticeably 'adolescent' male agency that initiated an ecological sensibility, later examples in the 1970s and 1980s, when contextualised through an eco-feminist analysis, can be read as more sophisticated, even mature. Many cultural historians affirm that ecological thinking in the 1970s emphatically transcended 'protection of nature'. It was more concerned with a 'conceptual change in understanding of the environment' and the interrelations embedded in humanity, urged on by a threat to the health and life of people resulting from technological developments and industrial global effects, which dramatically (re)present the 'ill-conduct of humanity' (Talshir 1998: 16).

The feminist sociologist Angela McRobbie effectively traces these utopian possibilities within the amorphous plurality of postmodernist discourse and wholeheartedly endorses their 'attraction' and 'usefulness' because they offer a 'wider and more dynamic understanding of contemporary representation' (McRobbie 1994: 13). Utopian ideals, she continues, serve 'to deflect attention away from the singular scrutinising gaze of the semiologist'. Instead she proposes that this approach be 'replaced by a multiplicity of fragmented, and frequently interrupted, "looks"' (McRobbie 1994: 13). The breakdown of these 'looks' will be extensively analysed across a range of genres in the following chapters.

Light versus Dark Ecology

Light versus dark ecology can loosely be compared using Jonathan Porritt's simplified structuralist binary opposition model to expose the 'regressive' aspects of industrialism as opposed to the 'progressive' attributes of ecology. This distinction can be recognised throughout this study and used to illustrate primary nature/ culture conflicts from an ecological perspective.

The Politics of Industrialism	The Politics of Ecology
a deterministic view of the future	flexibility & personal
aggressive individualism	co-operative/communitarian
materialism	move towards the spiritual
divisive/reductive	holistic synthesis
anthropocentrism	biocentrism
rationality	intuition and understanding
outer-directed motivation	inner directed motivation
patriarchal values	post-patriarchal, feminist
institutionalised violence	non-violence
economic growth and GNP	sustainable and quality
production for exchange	production for use
high income differentials	low income differentials
free market economy	local production
ever expanding trade	self reliance
demand stimulation	voluntary simplicity
employment as a means to an end	work as an end in itself
capital intensive production	labour intensive production

technological fix	discriminating technology
centralised economies of scale	decentralised human scale
hierarchical structure	non-hierarchical
dependence on experts	participative involvement
representative democracy	direct democracy
emphasis on law and order	libertarianism
sovereignty of nation state	internationalism and global
domination over nature	harmony with nature
environmentalism	ecology
environment managed as resource	resource - finite
nuclear power	renewable sources of energy
high energy/ high consumption	low energy/ low consumption

(Porritt 1984: 216-17)

In Porritt's and other ecological writings, where 'light' tends to provide a more 'environmental/managerial' approach to the environment with the status quo almost implicitly accepted, deep ecology is considered to be more progressive if somewhat abstract and idealistic. While a compliant resolution to problems is shunned by many purist deep ecologists, its expression nevertheless reflects a growing awareness of ecological issues in Hollywood.

Ecological critics like Button tend to dismiss 'environmentalism' as equivalent to 'light' ecology and the propagation of ideas and practices of conservation, which propose little intrinsic change to the status quo. This is in contrast to the taxonomy of 'ecological thinking' cited by Porritt, which demands deep change in the fabric and structure of society.[18] The founding father of 'deep ecology', Arne Naess, considers it as having fundamental ethical implications which include:

- Biospherical egalitarianism: the equal right of all creatures to live and blossom.

- Principle of Diversity and symbiosis: the richness of forms as ends in themselves both within human cultures and in the natural world.

(cited in Allison 1991: 25)

Deep ecology evidently goes beyond the transformation of technology and politics to a transformation of humanity. Its holistic view breaks down any boundaries between man and nature (Eccleshall 1994: 237) and has come to be understood by some cultural critics as more radical than the Copernican revolution. What can be described as 'evolutionary ecology' displaces humankind from a position of centrality in the universe and on the planet. This notion, evoking a new holistic eco-consciousness, will be applied throughout the range of textual analysis in this book, focusing in particular on the transformation of human protagonists as they begin to appreciate and learn from their symbiotic environment.[19]

Contradictory positions between light and dark ecology can initially be reconciled by focusing on the seminal writings of the environmental guru Aldo Leopold. He attempted to 'mediate the perennial American conflict between holistic and material attitudes towards nature' (Barillas 1996: 61) and spoke of how the 'land ethic' rests upon a single unifying premise: 'that the individual is a member of a community of interdependent parts'. His vision served to enlarge the boundaries of community to include soils, water, plants, animals and so forth (Leopold 1947: 204). Especially since his 'rediscovery' in the 1960s, Leopold's 'land ethic' thesis has become a central tenet of environmental thinking and the symbiotic relationship he proposes between man and nature has remained the dominant orthodoxy of much ecological thinking.[20]

While at first sight Leopold's definition may appear essentialist and ahistorical, critics like Scott Lash and John Urry apply a notion of 'glacial time' to offset such criticism. They contend that 'the relationship between humans and nature is very long term and evolutionary' (Lash and Urry 1994: 242). Manuel Castells also endorses ecological thinking and recognises the 'interaction between all forms of matter' within an 'evolutionary perspective' (Castells 1997: 125). It is this 'unity of the species' and its 'spatio-temporal evolution' that is privileged most explicitly by deep ecologists and eco-feminist thinkers. 'Ecologists induce the creation of a new identity, a biological identity, a culture of the human species as a component of nature' (Castells 1997: 126). At one level, ecology as a discipline appeared impossible until the development of such a systematic concept of evolution; while at another level, non-Enlightenment sources, especially native American cultures, also helped forge a western ecological consciousness. Consequently, eco-sapiens' understanding and appreciation of (their) ecology has evolved and become more systematic over time.

Philosophical theories of the value of nature most specifically address these light and dark gradations of ecology and help provide an effective starting point to position a reading of Hollywood films. These can be grouped into the following broad categories.

a) Anthropocentrism. This position recognises nature primarily as a resource, which contributes to human value. This pervasive notion will be explored in detail, especially through the exposition of animism in the Spielberg oeuvre as providing a fruitful site of light eco-utopianism.

Many ecological critics of anthropocentrism have argued that the dominant tendency in western culture (for instance Christianity) has been to construe difference in terms of hierarchy and that a less colonising approach to nature does not involve denying human reason or human difference but rather ceasing to treat reason as the basis of superiority and domination. An ecological ethic must, according to Val Plumwood, always be an 'ethic of eco-justice that recognises the interconnection of social domination and the domination of nature' (Plumwood 1993: 20).

However, the social ecologist Murray Bookchin asserts that the denial of hierarchy over nature results in a form of essentialism which accepts the denial of human distinctness and the rejection of 'colonising forms of reason', even the rejection of all rationality. He believes that current ecological crises are a direct result of the failure of human society to recognise and value the continuity, rather than the divisions, between nature and culture (cited in Gruen *et al.* 1994: 112). Bookchin affirms that human beings have a vital role to play as 'ecological stewards' in the evolutionary process, consciously engaged in the negotiated relationship between society and nature which is echoed in the other major philosophical theory of inherentism.

b) Inherentism. This position recognises that the very concept of value is innately human. This philosophical notion appears to be at odds with deep ecology and so any attribution of such ecology to nature is dependent upon human consciousness and the constructions which that makes. Apparent contradictions within ecological values in general demand careful negotiation, especially warning against human complicity in eco-narratives which are often seen 'not as liberating but as a call to caution' (Campbell in Glotfelty 1996: 131). Consequently, a historical study of the evolution of these ecological precepts exposes the changing wishes, fears and desires of the human organism as part of a planetary eco-system.

In this study human agency as depicted in Hollywood film will serve to illustrate how some of the ecological values promoted evolve more specifically from a holistic notion of nature itself rather than affirming a conventional belief in inherentism.

At one extreme this can be compared with the Gaia thesis where the environment is unconditionally believed to have inherent value, having little to do with anything human. Knowledge of its deep ecological value, therefore, is independent of all human experience and acknowledged to be intuitively 'true' (Simmons 1993: 184).

Eco-philosophical debates helped redefine what it meant to be 'human' at the end of the last century. As Campbell asserts: 'At the core of our sense of self is our feeling of loss and the desire for unity that is born of loss' (in Glotfelty 1996: 134). Such universal, mythic expressions of loss and the desire for ecological unity can be found in popular cultural texts like *Titanic*. The desire for a utopian form of ecological symbiosis and harmony with nature is explored from different perspectives in subsequent chapters. Special emphasis will be placed throughout the study on the more recuperative forms of ecological hope, embodied in 'Othered' figures such as native Americans, female protagonists and a number of post-human life forms. These filmic agents question the ecological status quo and often affirm the need for more radical assertions of post-human consciousness, especially through their relationship with their environment. Finally, however, I wish to focus upon western eco-feminism, which has had the most pervasive historical and academic influence on ecological debates and has helped shape the perspectives taken in this study.

Eco-feminism

The term 'eco-feminism' was first used in 1974 by the French writer Francoise d'Eaubonne, who called upon women to lead an ecological revolution to save the planet (Merchant 1995: 5). The evolving parameters of eco-feminist discourse embrace various positions in relation to nature, rejecting both the view of humans as apart from and outside nature and of nature as a limitless provider of man's needs.[21] Consequently, feminist discourse incorporated an inherent critique of masculinity and its 'values' (for example, Chodorow 1979), as well as a critique of rationality and the 'overvaluation of reason'. It was also promoted as a critique of 'human domination of nature, human chauvinism, speciesism, or anthropocentrism' (for example Naess 1973; Plumwood 1975) together with a critique of the treatment of nature in purely instrumental terms (Plumwood 1993: 24).

Sue Thornham clarifies a primary dilemma of essentialism when she affirms how feminist theorists suffer from having to 'speak as a woman' (Thornham 1997: 2), a problem which remains central to debates about how to find a voice and an appropriate language for oppositional discourse.

Not surprisingly, ecology as the study of the balance and interrelationship of all life on earth maps onto the essentialising impulse of the 'feminine principle' and the striving towards human 'balance and interrelationship' which is the stated claim of many feminists. Consequently it follows that if these principles are accepted, feminism and ecology are inextricably connected. From earliest times nature, and especially the earth, was represented as a kind and nurturing mother or alternatively, according to Capra, 'as a wild and uncontrollable female' (Capra 1983: 25). Much later, under the dominance of western patriarchy, the apparently benign if always ambiguous image of nature changed into one of 'passivity' (*ibid.*).[22]

Later eco-feminists especially sought to analyse environmental problems within their critique of patriarchy and to offer alternatives that could liberate both women and nature. This was particularly popularised in the late 1960s and 1970s with writers such as Mary Daly with *Gyn/Ecology* (1978) and Adrienne Rich with Of *Women Born* (1977) who promoted a response to the perception that women and nature have been mutually associated and similarly devalued in western culture.

Environmental equality continues to be regarded by feminists like Carolyn Merchant as a primary ecofeminist issue. 'The body, home, and community are sites of women's local experience and local contestation.' For example, 'women experience chemical pollution through their bodies' (as sites of reproduction) (Merchant 1995: 161). Rachel Carson's *Silent Spring* (1962) effectively expressed this paradigm for America in particular, exposing the 'death producing effects' of chemicals and helping to make the question of life on earth a public, ethical and political issue (Naess in Gruen *et al.* 1994: 116).

Merchant promotes a form of 'partnership ethics' which can be seen as a more robust form of liberal eco-feminism, avoiding the gendering of nature as a nurturing mother or a goddess, while also avoiding the ecocentric hierarchic assumptions that humans are part of an ecological web of life and thereby 'morally equal' to a bacterium or a mosquito. She endorses this form of ethics as grounded in relations between humans and nature and based on:

1) Equity between humans and non-human communities.

2) Moral considerations for humans and non-human nature.

3) Respect for cultural diversity and biodiversity.

4) Inclusion of women, minorities and non-human nature in the code of ethical accountability

(Merchant 1995: 217).

Merchant's ideas contrast with Leopold's 'extensionist ethic', in which the community is extended to encompass non-human nature, whereas:

> partnership ethics recognises both continuities and differences between humans and nonhuman nature. It admits that humans are dependent on non-human nature and that non-human nature has preceded and will post-date human nature . . . and recognises humans now have power/ knowledge/ technology to destroy life as we know it today

(ibid.: 217).

In spite of carefully outlining the various, often confused, nuances of feminist discourse, Merchant finally hopes that there is more to unite the various contradictory strands of eco-feminist thought than there is to divide them.

> Marxist feminists assume that non-human nature is the material basis of all of life and that food, clothing, shelter, and energy are essential to the maintenance of human life . . . Nature is an active subject, not a passive object to be dominated, and humans must develop sustainable relations with it

(Merchant 1995: 6).

Ecological critics have to overcome this divisive ideological and gender polarisation of positions and to establish non-instrumental relationships with nature, where both connection and otherness become the basis of interaction.[23] Merchant remains optimistic regarding the links between feminist and ecological politics and claims that:

> Both movements (eco and women's movement) have been liberatory and democratic in their outlook and reformist or revolutionary in their politics. Yet both pose a threat to reinforce traditional forms of oppression

(Merchant 1995: 139).

New feminist discourse is setting the tone for a more 'transgressive' form of utopianism, which effectively counters many of the concerns of an ideological critique. In particular, Lucy Sargisson, a critical optimist, reclaims the radical importance of utopian thought and affirms that it:

creates a space, previously non-existent and still 'unreal', in which radically different speculation can take place and in which totally new ways of being can be envisaged. In this space transformative thinking can take place, and paradigmatic shifts in approach can be undertaken

(Sargisson 1994: 63).

Sargisson rejects 'conventional' feminists who tended to endorse Derrida's notion that 'utopianism is a masculinized construct in the libidinal economic sense and that the (universalist, blueprinting and perfectionist) utopianism created by some approaches is disempowered to all but those who construct it' (Sargisson 1994: 87). Feminist utopianism, on the other hand, sets the tone for a post-Enlightenment utopianism and 'replaces the old standard with something more flexible, more interesting and more appropriate' (*ibid.*: 64). She convincingly argues that it serves to create a form of 'transgressive/(transformative) thinking' (*ibid.*: 76). This new form of utopian optimism can also be detected in Hollywood films, as evidenced through a range of readings to follow. In the creation of a new conceptual space, this form of eco-utopianism helps to provide a potentially more effective blueprint for theorising possible eco-readings of Hollywood texts.

To reiterate, this analysis is premised on the importance of not dismissing the utopian, even therapeutic, articulation of ecological issues within popular culture which Jameson suggests is difficult for the 'Left' to appreciate. The Gaia model, for instance, together with conventional structuralist film theory, can be used to explore light as opposed to deep ecological textual readings; but at the outset both tendencies remain productive and feed into the debates about ideology and utopianism discussed above. Finally, this study seeks to endorse Norton's proposition that environmentalists must learn to educate the public to see problems from a 'synoptic and contextual perspective' and help develop and promote a range of 'ecocentric ethics' (Stavrakakis 1997). Eco-feminist discourse in particular provides a tangible trajectory and scaffold for this ecological reading of Hollywood film.

The following section will explore how conventional ideological textual analysis together with philosophical and ethical methodologies already highlighted can be applied to an ecological reading of films.

Section Two

Ecological Textual Analysis: A Rationale?

David Harvey in *Justice, Nature and the Geography of Difference* concludes:

> It is dangerous in academia these days to confess to being meta about anything, for
> to do so is to suggest a longing for something mystically outside of us (or within us)
> to which we can appeal to stabilize the flood of chaotic images, ephemeral represen-
> tations, contorted positionings, and multiple fragmentations of knowledge within
> which we now have our collective being

(Harvey 1996: 2).

While academic theory has enormous difficulty articulating, much less legitimising, various foundational beliefs, Hollywood has no qualms whatsoever in promoting them. However, because the utopian ecological impulse in particular can appear more prevalent within Hollywood, there is a danger of critical slippage, resulting in total ambiguity and confusion. Consequently, and for the sake of clarity, it is essential to (re)construct a clear and robust rationale and framework for analysis that begins by legitimating audience pleasures.

Unlike the theorists of the Frankfurt School, who can simplistically be read as contending that commercial culture robs the arts of their critical ability to negate the status-quo and creates passive viewers who uncritically accept the ideas and values sold in the cultural market place, audience theorists assert the primacy of readers in the reading process and their pro-active ability to engage with such texts.

> Particular genres tend to be popular at certain points in time because they somehow
> embody and work through those social contradictions which the culture needs to
> come to grips with, and may not be able to deal with, except in the realm of fantasy
> - the same way as myth functions - to work through social contradictions in the form
> of a narrative so that very real problems can be transposed to the realms of fantasy
> and apparently solved there

(Angus and Jhally 1989: 187).

But in spite of the recent growth in reception theory there remains an almost innate and pernicious criticism of Hollywood cinema and, by extension, of its audiences. Richard Schickel exaggerates many of these more recent criticisms when he dismisses the audience as follows:

Essentially a youthful crowd, this audience does not have very sophisticated tastes or expectations when it comes to narrative. Given this lack, they may never ask for strong, persuasive story-telling when they grow up. What they get . . . is not narrative as it has been traditionally defined, but a succession of undifferentiated sensations . . . there is in fact no authentic emotional build-up, consequently no catharsis at the movie's conclusion

(Schickel in Collins 1995: 141).

But, as Collins rightly asserts, Schickel is nostalgically evoking traditional notions of narrative that depend on 'coherence, plausibility, authentic emotional build-up, natural outgrowths and catharsis'. This list of requirements grows out of conventions first developed in classical tragedy, codified most obviously in Aristotle's *Poetics* and then expanded in realist theatre and literature through the nineteenth century. According to this model, 'virtually all modernist and postmodernist narratives would be deficient' (Collins 1995: 142).

John Fiske, a 'high priest' of audience reception theory, lays down the gauntlet for the 'progressive' potentiality of popular, commercial texts by affirming that all films and other mediated texts must, 'in order to be popular, contain within them unresolved contradictions that the viewer can expect in order to find within them structural similarities to his or her own social relations and identities' (cited in Angus *et al.* 1989: 186). While other critics such as Robert Stam correctly highlight some very pertinent institutional questions which can undermine this textual position,[24] Fiske's assertions remain a starting point for this valorisation of the progressive potential of Hollywood utopianism.

Norman Denzin also affirms what can be described as an 'existential aesthetic perspective', which decodes the popular as containing 'multiple, contradictory, and complex positions' (Denzin 1992: 139). While these contradictions remain unresolved within popular texts, they can serve to expose and dramatise the core concerns of the age. Ecological meta-narratives flourish within this cultural and aesthetic milieu.

But, first of all, issues of relative value and progressive potential must be fully addressed if not systematised within a textual analytical framework. It is commonly asserted that there have been two basic approaches to interpretation: 'thematic explication' and 'symptomatic reading'. Both avoid audience consideration yet intend to go beyond simple comprehension. Explication explores meaning, which is covert or symbolic and is often artist-centred, intending to reveal an individual director's underlying vision, whereas symptomatic interpretation looks for repressed (ideological) meaning in the text, such as gaps between its explicit moral framework compared with aspects of its style or semantic structure.

The explicatory critic searches for underlying meaning, a search which is premised, as David Bordwell points out, on Sartre's maxim that 'every technique reveals a metaphysics' (Bordwell 1989: 47). The practice of symptomatic interpretation emerged in the early 1970s as a reaction against *auteur* and *mise-en-scène* criticism, which by that time had reified into a routine activity of searching for unity in a director's films. One of the strengths of symptomatic interpretation, at least as initially conceptualised, lies in its oppositional reading of mainstream narrative films. But according to critics like Bordwell and Carroll, such methodologies have become overly 'abstract' instead of encouraging 'concrete' and 'empirical' interpretation.

The dominant assumption famously promoted by Bordwell is that one's theory, of whatever sort, determines one's criticism.[25] Criticism consciously derives its mode of interpretation from a 'comprehensive and coherent theory' (Bordwell 1989: 104). While cultural critics continue to expose the ever present 'sleight of hand' of ideology, feminist writer Jackie Byars asserts that one of the main functions of textual analysis is 'the articulation of interpretative stances in the critical struggle over differing explanations of how we construct what we know to be "real"' (Byars 1991: 261). Reading 'against the grain' has been more successful in recuperating marginal/outsider positions and utopian possibilities than more conventional analysis, which effectively aims at exposing and debunking dominant ideological positions buried below the surface of popular texts.

While marginality and otherness will continue to be used as effective objects and instruments of analysis, the primary target of the ensuing textual analyses is to explicate a range of more universal (post)human ecological values embedded within a 'bottom-up' validation of film audiences' prototypical utopian beliefs, which overlay and sometimes transcend the divisive inequalities within and between humans. This aim echoes Harvey's provocative affirmation of the need for academic discourse to more positively engage with a range of meta-beliefs which continue to make 'interpretation and political action meaningful, creative and possible' (Harvey 1996: 2).

Referring to ethnographic research, Clifford Geertz speaks of the need to produce 'thick descriptions' that capture the 'multiplicity of conceptual structures', many of which are 'superimposed upon or knotted into one another' and which are 'at once strange, irregular and unexplicit'. Ethnographic research nominates the 'making and taking of meaning as its special focus, and lays claim to particular expertise and authority in this area' (Geertz 1973: 10). It is frequently asserted that 'thick description' plays 'a central role in cultural analysis' (Murdock cited in McGuigan *et al.* 1997: 179). How to unpack the richness and polysemic nature of a film remains the primary methodological difficulty for which thick descriptions can provide an initial starting point. While this study does not set out to produce primary audience research, it can apply interpretative techniques such as those mentioned above to enrich an otherwise abstract theoretical methodology.

To determine a reading strategy and overall method, which takes on board the complications cited above, various issues will be looked at using detailed examples. In particular, the stylistic application of poetic or thick descriptions will be used to examine how spatial metaphors and excessive visualisation is adapted in film. Special emphasis will be given to excessive scenography evidenced through the sublime evocations of landscape, which often helps to promote an ecological discourse. Furthermore, feminist theory will be incorporated to anchor these textual readings. This conjunction begins to address the dilemma of theory/interpretation and provides a fruitful starting point for this book's focus on narrative closure and other key visual moments.

Nature and Agency

While citing the evolving historical and political representation of romantic landscape in western culture, this study will concentrate on how Hollywood draws on the therapeutic power of raw nature and landscape and how this becomes more ecologically charged and potent when coupled with human agency. This is most evident within the representation of the 'other' in Hollywood film, encoded particularly in the 'savage' native American who came to embody the role of universal visionary and protector of the primary eco-system.

The myth of the pure native American is summed up by the final shot of *The Last of the Mohicans* (1992),[26] as the last survivor, Chingachgook, looks over the majestic unspoilt landscape. He alone now holds 'the conscience of his people', symbolised by his statuesque pose and affirmed by the attention-seeking celebratory music which revalidates his mythic harmony with nature. He pronounces: 'The frontier moves with the sun and pushes the Red man of the wilderness forests with it, until one day there will be nowhere left . . . no more frontier'. The romantic and nostalgic recreation of the mythic age of ecological innocence remains a potent one for an audience unable to attain a tangible sense of ownership or responsibility for the planet of which they are the inheritors. However, as *The Last of the Mohicans* suggests, at least ecological sanctuary can be (re)discovered and expressed inside the fantasy world of Hollywood.

The western in particular provides a primary site for ecological themes, since its generic structures directly involve spatial exploration. The uses and abuses of landscape provide the feeding ground for much narrative construction and visual exposition. While there is often little explicit reference to the geo-politics of ecology, the genre nevertheless addresses the right of the human species to own and control the landscape, together with what this means for social organisation.

This thematic preoccupation, explored in Chapter 2, dramatises the universal tensions of humankind's relations with nature and ecology.

This phenomenon is clearly recognised in the closure of *Grand Canyon* (1991), to be explored in detail in Chapter 3. Danny Glover, the black auto-repair man and saviour-figure of the film, makes several references to the power of the canyon. He describes his feelings when he first visited the site: 'The rocks are so old, it makes my problems seem so insignificant. I felt like a gnat on the ass of a cow.' At last, in the final closing set-piece of the film when the main protagonists re-visit the site, its sublime power becomes realised. 'It's wide, like the gulf between different sections of society, but it can also bring us together in awe of its size and beauty.' While such a closure may be unconvincing for many critics, its romantic utopian impulse - what Kant called the sublime -is what Hollywood has always been good at exploiting. This transcendental power should not be underestimated, in spite of the danger of also appearing naive as a utopian fantasy projection of the film's protagonists.

The liberal constituency addressed in *Grand Canyon* and in many recent Hollywood films needs and craves absolution within a post-colonialist, post-industrial environment, when all that finally matters is the eco-self. Glover, embodying the eco-seeing 'other', is capable of transforming the white, liberal, middle-class protagonist's perspective to concur with his vision. Particularly within American cultural debates, there remains a major ideological dispute between determinists who believe that 'human behaviour is primarily determined by outside forces' and would-be 'voluntarists' like Glover who believe that 'humans possess free will and can act as they wish' (Haralambos *et al.* 1990: 817). This independence of mind allows him to see the 'bigger ecological picture' over and above the ecocidal disharmony of his city space.

The film's closure can be compared with the famous selfless egalitarian speech at the end of *Casablanca* (1942), when Bogart subordinates his private needs to the common good, a high point of wartime voluntarist sensibility, which finally legitimises American interventionism in World War Two (see Ray 1985). But in *Grand Canyon*, closure presents our heroes gathering around the apex of the canyon, appreciating for the first time their own insignificance while promoting a new form of eco-praxis by showing them beginning to accept their communion with the cosmos. This contrasts, for instance, with the artificial fog in the final scene of *Casablanca* (1942), which never obscures Bogart, who does not lose his individuality in spite of his heroic transcendence for a common cause. In *Grand Canyon* the silent, majestic landscape of the canyon remains central both aesthetically and narratively to the meaning and potency of its closure. In contrast, the closing *mise-en-scène* of *Casablanca* does not envelop, much less obscure, the human agents who always keep centre stage both thematically and aesthetically.

While the critical danger of using manipulative imagery to resolve social and political contradictions is ever-present, contemporary Hollywood especially appears more than willing to de-centre its protagonists and present a meta-discourse on 'nature' to the audience outside of the strict narrative requirements of the text.

Grand Canyon's closure, focusing on the grandeur and natural beauty of the landscape, provides a potent signifier for audiences to engage their own fantasies of a utopian ecological environment, above and beyond the narrative specificity of the text. Instead of discovering the restrictions of classical closure, an eco-utopian reading would suggest that audiences are presented with an excess of signification, reminiscent of so-called 'primitive' cinema, which allows for an almost metaphysical engagement with holistic spatial identity. This, of course, must be placed in opposition to a more cynical 'top-down' ideological reading, which might suggest that 'nature' is constructed as a therapeutic palliative and is falsely exploited to resolve the psychic and social conflicts of urban modernity.

The outline of an ecological reading suggests, however, that as the protagonists construct a tableau standing at the canyon's edge, staring into the abyss of spatial continuity, they overcome their anomie, their feelings of impotence, and acquire a newfound communality with each other, having been enriched by their co-presence with and in landscape. I will illustrate this reading in greater detail in Chapter 3 to explore how these protagonists have, at least potentially, acquired the ability to give up their preconceived notions of place and identity to actively endorse an eco-utopian sensibility. *Grand Canyon* presents a potent example of the way narrative space especially has been used to articulate various contradictory forms of eco-utopian values and attitudes.

Film Spectacle

More recent forms of excessive visualisation are heightened through the use of special effects in mainstream Hollywood cinema, which in turn creates the potential for new ways of articulating ecological expression, assisted and often embodied by helpful agents. Yet Marxists critics traditionally reject spectacle as encouraging audiences to remain passive consumers and similarly tend to dismiss blockbuster films because 'they emphasise style, spectacle, special effects and images, at the expense of content, character, substance, narrative and social comment' (Strinati 1995: 229).

Nevertheless, cinematic spectacle probably remains the most important pleasurable aspect for blockbuster audiences, 'much like the cinema of attractions' of early cinema (see Friedberg 1993: 59). As the success of films like *Titanic* illustrate, this form of spectacle need not necessarily be empty and vacuous and can even provoke a spiralling range of ecological debates.[27]

Film theorists have tried to grapple with how the cinematic medium reflects this romantic sublime with varying degrees of success. David Bordwell speaks of the 'scenographic' space, which can be reinforced or modified by camera movement. He explores the ability of the subjective camera movement to endow static scenes with depth, which he calls the 'kinetic depth effect' (Bordwell in Burnett 1991: 232). This result is certainly achieved in the closing sequence of *Grand Canyon*, for example, as the camera majestically moves across the extensive vista, continuously framing the 'look' of the protagonists. Stephen Heath also speaks of how camera movement operates in that zone between the spectator's 'look' and the camera's 'look' with perceptual cues serving to identify the two (cited in Burnett 1991: 232).[28]

Men in Black

A playful yet far from mindless example of the use of special effects using a form of excessive visuality and eco-mapping can be seen in the exciting opening shot of *Men in Black* -the extremely successful blockbuster from 1997 which spawned a very disappointing sequel in 2002. It begins with the representation of a 'natural dragonfly' in flight, closely tracked by a moving film camera. This point-of-view opening positions the audience as active observers through the long tracking shot, with the 'bug' superbly avoiding various obstacles in its path. Like a Disney fairground ride or an advanced video game, audiences are engaged with both the thrill and sensation of continuous controlled movement. However, this kinetic movement is savagely if humorously terminated when the bug crashes into a truck's windscreen, designed for human visibility and protection. The organism is transformed into a colourful splat, as its body becomes crushed on the translucent glass. For the driver, this highly developed aerodynamic organism represents mere 'dirt' that simply impedes visibility, as he tries to dislodge its body with his screen wipers, to the audience's unsettled delight and disgust.

The lorry is carrying 'scruffy' illegal Mexican immigrants, a human form of aliens (bugs), into the land of the free-America. The contrasting range of alien bodies represented in the film, from the humble bug and the illegal alien immigrants to the more humanoid aliens exposed later, humorously serves to dramatise the complexity and range of interconnected life-forms on the planet while also, if only tangentially, articulating a critique of racism. This counterpointing of complex planetary and universal eco-systems exposing the irreducible nature of various organisms, also helps to demonstrate the potential insignificance of human nature, while at the same time continuing the narrative convention which requires that heroic outsiders clean up the mess and resolve the primary enigma of the narrative.

The elite eco-sapiens chosen by natural selection, who serve to protect the planet, must freely sacrifice their individual human past lives for the corporate 'common good'. All they have left to define their 'individuality' is their unifying black suits and sunglasses.

Conventional 'ideological' critics might dismiss this 'playful' over-determinism of uniformity and rigid belief system - in spite of its ironic postmodernist surface -as signalling the re-emergence of a dominant ideological corporatist super-structure that promotes institutional rather than individual values. But such criticism avoids appreciating the poetics (much less the entropy) of the text in all its formal, aesthetic and cultural richness, which privileges a pervasive humanist framework. My reading illustrates that a potent ecological dimension also remains at the heart of the text, which is at best under-represented within a strictly ideological reading that emphasises corporate power politics and 'aliens', who can only be connoted as 'illegal' and thereby harmful to the body politic. This reading suggests, however, that the film playfully constructs a more provocative yet incomplete position for audiences to engage with and questions what it means to be human and part of a planetary eco-system.

Class, race and gender issues cannot be avoided within film and in any case these more obvious constituents are necessary to attract audience attention and drive the narrative forward. However, the ethical and philosophical concerns of the text overlay these more obvious signifiers and underpin my reading of the film.

For example, the film's dramatic opening is superbly counterpointed by the mythic signification at the end of the film and helps to exemplify Merchant's earlier call for partnership ethics to resolve conflicts between humans and other forms of nature (Merchant 1995: 217). Race and gender issues are clinically resolved with a woman becoming a full partner and member of the elite 'men in black' team. More significantly, the finale articulates the deep ecological meaning of the text. Focusing on the cat's collar, which contains the much sought-after object of the quest, 'a miniature planetary complex', the audience is finally allowed into the visual spectacle of this astronomical other-world. The camera pulls out of the representation of New York and the planet into the solar system surrounded by several others, which end up making a slight speck on the screen. When all of the specks are combined, collectively they represent a cosmic super-system. Overseeing all this hyper-visualised 'space' is a strange cat-like deity, who juggles several other similar 'universes' and proceeds to playfully put them in a large unmarked bag that is drawn closed.

This technically complex but playful closure both demonstrates and dramatises human insignificance, which is the ultimate message of modern astronomy and, as such, remains philosophically awesome. But at the same time the ending also supports a reading that dramatises the precarious ecological balance in nature. The use of extra-terrestrials as the ultimate expression of both ecological harmony and imbalance in nature remains emblematic of 'progressive' (post)human agency. Within what is conventionally regarded as a postmodern world, which is defined by a cessation of controlling meta-narratives, what better way for western popular culture to engage with fundamental debates concerning humans and their overweening eco-system than through widening the symbolic (human) genome template to include bugs and aliens.

Conclusion

Grand Canyon and *Men in Black* in varying ways serve as broad illustrations of a range of ecological concerns by focusing in particular on environmental representations of raw nature and the use of alien/human agency to promote evidence of a deep ecological discourse.

Each following chapter will focus on related popular textual examples to investigate and develop specific responses that address their ecological representation. Taking on board Bordwell's broad considerations,[29] the examples chosen will finally be based on ecological use-value, which nonetheless reflects a broad spectrum of Hollywood film across the genres discussed. John Thompson succinctly affirms that cultural interpretation begins with the proposition that symbolic forms are 'referential' - 'they represent something, refer to something, say something about something' (see Thompson 1990: 289). Interpretation as applied here seeks to grasp this referentiality and, through a synthesis of formal and socio-historical analysis (Peck 1996: 6), to construct possible meanings of 'use' for an eco-utopian project.

Bordwell continues to throw down the gauntlet with regard to the standards necessary to be consistent and even 'scientific' when analysing film, and while one could argue against the illusion of scientific certitude, I would endorse his principled position. Carroll, Bordwell and others must also be commended for the way they push textual analysis towards a more philosophical realm by affirming that 'film is a way of thinking', and also 'a way of doing philosophy, but in purely filmic terms' (cited in Carroll 1990: 143). As Daniel Frampton succinctly states, 'Film study must progress conceptually to survive' (Frampton in MacCabe *et al.* 1996: 86). I fully endorse this proposal for a form of 'filmosophy', which elucidates both the critic's thinking and the film's thinking, and this strategy will be used to deepen the resonant meaning(s) of the films discussed. According to Frampton, the resultant discourse would be 'a poetic translation of those joined "thinkings"', and

chat that leaves the film purer, not hidden behind a mass of industrial workings, but out in the open as a world-mind-life-thought. Filmosophies should point back to the film to let its whole voice be heard. The study of film needs these new concepts, and in one sense to do that it needs to become philosophical - that is . . . to consider (to mistrust) inherited concepts and terms

(Frampton in MacCabe et al. 1996: 106).

Christine Gledhill, a feminist theorist and critic, tempers such philosophical reflections with radical ethical politics and strongly argues that 'meaning . . . is neither imposed, nor passively imbibed, but arises out of a struggle or negotiation between competing frames of reference, motivation and experience'. These can be analysed at three different levels: 'institutions, texts and audiences' (in Pribram 1988: 68). This study will concentrate almost exclusively on textual analysis from a broadly cultural, philosophical and eco-ethical perspective without necessarily undervaluing the other possible areas of analysis, especially reception theory.

Sue Thornham contends, however, that established feminists like Gledhill must perform a 'dual function'. Initially, they must 'open up the negotiations of the text' in order to determine the possibilities that exist for a gendered reading, but they must also 'enter the polemics of negotiation, exploiting textual contradictions to put into circulation readings that draw the text into a female/or feminist orbit' (cited in Pribram 1988: 75). I would contend that feminist theorising most especially anchors supposed universal meaning(s) and serves to alleviate the danger of grand philosophical theories having little connection with concrete social, cultural and ethical problems for the human race. Ecological readings and criticism explored in this book must also perform this dual function and can learn a lot from such a position.[30]

Positioning texts across the 'shallow versus deep' matrix, as explored earlier, may not finally be able to provide clear measurements of the effective potency of a range of ecological themes and aesthetic strategies used in film. Nevertheless, this crude framework is at least initially helpful in breaking down divisions and beginning the process of an ecological reading of film. In particular, the play between oppositions in Hollywood texts can highlight the apparently superficial and sometimes parochial evocation of nature which appeals to be light, transitory here and now, as opposed to more resonant, deep evocations. It is from within these interconnecting and often contradictory avenues of investigation that a methodology appropriate to an ecological textual analysis becomes feasible.

Finally, however, this methodological approach seeks to engage most critically with the symptomatic (or political/ideological, top-down discourses) alongside the aesthetic (or technical, bottom-up) reading strategies, with the primary aim of validating an ecological method of reading film. Each chapter will continue to develop and clarify a specific aspect of this necessary dual process, involving theorising and interpretation, which underpins this analytical strategy.

Notes

1. For example see my review of *Cultural Ecology: the Changing Dynamics of Communication*, edited by Danielle Cliche in Convergence, 3, 3, Autumn 1997: 148-50.

2. The phrase is borrowed from Robert B. Ray's (1985) study 'A Certain Tendency of the Hollywood Cinema'.

3. Tom Gunning's important term 'cinema of attractions', coined to evoke so-called 'primitive cinema', remains pertinent and becomes more relevant with the growth of contemporary special effects-driven films.

4. Peter Kramer, in an essay entitled 'Women First' in the *Historical Journal of Film, Radio and Television*, exposes how Cameron was looking for an opportunity to do an epic romance in the tradition of *Gone with the Wind*, what *Newsweek* described as a 'chick-flick period piece'. Women (mature) had become the new target audience, breaking a trend of addressing blockbuster special effects films primarily at (male) adolescent audiences. The strategy worked, at least in the short term, with 'over 60% of all ticket sales by women - many for repeat viewings' (Kramer 1997: 612).

5. David Lubin's engaging BFI monograph on the film makes an interesting connection with John Kasson, the historian of Coney Island, who explains: 'In its very horror, disaster conferred a kind of transcendent meaning to its victims' lives, transforming commonplace routine into the extraordinary. Sensationalised re-creations of such disasters gave a vicarious sense of this transcendence to their audience - with of course the inestimable advantage of allowing them to emerge from the performance unharmed' (cited in Lubin 1999: 112).

6. Friedrich Ratzel (1844-1904) is often considered the father of environmental determinism and first argued how the natural environment was immutable, underlying all human activity. In turn, Ratzel was influenced by George Perking March, who in 1864 published his very influential Man and Nature (just five years after Darwin's *The Origin of the Species*), which considered humans as active agents effecting change in the environment.
'Nature' within this discourse provides a rich reservoir of socially constructed, historical and philosophical attitudes and beliefs concerning ecology. Most notably while the seventeenth-century philosopher Thomas Hobbes viewed the 'natural human condition', prior to the emergence of civilised society, as 'nasty, brutish and short', his contemporary John Locke considered that nature embodied a state of 'humanitarian bliss' and affirmed that 'natural laws' must form the basis of a just society (cited in Anderson 1996: 5). Descartes, on the other hand, construed nature as 'the Other' and in so doing reified nature as a thing -an external other - entirely separate from the world of thought. Nature became, as Heidegger later complained, 'one

vast gasoline station for human exploitation'. Adorno in Revolt of Nature continued in this vein and prophetically contended that mastery over nature inevitably turns to mastery over men (cited in Anderson 1996: 134).

7. In particular in the early nineteenth century, German Romantics, 'in protest against Enlightenment rationality', called for a rebirth of mythology and what Schelling termed a new 'universal symbolism' based on the 'things of nature' which 'both signify and are' (Buck-Morss in Levin 1993: 317). This form of nature romanticism had disastrous consequences for the first half of the twentieth century, most notably with the evolution of Nazism.

8. The word 'biosphere' has three meanings: 'the totality of living things dwelling on the earth, the space occupied by living things, or life and life-support systems, atmosphere, hydrosphere, lithosphere, and pedosphere'. The term was invented by Eduard Suess (1875), who wrote of a sphere of living organisms or biological processes (Huggett 1995: 8).

9. Nature as female became a root metaphor for sixteenth-century Europeans but such an all-encompassing metaphor can be a double-edged notion, often rendering both women and nature as passive and submissive (Merchant 1995: 142). However, Patrick Murphy's argument that James Lovelock's original Gaia hypothesis can be regarded as an essentially sexist one is possibly over-stretching its intended meaning.
In 1980 at a 'survival gathering' of native Americans in the Black Hills of South Dakota, a 'Declaration of Dependence on the Land -Mother Earth' (see Akwesasne Notes, Summer 1980) was issued which declared: 'We call for the recognition of our responsibilities to be stewards of the land, to treat with respect and love our Mother Earth who is a source of our physical nourishment and our spiritual strength. We are people of the land. We believe that the land is not to be owned but to be shared. We believe that we are guardians of the land' (cited in Merchant 1995: 155).

10. Consequently sales of Leopold's 'bible of this new environmentalism' reached over 270,000 copies in 1973 alone. Most variations of radical ecology also tend to assume this holistic ethic of creation.

11. The polarising beliefs that form the core of this biocentric ethical outlook, include 'the belief that humans are members of the earth's "community of life" in the same sense and on the same terms in which other living things are members of that community' (Taylor in Gruen 1994: 43).

12. Ecological historians often attempt to (re)construct a master eco-narrative to help replace, or supersede, what they regard as 'reductive' and 'outworn' controlling ideological categorisations, namely: 'red/blue' or left/right oppositions, which some argue have become less relevant to the globalised West. We have, according to the more pessimistic critics like David Pepper, become trapped within an apparently relativist, postmodernist culture which unintentionally promotes exclusivity.

13. Utopianism gets its name from Sir Thomas More's fictional Utopia. Geoghegan begins his book on this topic with a plea which this study endorses: 'I wish to defend that unrealistic, irrational, naive, self-indulgent, unscientific, escapist, elitist, activity known as Utopianism' (Geoghegan 1987: 1).

14. The Frankfurt School postulated at least four major interrogative positions which, tangentially at least, need to be addressed by this study, most specifically with reference to science fiction films:

    1) The role of scientific enquiry as a liberating force is called into question - they fought against Positivists and Newtonian/Cartesian scientific methods.

    2) They challenged the hegemony of instrumental rationality and argued for an 'alternative' rationality, with power to give a deeper sense of meaning to life.

    3) They asked what kinds of aesthetics were possible after Auschwitz. Many agreed that 'purity' in art was the only guarantee against co-option and corruption.

    4) Their idea of the human domination of nature as 'other' was especially taken up by (eco) feminists (Harvey 1996: 137).

15. Karl Popper continues in this pessimistic vein by discounting utopias as leading to totalitarianism. Such a theoretical position was realised, for example, by the poet and (ex-) President of the 'new' Czech Republic, Vaclav Havel. He asserted that the 'death of utopian ideals' are essentially good, since he and many others equated these ideals with Marxism and Stalinism, which served to keep his people suppressed for so long. Such outright rejection effectively promotes the current orthodoxy, which affirms that there is little alternative to free market capitalism.

16. At the same time critics like John O'Neill in *The Poverty of Postmodernism* (O'Neill 1995) continue to dismiss postmodern culture in particular for not expressing any form of 'authentic' utopian values. For example, Rushing *et al.* insist that postmodernism 'ultimately offers no cure because the malady is all that it can see' (Rushing *et al.* 1995: 12). We cannot, they conclude, return to modernist theories - 'the very ones that infected us with the plague that postmodernism describes . . . but we still need a theoretical perspective' (Rushing *et al.* 1995: 29). Consequently they collapse the two primary and totalising concepts to create a more appropriate notion to suit their 'essentialist' aims - 'transmodernism'.

17. Yet it was not until 1980 that the first major report on environment and development was published. *The World Conservation Strategy* (IUNCN 1980) emphasised the global scale of ecological imbalance, 'the impact of human endeavours on the carrying capacity of the planet as a whole, and the need for a global agenda for change' (cited in Cooper *et al.* 1995: 32).

18. Lincoln Allison similarly asserts that 'shallow' and 'deep' are fundamentally opposed ethical

systems with the former affirming a dualistic notion of human nature as opposed to other life forms and the latter attempting to create a holistic appreciation of life and nature (in Eccleshall 1994: 237).

19. In contrast to Button and Allison, other, more conciliatory, green speakers argue that ecology requires the theoretical underpinning of environmentalism, which provides the practical application of theoretical ecological thinking. One critic goes even further by asserting that light ecology is:
'dualistic or pluralistic, compartmentalistic rather than holistic, and definitely mechanistic. Like deep ecology however, shallow ecology allows both materialism and idealism and it does not presume any view on causation. Finally unlike deep ecology, shallow ecology allows both an evolutionary and an equilibrium perspective on nature' (Wissenburg 1997: 6).

20. See for example populist eco-thinkers such as Fritjof Capra, who has remained on the best-seller lists since the late 1970s with *The Tao of Physics* (Capra 1979) and *The Turning Point: Science, Society and the Rising Culture* (Capra 1983).

21. 'Feminists argue that most contemporary political theory, whether liberal, Marxist, or Frankfurt School, works from a model of man which is universal, uniform, ahistorical and transcendent, excluding a model of woman which is contextual, relativistic and particularistic. Ecofeminists add that the traditional model of man is alienated from natural contexts too' (Gruen *et al.* 1994: 161).

22. This image of nature is probably the most common preoccupation in much Hollywood cinema. Critics especially cite Walt Disney's fixation with a two-dimensional representation of nature. Bambi (1942), for example, illustrates the classic Disney(land) view, as all the animals troop down to see the 'miracle' of a new baby deer. Such a mise-en-scène evokes and serves to reinforce the idyllic co-existence of all animals. Only 'man' can upset this utopia. Bambi's mother is killed by Mr Man and his sweetheart by Mr Man's dog; finally his terrestrial paradise is destroyed by Mr Man's fire. This potent 'eco-trope' is probably one of the major reasons why Disney narratives are so successful. Everyone, especially children (and the child in all of us), wants to believe that humans and all animals can happily co-exist, even if little thought is given to the implications of this sentimental but benevolent representation. This primal fantasy, while dramatically evoked, is never consciously problematised.

23. The failure to affirm difference is characteristic of the colonising self, which denies the other through the attempt to incorporate it into the empire of the self and is unable to experience sameness without erasing difference.

24. For instance, he poses the question: to what extent, we must ask, is the televisual popular spectacle the 'product of oppositional culture of the oppressed and to what extent is it a bread-and-circuses show managed from above for purposes of profit?' To what extent (also) does such

spectacle merely provide an arena for the acting out of the ambient aggressivity of late-capitalist culture? (Stam 1992: 227).

25. Bordwell continually reiterates and endorses two theoretical clichés, namely, 'meanings are not found but made' and the assumption that theory neither inductively nor deductively guarantees an interpretation.

26. Brian Jarvis affirms that Cooper's original novel indulges in 'the classic romantic trope of feminising the land, of imagining space as Mother Nature'. Space is perceived as 'dizzy, confused and overpowering' (Jarvis 1998: 186).
The novel is concerned with the: 'struggle between white men and red men for the possession of women's bodies (the narrative is structured around a series of kidnappings) and it is set against the historical backdrop of the struggle between white men and red men for the possession and ownership of the wilderness . . . in Cooper's world both the land and women are seen essentially as forms of male property' (*ibid*.: 187).

27. Consequently I will seek to validate and legitimate commercialised spectacle, which is usefully described by Robert Baird in an essay on Jurassic Park as a 'return of the cinematic spectacular sublime' (Baird 1998: 97).

28. Gilles Deleuze argues that this 'movement is a translation in space -movement [which] always relates to a change' (Deleuze 1986: 8). Anne Friedberg, adapting the notion of the urban-based flaneur, goes even further and asserts that motion pictures have constructed 'a virtual, mobilized gaze by means of which the spectator would travel through an imaginary spatial and temporal elsewhere and elsewhen' (Friedberg 1993: 2).

29. Even if critics can overcome various 'philosophical' problems concerning textual analysis, Bordwell argues that they face several more immediately tangible difficulties before they can actually write up concrete examples on particular films. These include:
- appropriateness (picking a film that is an acceptable candidate for interpretation)
- recalcitrant data (adjusting elements of the film to match reigning notions of what ought to be interpreted)
- novelty (making the interpretation fresh)
- and plausibility (i.e. making the interpretation persuasive).
In learning to solve these problems the critic has acquired skills in seeking out significance, interpretability, salient patterns and exemplary passages (Bordwell 1989: 133).

30. Thornham suspects that Gledhill's stance is neither 'redemptive' nor 'recruitist' - indeed she suggests that such an opposition is 'over-simplistic'. Feminist textual analysis nonetheless seeks to distinguish between the 'parochial' representations of 'women' and the 'universal' which seeks to explore the historical, socio-cultural experience of 'woman' (Thornham 1997: 2).

2 NATURE FILM AND ECOLOGY

Prologue

From simple descriptions of nature in the familiar settings of the New England landscape, inspirational nature poetry was initiated by Emerson, Dickinson and Whitman. Emerson expressed his transcendental ideals as much in poetry as in prose and his poetic celebrations of the restorative powers of nature, where 'the gods talk in the breath of the woods', were widely published and did much to make him the icon of mid-nineteenth-century nature worship. Such natural idealism continues to infiltrate the film medium. This rise of nature worship in many ways reflects a 'foreboding of impending loss; a melancholic anticipation of the advance of civilisation' and the 'disappearance of the natural world' (Bunce 1994: 191).

In a survey essay entitled 'The Genre of Nature', Leo Braudy taps into this preoccupation and draws comparisons with Hollywood film when he asserts that the 'lost natural innocence celebrated by the romantic poets as a reproach to the industrial' has 'metamorphosed into a late twentieth-century dream of renewing that innocence and thereby evading the twin nightmares of being swallowed up by either an unappreciated past or an unknown future' (Braudy 1998: 294).

In many ways the domination of nature coupled with the romanticisation of nature became a defining aspect of western civilisation from around the eighteenth century. Because of this importance, it is necessary in this chapter to sketch the contrasting ecological connotations of nature through Hollywood film from the post-war period to the end of the century. To schematise this mammoth task a number of key films are analysed to highlight a range of comparisons and thematic ecological continuities and transformations. *The Yearling* (1946) is examined as a film that signalled the consolidation of post-war normative values regarding nature and is contrasted with the more overt and contemporary expression of ecological values in *The Emerald Forest* (1985). A major part of the chapter is taken up with a case study of Steven Spielberg, who can be regarded as the most important ecological film-maker in Hollywood. While recently nature romanticism has become aesthetically transformed through the use of special effects, as exemplified within natural disaster movies like *Twister* (1996), more evocative traces of the well-worn nature/romantic trope can be found in *Jurassic Park* (1993) and *The Lost World* (1997).

Introduction

Over many centuries the dominant image of civilised pleasure in painting, which remains an often untheorised aesthetic influence on cinematography, has been the Arcadian scene. The study of a nature *mise-en-scène* helps cross connect the two art forms. Typically, such a painted scene focuses on a gathering of people, either naked or in formal dress, enjoying themselves in the open air and signals culture preening itself in the presence of its opposite nature. These idealised representations can be seen most clearly through the paintings of Giorgione and Titian in sixteenth century Venice and, according to art critics, were evidence that the forest fears of the medieval world had at last been exorcised. Nature was newly represented as benevolent and therefore could be symbolically entered without any fear. Such representations of nature continue to be eulogised, while at the same time these 'medieval fears' have also persisted (in, for example, Peter Weir's *Picnic at Hanging Rock* 1973)[1] and become transmuted through Hollywood film within the confines of more contemporary relevant ecological fears.[2]

This conflation need not be reduced to a pure aesthetic valorisation of a utopic landscape that in turn militates against reflective and critical distance. Marcia M. Eaton affirms in an essay on the aesthetic appreciation of nature in the *Journal of Aesthetic Art*, that 'knowledge does not kill aesthetic pleasure' and continues to passionately proclaim how 'human valuing' is predominantly 'holistic'. We rarely experience something 'purely aesthetically or purely ethically or purely religiously or purely scientifically' (Eaton 1998). This is true also of the various pleasures and knowledge afforded by popular film which cannot be reduced to a few discrete variables.

The Primary Elements of Nature

The primary expression of such classical pictorial representation of raw nature can be traced in film studies through the evolution of the quintessential American genre -the Western. Frederick Jackson Turner, in particular, suggests that the story of America echoes the ascending stages of European civilisation in producing a uniquely democratic and egalitarian community. Turner regarded the transformation of the American landscape from wilderness to commercialised urbanisation as the central saga of the nation.[3] The genre became most heavily theorised in film studies when anchored within polarised debates between 'nature' and the agency of native Americans as opposed to 'culture' and the agency of white settlers. In crude terms, the apparently greater appreciation and harmony of the natives with their eco-system is often dramatically counterpointed with the corrupting nature of various colonialist settlers. This sometimes obtuse endorsement of 'otherness' as a key signifier remains most significant for an ecological reading of the classical nature genre. Conceptually, however, because the genre remained preoccupied with mobility and the goal of traversing landscape, discussion of the western is carried out in the following chapter.

Heraclitus, the pre-Socratic philosopher, spoke of the common principle underlying all matter as being endless change and transformation. He is probably the first western philosopher to appreciate the holistic connections between all the primary elements, which he reduced to earth, air, fire and water. These elemental forces infuse and help to structure the comparison of filmic examples used in all chapters in this study. In many of the films discussed in this chapter, tensions between the four elements are foregrounded to an almost extreme level, dramatising the innate symbiotic connectivity between all natural forces in sustaining an evolutionary ecology which is not always predetermined by human agency. From the preoccupation with earth and air in *The Yearling* (1946), to fire and water in *The Emerald Forest* (1985) and water alone in *Jaws* (1975) and *Waterworld* (1995), the chapter concludes with an exploration of synthetic special effects which result from the manipulation of primary elements excavated from the earth to create a long extinct range of dinosaur species in the *Jurassic Park* (1993) phenomenon.

American Romanticism and Nature

When the desire to represent and foreground the countryside as a distinct entity first manifested itself, this aesthetic interest in the land appeared to run parallel with its unceasing exploitation for the purposes of agriculture, hunting and travel. More recently, literary and cultural analysts have drawn on the writings of Lévi-Strauss and continue to apply rather crude binary oppositions between 'nature and culture' and 'rural and urban' as the primary structuring rationale for all art.[4]

The dominant ideology, which incorporates a predisposition towards scientific materialism at the expense of the total environment, can most clearly be traced to the profound changes initiated by the Industrial Revolution. For instance, the romantic scientist Jacob Bronowski, in his classic television series *The Ascent of Man* (1973), optimistically concluded that while the Renaissance established the 'dignity of man', the Industrial Revolution established the 'unity of nature' (Bronowski 1973: 260). All of this was promoted, he argued, by scientists and, equally importantly from a cultural perspective, the romantic poets, who saw that the wind and the sea and primary sources of power like coal are all created by the heat of the sun, which is the source of energy (*ibid.*: 286). Bronowski and others regarded the pure scientific urge towards invention and knowledge as ennobling the 'human spirit', echoing the utopian agenda of the romantic poets. Nevertheless, the functional and economic imperative to which such inventions were used, could not by any stretch of the imagination be regarded as serving the demands of such utopian idealism. Philanthropic socialist beliefs, as espoused by

Bronowski, have primarily concerned a small number of entrepreneurial idealists who, whether by choice or not, remained outside the mainstream expansion of industrialism with its ceaseless exploitation of natural resources. The deep ecological message of the 'unity of nature' was consequently not learned or endorsed by the forefathers of industrialisation on either side of the Atlantic.

The Industrial Revolution as a new economic and ethical manifestation mapping out how humans should relate to their environment was underpinned by notions developed through thinkers like Francis Bacon, who foresaw the need to combine knowledge with invention to give humankind control of nature. Bacon spoke of 'victory' over nature, which was conceptualised as incomplete and potentially corrupt without the controlling benevolence of 'man'. Even more significant for extending the connections between humans and nature was Charles Darwin's core theory of natural selection, transformed by writers like Herbert Spencer into the doctrine of the survival of the fittest, which in many ways became the new orthodoxy for human survival. Nature and the environment became simply the unanimated space for higher order species like humans to evolve and become dominant over all other sentient life forms.

As evidenced by a strong European romantic tradition within western culture, there has also been a continuing historical danger of 'nature idolatry'. Historical romantics such as William Wordsworth sought to 'ennoble and spiritualize nature' and even 'derive a transcendent nature from an ecological nature' (Gerard 1996: 457).

Historically in America, Ralph Waldo Emerson felt so strongly the need to appreciate and understand nature that he urged his fellow Americans against the intellectual dependency on books which could make them into 'bibliomaniacs'. Instead he urged others to use nature as their dictionary (Bronowski 1973: 156). As a romantic thinker, Emerson articulated the polarity between nature (the green world and the actual earth of value) and culture (the print world and the mind of Europe) and threw his support behind the former with the hope of redressing the emerging 'industrial era's radical bias towards the abstract symbolisation of thought and knowledge' (Marc 1992: 157). This romantic aesthetic agenda has remained prevalent within American culture ever since. As Emerson never tired of asserting, Americans were and ought to be 'nature's nation' (Braudy 1998: 280). Leo Braudy historically defines nature as 'the primitive essence of what it means to be human; the animal world over which we strive to dominate; and sometimes it is the inanimate world of vegetation, rock, and earth' (*ibid*.: 278).

Braudy affirms that, in recent years, the myths, metaphors and motifs of nature have become more prevalent in Hollywood and concludes that with:

their dystopian gloom or utopian optimism, these films similarly assert the need for a reconnection to what is vital in nature in order that we might escape from the dilemmas history has forced upon us. Whether their settings are the primitive world of the past, the natural world of the present, or the unexplored world of the future, their common impulse is to begin again, to have a second chance at creation

(ibid.: 305).

While Hollywood could never be accused of suffering from 'bibliomania', to all appearances 'nature' remains remarkably potent and evocative within both the form and content of film history. 'Nature' is most certainly central to the aesthetic vocabulary of western culture, with most audiences having tangible knowledge and experience, and a few even moved to defend its sanctity at great personal risk. Yet while nature is very much a part of popular culture, a difficult question remains - which 'nature'? Ulrich Beck agrees that the term 'nature' can mean almost anything you want, which can be extremely dangerous when co-opted for pernicious political use as in Germany and Russia in the twentieth century.

A framing structure, which is useful for schematising the evolution of various, often competing, notions of nature as Beck suggests, is posited by Val Plumwood.

The first step in the evolution of human/nature dualism is the construction of the normative (the best or ideal) human identity as mind or reason, excluding or inferiorizing the whole rich range of other human and non-human characteristics or construing them as inessential. The construction of mind or reason in terms exclusive of and oppositional to nature is the second step. The construction of nature itself as mindless is the third step, one which both reinforces the opposition and constructs nature as ineluctably alien, disposing of an important area of continuity and overlap between humans and animals and non-human nature

(Plumwood 1993: 107).

Plumwood pessimistically concludes that in many ways this 'removes the basis for an ethical response to the world' *(ibid.: 118).* More constructively however, from a cultural analysis perspective, Ronnie Zoe Hawkins asserts that an ecological framework 'provides a snapshot, a temporal cross-section of current relationships among different kinds of organisms' (Hawkins 1998: 165). Donna Haraway, in a 1995 essay 'Otherwordly Conversations, Terrain, Topics, Local Terms', also affirms 'we must find another relationship to nature besides reification, possession, appropriation and nostalgia' (cited in Shiva and Moser 1995: 70). Before dealing with more contemporary films, it is necessary to clarify the normative baseline for post-war representations of nature in Hollywood cinema.

Pre-Ecological Evocations of Nature: *The Yearling*

Clarence Brown, who directed *The Yearling* (1946),[5] learned his craft from the great European master Maurice Tourneur, whose aesthetic values of pictorial quality and romantic evocation were continued in many of his films and typifies this strand of film-making as it developed in Hollywood. As a director Brown became preoccupied with 'rural Americana' in films like *Ah Wilderness* (1935), Of *Human Hearts* (1938), *The Human Comedy* (1943) and *Intruder in the Dust* (1950), among others. While very popular at the box office, critical appraisal of *The Yearling* remains somewhat dismissive. For example, Ephram Katz's encyclopaedia of film is typical when it says that 'for the most part Brown subjugated his themes to his pictorial vision and was unabashedly sentimental in his celebration of romanticism' (Katz 1982: 171). Based on a Pulitzer Prize-winning novel by Majorie Kinnan Rawlings, the film uses many melodramatic conventional ingredients framed within an idealised landscape which appear to pre-echo a later Disney aesthetic. A beautiful blonde farmer's boy (Claude Jarman, Jr.) falls in love with a fawn, much to the consternation of his parents (Gregory Peck and Jane Wyman), who have great difficulties to contend with in their collective struggle for survival on a small farm in Florida. Most notably, lighting and music are continuously used with powerful effect to evoke the romantic majesty of the wilderness.

The act of hunting becomes the focus for engaging with nature. In one memorable scene Gregory Peck is ineffective in his attempts to kill a dangerous bear, being let down several times by a defective shotgun. Marti Kheel writes how the creation of a type of 'holy hunter' promotes the notion that hunting is a positive spiritual experience. In turn, this establishes or reinforces an identification with the natural world and often shows the killed animal as somehow making a 'gift' of his or her life, almost as a symbolic sacrifice.[6]

The film continually sets up oppositions between 'primitive nature' and 'modernity', with Peck as a farmer trying to take control of his habitat and develop the land through more effective stewarding systems. Nevertheless, nature's primacy and indeterminacy is affirmed in a memorable static scene immediately after 'wild nature' has destroyed all their belongings. The family stand together in a tableau-like pose, surveying the desolation with great humility, which is effectively signalled through dirt and a pervasive sense of awe in their faces. This evocative form of empathy is encapsulated in the *mise-en-scène*, with the protagonists looking out into the dramatic landscape, which represents a recurring visual motif. Peck speaks for all when he says that they must accept nature's power to control their lives but also learn to pick up the pieces, as was demanded of a post-war generation.

The focus of conflict in the film centres on a fawn, the yearling of the title, which serves as a pet for the young boy. Throughout the narrative the fawn remains closely linked with untrammelled nature. This can be seen through a recurring visual moment of the boy gambolling in harmony with the fawn as they traverse the wilderness. Both are drinking *au naturel* from the river while being observed, not by an omniscient narrator in a television nature documentary, but by other 'wild' animals. Wilderness, particularly within an American context, is 'a metaphor of unlimited opportunity, rising from the tribal memory of a time when humanity spread across the world . . . firm in the belief that virgin land went on forever past the horizon' (Wilson 1992: 335). Both child and animal became harmonised and (re)presented in natural ecstasy. But the nascent child farmer has to learn, as his screen father pontificates, that wild animals cannot coexist with, much less endure, man's ultimate economic demand to tame and control his environment. In the end, the boy must grow up and accept the post-war primary function of nature as raw material within a capitalist system, instead of endorsing a 'naive' romantic ecological predisposition, which privileges an emotional harmony with nature.

Such a closure is, however, unlike the synthetic harmony of the Disney oeuvre, where the forces of innocence and nature appear to win out in the end and conflict is resolved. The yearling boy learns to capitulate to the laws of agricultural capitalism which are necessary for him to survive within an American post-war mind set. Like the prodigal son, he comes back to accept his inheritance and the possible future delights of creating a spring-well for his mother while carving a farm out of the wilderness.[7] By the end he has matured and grown to accept the impracticality of his former naive pastoral coexistence with nature, while at the same time, like his teacher and father, maintaining respect for its potency to control their lives. The hegemonic post-war valuation of production and fruitful labour, as opposed to the otherwise passive delights of pastoral harmony, have to be finally vindicated, at least thematically.

While *The Yearling* most certainly validates the taming of the landscape and concurs with the frontier ethos of the western, the evocation of a 'progressive' sublime nature/ecology is most cogently articulated when ecological lessons become more widely communicated with the growth of the Green movement from the 1960s onwards. Nonetheless, echoes of a conventional use of nature remain embedded within Hollywood, which regularly foregrounds visual images that unashamedly support beautiful and healthy environments for recreation and the glorification of landscape. It has become almost axiomatic for Hollywood that land and nature should not be 'abused' or 'violated', since humans owe it to their children to maintain their birthright. This truly radical extension of the traditional conservative concept of lineage over land and property to include all children and their children at least potentially serves to subvert the ideological polarities of the class system bolstered on inherited property and individual wealth. Natural beauty can no longer be 'owned' exclusively by the aristocracy and becomes the birthright of everyone who has 'eyes to see'.

More recently Hollywood and nature films in particular appear to recognise their role in teaching mass audiences throughout the world both to perceive and appreciate this natural birthright. While *The Yearling* sought to foreground nature primarily for aesthetic reasons, the evolution and growth of an ecology movement in the 1960s encouraged a more explicit critique of the exploitation of nature. This became most easily and effectively demarcated by the problem of erosion in the great forests of the Third World - perceived as the last frontier maintaining ecological purity beyond the now outdated Hollywood western with no frontier remaining to be conquered.

The Emerald Forest

After the post-war project of reaffirming nationhood, as undertaken in *The Yearling*, was completed, few Hollywood texts apart from the western and road movie genres explicitly dealt with the romanticisation of nature. But with the more recent questioning of this romantic consensus fuelled by a growing debate over ecological issues and beliefs, representations of mediated raw nature have again become explicitly foregrounded throughout the 'public sphere' of Hollywood. This more contemporary ecological questioning of the abuse of nature can be clearly appreciated in apparently 'committed' green films like *The Emerald Forest* (1985).

Almost 40 years separate the post-war evocation of nature in *The Yearling* and more contemporary valorisations, which have created a rich seam of ecological representations. *The Emerald Forest* in particular coincided with the consolidation of radical ecological thinking which has exploited this contemporary consciousness. Yet many critics have dismissed the film as reminiscent of the 'chocolate box' romanticism of *The Yearling* and looking like a Third World charity appeal or a public relations exercise in 'ecological political correctness'. Nonetheless, such overtly ecological narratives help foreground major natural disasters, even if only as a pretext for thematic originality and contemporaneity.

The director John Boorman has remained preoccupied with the narrative format of the quest,[8] which in this instance involves an engineer who loses his son while playing in the Amazonian forest, where he is helping to harness and control its power by constructing a dam. As a consequence, the father spends almost ten years attempting to find him. The quest, as in the quintessential *The Searchers* discussed in the next chapter, becomes a suitable Hollywood peg on which to hang the theme of ecological disaster. Ecology is dramatised by the rainforests becoming eroded over time with the construction of a dam, which signifies the white man's continuous efforts to control nature, ostensibly for the betterment of all mankind. But the film finally makes explicit how such technological advances and developments help few, except the money men.

For Hollywood myth-makers, the pure, dense and holistic African rainforests have become a rich source of ecological expression. Other examples include *Gorillas in the Mist* (1988), which swaps 'primitive' humans and the mythic potency of dams for a closer inspection of animals in their own natural habitat. Apted's biopic about the late Diane Fossey's mission to save the endangered mountain gorillas similarly provides a suitable platform for ecological exposition. Liberal ethical exposition using earnest didactic soul-searching often fails to recognise the potential of popular cultural discourse which requires subtlety and sophistication in its delivery, more so than is often recognised by the predominantly high-cultural intelligentsia.

Other examples of didactic eco-soul-searching can also be detected in Medicine Man (1992), with the forest again under threat. Sean Connery, who plays the role of Dr Campbell, finds a cure for cancer within the organically rich yet so-called 'primitive' rainforest. The film's narrative concerns his attempt to find the formula cure again after losing it. This becomes a race against time before the forces of western destruction achieve their 'civilising' goal by constructing a road through the forest.9

Within the narrative Dr Campbell must learn that his wild, often obsessional behaviour to 'save humanity' is directly proportionate to the guilt he suffers from being part of the Ashton corporation, whose *raison d'être* is to maximise profits at the expense of the rainforests. Coincidentally Connery is also responsible, like the otherwise benign agent in *At Play in the Fields of the Lord* (1991) for a 'swine flu' that kills off an entire village.

The screenplay of *Medicine Man* by Tom Schulman is similar in many respects to Peter Weir's *Dead Poet's Society* (1989), which he also wrote.[10] Nevertheless, while this may summarise the ecological context of the film, the controlling narrative concerns a love affair between an ageing pony-tailed adventurer and a fiery young female (Lorraine Bracco) as they work through a screen romance within an exotic background. The ecological message, as with many similar Hollywood films, remains simply a 'hook' on which to hang a conventional love story.

All these forest-centred narratives appeal to a utopian sensibility but seldom explore, much less deconstruct, the ideological conflicts inherent in these enclosed ecological environments. The dams and the roads being constructed in the jungle are shorthand signifiers which are dramatically necessary to expose and explore the heroic potential of Connery *et al*. In the end, the system is not defeated, as it was never intended to be, which remains a dominant criticism of Hollywood narratives. At best the ideological system incorporates and accommodates some of the criticisms of the 'light' ecological message without necessarily having to compromise or undermine the dominant ideology of 'natural progression'.[11]

Nonetheless, such otherwise superficial ecological texts at least expose a range of utopic issues, even if they rarely create the screen space necessary to fully develop many of the implications of such a discourse.

Because films like *Medicine Man* remain overtly didactic and outwardly ecological in their thematic concerns, they continue to work within existing socio-political systems rather than promote a more holistic and radically deeper form of ecological expression. Nevertheless, though the potent evocation of nature imagery may appear crude to 'sophisticated' viewers, it helps consolidate and dramatise inherent ecological and human conflicts. In *Emerald Forest* the (post)colonial clash of cultures is strongly visualised by the foregrounded image of a 'naturalised' Charlie climbing the outside of his father's apartment block in his quest to save *his* people. The incongruity of his ascent, which is more usually associated with conquering a 'primitive' natural obstacle, serves in this example to dramatise the clash of these mutually opposing cultures while also becoming metaphorically and visually resonant over and above the diegetic requirements of the text. Urban sophistication and architecture counterpoint the more primal and primitive beauty of the forest.

Jerry Mander simplistically suggests that such sequences and films attempt to show white people from the point of view of natives. The native Americans call the whites 'the termite people' because of how they destroy the forest. As a consequence, white society conjures up the 'dead world' because of the concrete environment it creates where nothing grows (Mander 1992: 225). How to represent native indigenous peoples in Hollywood film is always problematic. If presented as radically different, with their 'otherness' fully articulated, scriptwriters often presume western mass audiences would not respond, much less understand. Consequently their representation becomes more uniformly like Walt Disney's anthropomorphic 'human' animals and even caricatured as two-dimensional and thereby either appealing or repulsive to audiences. Hence they remain typecast as exotic and alien or idyllically innocent and primitive.

This criticism can most readily be appreciated through the almost obligatory ritualised and idyllic scenes of native nubile bodies bathing and grooming, as evidenced in many western romantic paintings of nature. Old wrinkled bodies are rarely if ever displayed in films of 'primitive' societies, which are linked to the erotic evocation of easy and available sexuality through the promotion of exotic rites-of-passage rituals. *Fatimah Tobing Ront* (1996) speaks of the 'Rousseauesque study' of remaining 'primitive peoples which have survived as a taxidermic mode of ethnographic cinema' that began with Robert Flaherty's *Nanook of the North* (1922). Yet in many of the films mentioned above, and especially in the extremely successful *Dances with Wolves* (1990), to be discussed in detail in the following chapter, concessions are made to the native culture's unique, authentic language, with subtitles extensively used. But as many cultural critics assert, even this form of verbalisation can further increase the surfeit evocation of exoticism. There appears to be no easy, much less formulaic, representational method of avoiding such polarising (mis)representations between so called western 'civilised' and 'primitive' societies.

Nonetheless, for Boorman and many other romantically inspired film-makers, the 'primitive' embodies all that is ecologically enviable. Charlie, the little white boy, is kidnapped because he has a 'love of the forest in his eye' and learns to be at 'one with nature'. Only patriarchal white culture brings disease and disharmony, which results in the corruption of the natural world. Boorman (like Kevin Costner in *Dances with Wolves*) avoids any fears of contamination by reinforcing a simple opposition between 'good' natives and the 'fierce' people who, owing to the erosion of their lands, are forced to adopt western ways and end up acting as pimps for girls kidnapped from other tribes. White imperialist culture is shown to corrupt absolutely.

In the end the main protagonist and engineer comes to the realisation that white men and their dams must be stopped not only for the survival of the natural ecology of the area but also for the protection of his son's chosen people. Like most western 'non-believers', he rationalises that he must help nature fight the enemy and consequently sets explosives to blow up the dam, which is affirmed as 'unnatural'. Unlike his son, who becomes like a primitive shaman,[12] the architect father does not have faith in nature's power. But the 'miracle' of the flooding which arrives suddenly to protect the ecological balance of the habitat succeeds in destroying the dam, leaving no need for the father's artificial and interventionist solution. As the Gaia mantra articulates, 'nature will find a way'.

Leo Braudy states that in *Emerald Forest* audiences are provided with two closely related endings, exemplifying that 'there is also often a syntactic disjuncture at the point of narrative closure in which the discourses of real (dystopian civilisation) and ideal (natural community) clash' (Braudy 1998: 291). This clash echoes theoretical positions affirmed by Jean Baudrillard and Ulrich Beck. Beck's 'overly pessimistic'[13] and gloomy prognosis regarding the prospect of environmental accidents and disasters like the ones used above can be compared with Baudrillard's and his notion of 'manufactured catastrophe', which somehow might be 'deliberate and experimental, triggered by our compulsion to generate something novel and marvellous', something 'which exceeds the nature which we have become so familiar' (Clark 1997: 79). Contemporary special effects driven disaster movies appear to promote Baudrillard's thesis; however, a more measured insight can be detected in the ostensibly cautionary ecological tales of *Jurassic Park* explored at the end of this chapter.

Threats to nature are transformed within the loose nomenclature of 'nature films' into human threats from nature as successful Hollywood films appropriate the potency of nature myths. Ostensibly the growth of nature disaster movies -as already signalled through a reading of *Titanic* in the opening chapter - can be read using Heraclitus's evocation of 'earth, air, fire and water' as the primary structuring elements of all natural eco-systems. This loose categorisation strategy is used to frame the readings that follow.

Disaster Movies (Water!)

Jaws and Waterworld

An 'unnatural' fear of the unknown is explored in Spielberg's seminal *Jaws* when the main protagonist, the newly-appointed Chief of Police Brody, in charge of an island community who has escaped from the grime of New York, reveals he also has a fear of water. *Jaws* serves as a prototypical nature text for later Spielberg films and, for many critics, the beginning of the 'high concept' successful blockbuster formula of film-making that dominated the latter end of the twentieth century. Derived from Melville's *Moby Dick*, the deep story in *Jaws* is not in the familiar, mythic story of the hero 'revitalising the civilised world by slaying the leviathan, but in the relationship among the male characters' (cited in Rushing *et al*. 1995: 83). Such relationship conflicts serve as a potent allegory of opposing methods and philosophies for dealing with nature and its aberrations.

An important mini-narrative within the film helps to frame the primary nature discourse of the film. Alone on the boat, filling time before the inevitable attack, the three men find time to reveal their past. Quint's story is by far the most revealing and is what Spielberg later asserted to be the most interesting aspect of the film for him, which, incidentally, was not in Benchley's[14] original novel. He tells the story about how he was a crew member of the ship which delivered an atomic bomb - the ultimate signifier of unnatural human potency. On the way home from their mission, they were attacked and their ship sank. Trying to survive in alien waters with constant shark attacks is effectively described by Quint's recounting of the incident. Soon their number was decimated as they floated in their supposedly lifesaving jackets - no wonder he refused to ever wear one again. This historical story, which can be allegorically read as nature's revenge against the 'unnatural' creation and use of the most destructive force ever developed, remains a potent back-story framing their current quest to destroy this 'natural' leviathan.

Extending a Jungian interpretation,[15] one can even read the shark as 'an over developed shadow', symbolising repressed (ecological) fears that an increasingly autonomous ego-consciousness would create. Such a reading echoes the ecological interpretation of *Titanic* in Chapter 1. Matthew Hooper, the biologist brought in to understand and capture the shark, implores Mayor Vaughan: 'What we are dealing with is a perfect machine . . . an eating machine. It really is a miracle of evolution. All this machine does is swim, eat and make little sharks and that's all' (cited in Rushing *et al.* 1995: 84). Hooper, who promotes technology while endorsing Ahab's awe for the power of nature, cynically remarks on the West's abuse of nature.

> It is the rich and famous who more often go 'back to nature' for it is they who can afford to buy their way out of a mechanised existence through expensive leisure activities . . . and a quest for the wilderness.

(cited in Rushing et al. 1995: 91)

Brody, the small-town sheriff caught up in this awesome struggle, has to learn both from the (pre-industrial) archetypal male hunter Quint and the 'weedy' scientist Hooper, while at the same time overcoming his fear of water. Not surprisingly, Quint truly hates sharks after his wartime escapades and becomes an outsider with apparent contempt for all. In many ways, he also represents a conventional rogue hunter who nonetheless remains exploitative of nature. Hooper, on the other hand, loves and respects sharks as 'miracles of evolution' and because of his family wealth can supply the latest technology to catch the shark which, predictably, proves to be of little use.

It is the least equipped and most fretful character Brody who finally kills the shark by blowing up an air canister in his mouth at the film's closure. In the final *mise-en-scène*, the two surviving heroes begin peddling their constructed life raft back to the shore after affirming their manhood and supremacy in their fight to remain at the top of the chain of life.

Kevin Costner's big-budget financial failure *Waterworld* (1995) continues to focus on water and addresses this 'monstrous nature' motif by imagining a possible future world ecological disaster with water levels rising as a consequence of global warming, resulting in human survivors having to exist in artificially created floating edifices. From an ecological perspective, the opening sequence in particular is one of the most effective visual signifiers of recycling of human waste ever captured on film. Our hero is first seen in silhouette from behind, urinating into a container, which is then poured into a machine that almost instantaneously recycles the impure liquid, allowing it to be safely consumed again. After washing his mouth, Costner pours the rest of the life-giving water on his 'precious' natural plant, which becomes a symbolic motif of the precariousness of life and natural growth.[16]

This narrative trope of nature becoming monstrous reaches its apotheosis with Spielberg's *Jurassic Park*, which is explored in detail later. Unlike more recent fleshed out ecological parables, *Jaws* does not attempt to transcend its generic roots and remains a primal horror text which rarely questions the supremacy of man over nature, much less attempts to understand the other. Nonetheless, the narrative cited above effectively provokes a critique of consumer capitalism and the eternal frailty and heroism of human nature, which is articulated in different ways in *Twister*.

Disaster Movies (Air!)

Twister (1996)

Since the wide open, flat planes of North America often provide little in the way of spectacle and scenic excess, natural phenomena such as tornadoes or earthquakes dramatise the landscape and create a focus of attention. Consequently such landscape becomes interesting and often 'excessive' from the perspective of the power of nature impacting on it. Focusing on the tornado belt in the mid-west or the San Andreas fault-line in California, which often produces dramatic earthquakes, the landscape becomes particularly resonant and fully alive when affected by such massive energy rushes.

Twister,[17] a relatively recent 'nature' movie, veers between a disaster sub-genre and an explicitly ecological road movie, which has attracted a particularly bad press. In a negative review for *The Observer*, Charlotte O'Sullivan wonders why the 'disaster genre' was so prevalent in the 1970s and suggests that this is due to

> political disillusionment with assassinations and cover-ups galore . . . Never mind problems within society, never mind the dwindling role of nature in our day to day lives -here characters assumed once more the famed heroism of America's pioneers, setting their wits against the age-old wicked witch of the north . . . Putting survival first . . . In *Twister*, the hurricane is neither neutral nor benign, with references made to its 'ugly face' . . . [and] despite the fact that the goodies are a bunch of Nirvana-lookalike hippies, there's no talk of ecological abuse - i.e. the dark side of human nature. For what *Twister* is in the business of promoting is a never-never land of timeless, home-grown wisdom. There's never any mention of social or financial depravation

(O'Sullivan 14 July 1996).

Such 'ideological criticism' has been similarly levelled at many science fiction, action/adventure dramas. But as suggested in Chapter 1, critics often collapse conservative ideological analysis of human nature with Hollywood's more pervasive mythical evocation of raw nature which can often signal a regenerative evocation of natural energies. Such apparently regressive representation and politics need not predetermine the effectiveness or even progressiveness of an ecological agenda expressed in such texts. While such evocations of 'nature' often remain a narrative ploy embedded in the background, I would again suggest that dramatic, even excessive foregrounding moments help to reveal aspects of nature which are often ignored by textual analysis and undervalued as a site of critical exposition. The use of natural sublime landscapes and directly 'unmediated' evocations of raw nature is becoming more successfully foregrounded within generic popular texts like *Twister*.

The pretext of the narrative involves attempts to get a piece of scientific equipment -significantly called Dorothy - directly up into the core of a twister so that it can measure its potency. The machine's name explicitly references the child protagonist in *The Wizard of Oz* (1939), who had to ascend through a twister into another world to find her true identity and achieve a rite-of-passage transformation. Unlike the exposition of nature in *Wizard of Oz*, which produced an allegorical magical/fantasy world that must in the end be curbed, *Twister* more directly affords raw nature an excessive potency which is not determined by human psychological expression, yet is nevertheless used to signify indexically the emotional experience of heterosexual love.

This is evidenced at the climax of the film when the struggling couple have to face the awesome horror of the twister together. To observe such sublime nature they tie themselves to a pipe that runs deep into the ground and await their fate. The illogicality of this survival strategy (like the fantasy of escape in *The Wizard of Oz*) 'works' on a mythic and romantic level and is not questioned by the internal logic of the narrative. The faltering couple both visually and metaphorically consummate their love by looking up into the heart/eye of the twister. As a result the lovers and audience are treated to the ultimate experience ('money shot') of a twister's sublime core hovering above, as it fully engulfs them. This 'natural' (SFX) confrontation is reminiscent of finally looking into the mouth of the shark in *Jaws*, which was only illustrated/fetishised by static reproductions in nature books. While filmic mediation must remain somewhat artificial, nevertheless such a simulacrum has found a way of mapping and mimetically recording nature's potency. With the visualising power of special effects, discussed in detail below, human agents can begin to experience the unpredictable energy of 'wild' nature.[18]

Whereas conventional blockbuster special effects often capture a multiplicity of extrasensory experiences, nature films use special effects to augment more natural phenomena, like tornadoes in this instance. Extended moments of visual excess in the film give primacy to the awesome power of nature within the holistic eco-system of planet Earth. This primacy helps foreground narrative engagement with ecological issues rather than allowing nature to be represented simply as an undifferentiated background or a foil to frame human intervention to act out a heroic narrative. The experience of witnessing active twisters remains the key pleasure of the narrative, which in turn induces an appreciation of the power, even the therapeutic possibilities, of such natural phenomena.

Like many recent disaster movies, *Twister* contains an impressive array of unmotivated skyscape-shots, which is rare in fiction films, compared to the more character and narrative driven Hollywood evocation of nature. Geoff King confidently asserts that there are two types of photography within such nature/disaster films: the airy and exhilarating long shots from helicopters supported by the use of an upbeat score and the more tightly framed action sequences (as in Jan De Bont's earlier action adventure *Speed*) - often using an unsteady camera to create an impression of being right there and at one with nature (King 2000: 23). While at first glance this is true of many 'nature' films, I would suggest that the effect of such camera-work is more aesthetically reflective and provocative than King appears to infer.

King's extensive analysis of *Twister* positions the film within a conventional American frontier tradition, which suggests that the dangers of such a natural agency have to be tamed if the pastoral tradition is to be secured. King affirms that 'the continued proximity, or possibility of the frontier remain necessary if the pastoral is to maintain its ideal middle position' (*ibid.*: 29). This can be illustrated by the way a simple opposition is constructed between the fleet of sleek black vehicles headed by the egotistical Miller who believes that his more powerful technology will finally tame the chaos of tornadoes, as opposed to Harding and his decrepit but individualistic entourage who treat the quest like a celebratory western hunt. Harding and his loyal band of fellow explorers, however, remain true to their scientific calling, accepting their role as servants and students rather than controllers of nature. While initially unwilling to accept his true calling, symbolised by his more 'civilised' romantic love for a 'human fertility facilitator', soon the exotic lure of raw nature and the latent heroic agency of his ex-girlfriend draw him back into the quest for knowledge and adventure.

Like a nurturing farmer, Harding particularly learns most directly from experience and can read nature's signs without the often faulty aid of complicated technological devices. Simply by sniffing the earth and observing the sky, he can intuitively predict much more about the impending twister than by using an array of scientific instrumentation. Nevertheless the *raison d'être* of the quest, as already cited, is to provide accurate scientific information of nature's chaotic movements so that humans can have greater warning systems to protect them from what Ulrich Beck affirms is nature's great risk. To acquire this information they must accept, understand and even empathise with the power of nature at its most extreme.

Incidentally, Jean Baudrillard reads such human fascination with disaster - if only as a simulacrum of a tornado - not as conscious worry over being usurped by the forces of nature but almost as a desire for such excessive force and chaotic agency. While chaos and unpredictability are endlessly signalled, the goal of scientific understanding is finally 'tamed' by being replicated and mapped on a computer. Classic Hollywood closure is achieved but, as we learn from the chaos theorist in *Jurassic Park* to be explored presently, life, much less nature, is seldom totally predictable.

Spielberg: Eco-Auteur

The Steven Spielberg phenomenon and corpus of work - including directing, writing and, increasingly, producing - remains for this author the most successful embodiment of nature and ecology on film. Because of his enduring mass appeal and engagement with broadly ecological issues, he has helped to consolidate a uniquely Hollywood range of representations of nature, while not always promoting ecological praxis. Spielberg and Lucas in particular have most successfully adapted the romantic articulation of the child as 'nature's priest' and have made careers out of childhood 'vision', extending the Disney project to produce the most commercially successful films in the history of the cinema.[19]

According to Robert Baird, Spielberg has shown 'unprecedented sophistication in creating film structures that anticipate mass, even global schemata protocols. In doing so he has been the foremost author of the modern blockbuster' (Baird 1998: 88). And while many dismiss blockbuster success as primarily a result of the sheer force of capital investment and mass marketing within the powerful imperialist Hollywood system, Baird correctly perceives them as 'a thoughtful anticipation of human cognition and emotion', often with some special effects 'breakthroughs'. He concludes that 'blockbusters are artful, intelligent, and globally successful when they make a spectacle of cognition' (Baird 1998: 88).

Above all other film-makers, Spielberg continues to divide critics, often in spite of his enormous popularity and growing influence within the blockbuster Hollywood apparatus, having almost single-handedly constructed the template for the contemporary form. Such a lofty status increasingly leads to vitriolic criticism like Kolker's in *A Cinema of Loneliness* (1988), who argues that the ideological structures of Spielberg's films:

hail the spectator into a world of the obvious that affirms that what the viewer has always believed or hoped is (obviously) right and accessible, and assures the viewer excitement and comfort in the process. The films offer nothing new beyond their spectacle, nothing the viewer does not already want, does not immediately accept. That is their conservative power, and it has spread throughout the cinema of the 1980s

(cited in Rosenbaum 1997: 98).

Alex Sharkey, in a review in *The Independent,* articulates a growing consensus concerning this supreme populist film-maker which particularly applies to *Jaws* and *Jurassic Park*:

Spielberg is not a good director in the conventional sense. His characters assume recognizable human attributes only when they are dramatically endangered. He seems unable to represent emotions other than the primitive staples of terror, awe and sentimental yearning for the nuclear family with its clearly defined relationships . . . but when he cuts to the chase, he is peerless; his genius is for triggering the fight or flight response. In the universal language of fear he is fluent and voluble

(Sharkey 14 August 1993).

Other critics are even more dismissive of Spielberg's actors' performances, describing them as 'screaming, staring and scampering' and 'about as sinister as Walt Disney'. Even Wayne Knight's 'villainous Nedry in *Jurassic Park* is a complete caricature: an obese, jabbering wreck', he is the computer expert who sets up the destructive drama by turning off the system to give him a 'window' to get out stolen embryos to a paying competitor. However, he 'gets his comeuppance as is normal in moralistic Hollywood fare'. The stereotypical lawyer is also despatched for leaving the kids alone to face the danger. But as in *Twister*, characterisation and rounded human agency may not always be an indicator of value or be relevant for discussion within recent special effects driven nature films.

Adam Bresnick, in the *Times Literary Supplement* review of Joseph McBride's 1997 biography of Spielberg, provides a most provocative critique: 'At the deepest level of fantasy, Hollywood would like to believe that it is essentially a philanthropy, that what it offers its mesmerised public is the gift of pleasure and, at certain exalted moments, the gift of consciousness itself.' But for Bresnick, Spielberg, and particularly his alter-ego Schindler, hide behind the fantasy of philanthropy (the salve of liberalism's bad conscience) where a 'gift, can be an absolute good' with little need for any moral/ political context. Bresnick pushes his argument too far, however, when he contends that philanthropy is the only representationally accepted and 'viable way of solving society's ills - whether they be Nazi Germany or post cold-war America' (18 July 1997). This issue of philanthropy and finding a balance between 'benevolent' entrepreneurship and 'ecological' ethics becomes a dominant thematic tension particularly embodied in the character of John Hammond (Richard Attenborough), the owner/creator of *Jurassic Park*. His ecological sensibility, I will argue, becomes most pointedly transformed through the original blockbuster and into its sequel.

Jurassic Park

Jurassic Park, until recently at least, has been considered as the second highest grossing film of all time and is specifically about 'nature'. Like a Disney meta-project, the island is a man-made world, planned out like a large landscape garden and controlled by a computer centre with the minimum of staff. Like Walt Disney, the founder of the greatest simulacrum American culture has ever produced, John Hammond, the fictional entrepreneur of *Jurassic Park*, also plays God with nature, controlling every aspect of its evolution.[20] But as one of the protagonists ironically affirms, *Jurassic Park* is very unlike the benign reordering of nature in a Disney theme park where the 'animals' do not bite back and economics control the space.

Patrick Murphy raises some interesting points that go beyond the usual simulacrum debates when he affirms that

> escapism is based on denying wild nature as an integral part of the biosphere at the world level and as part of individual character at the personal level. The denial of wild nature serves the fabrication of a timeless, universal and unchanging order, articulated in part by means of cultural values and generalization

> *(in Bell et al. 1995: 125).*

Murphy continues that in ecology we speak of 'wild systems' and places as part of a process, 'with its active manifestations contingent, indeterminate, and contextually particularistic, and thus continuous demonstrations of the principle of difference'. The Disney ethos, on the other hand, Murphy claims, promotes escapism from the indeterminacy of these 'wild systems' through denial of process and difference. This is helped by the relative primitiveness of the mimetic animation aesthetic that consistently displays 'static' depictions of nature. 'Both are based on androcentric hierarchies and dichotomies with women and nature objectified for the benefit of the male subject' (in Bell 1995: 125B6). Murphy further claims that the 'androcentrism' of Disney animation is both ideologically consistent, yet at the same time incoherent. The consistency resides in the objectification and subordination of life forms, while the incoherence resides in the philosophical justifications and ideological formations that naturalise them.

Even if this criticism does accurately reflect the Disney aesthetic, the accusation is much more problematic with regard to the Spielberg oeuvre, which I suggest has less ideological, and especially anthropocentric, baggage to contend with. Yet obvious comparisons with Disney are certainly foregrounded in *Jurassic Park* with the story set in a theme park, which is paradigmatic of certain sorts of sensory experience. It is a place where the entire environment is designed for kinetic consumption and the film is certainly self-conscious about this setting.

Whereas pre-industrial cultures encountered plagues and natural disasters (as in *Twister*) that were out of their hands, classical industrial societies also have to concern themselves with the spatiality and temporally circumscribed hazards of mass production such as synthetic forms of nature/pollution. As a result, Beck and many 'right minded' critics continue to claim that 'we' are entering a new order of 'undelimitable' accidents which are not spatially controllable, whereas Jean Baudrillard mischievously affirms that western society in particular encourages the 'manufacture of catastrophes'. Baudrillard goes on to suggest that the danger threatening the human species has 'less risks of default (exhaustion of natural resources, dilapidation of the environment, etc.) than risks of excess: runaway energy flows, chain reactions, or frenzied autonomous developments' (Baudrillard 1993:103). Baudrillard incisively suggests that such 'pre-programmed catastrophes' might be 'deliberate and experimental', 'triggered by our own compulsion to generate something novel and marvellous, something which exceeds the nature with which we have become so familiar' (*ibid.*: 103). *Jurassic Park* certainly appears to fit into this framework.

Almost echoing Freud's 'death wish' theory, Baudrillard concludes his ephemeral ruminations with an assertion regarding human nature's ultimate amorality; 'We greet the worst and best with the *same* fascination' (*ibid.*: 103, added emphasis). Such a sweeping critical appreciation, which particularly applies to popular cultural texts like *Jurassic Park*, appears convincing at the outset. However, I would take issue with its overarching contention which displays Baudrillard's preoccupation with the hyperbolic conclusion that often hides and displaces a more complex and opaque discourse.

Simulacrum and Special Effects

The 'primitive' simulacra and effects of seminal texts like *King Kong* do not appear to 'work' for contemporary audiences, weaned on increasingly mimetically accurate and interactive mediated stimuli. David Nye's inclusive notion of 'technological sublime' can also be applied to the ur-horror and monster movie *King Kong* (1933),[21] which is continually invoked in *Jurassic Park*,[22] by questioning creative human potency through recreating 'extinct' life forces while exposing and even promoting a cautionary tale of evolutionary interdependence. Foregrounded special effects are required to encourage audiences to gasp and wonder at their own insignificance with humility and gratitude, while at the same time marvelling at technological innovation *per se*.

Yet surprisingly, such effects are often scientifically inaccurate. Stephen Jay Gould in particular provides a fascinating 'historical' analysis of *Jurassic Park*, which remains critical of both the book and its subsequent visual blockbuster. His criticism does not stem however from a didactic historian's perspective but captures the lack of 'authenticity' in this mass media world in an early anecdote. Having once asked Crichton why he had placed Tyrannosaurus, a Cretaceous dinosaur, on the cover of the book version, the author replied with absolutely candour: 'Oh migod, I never thought of that; we were just fooling around with images, and that one looked good' (in Carnes 1996: 31-5). Unlike the apparent verisimilitude of representational forms, scientific or historical accuracy has little intrinsic currency in the 'make-believe' world of Hollywood.

Gould, together with critiquing the derivation of a dinosaur's name,[23] continues to cite two major errors in the text which reflect an insufficient recognition of nature's complexity, embodying the worst 'stereotype of science as a reductionist solution' to a real problem and further cites the potency of this 'witches brew' in western cultural texts. The first error is that the fictional expert in *Jurassic Park* asserts, without evidence, that 'organisms are discrete and indissoluble entities, not simple sums of (imperfect) parts' (*ibid.*: 33). Gould concludes that we must debunk the 'silly idea'

> that scientists are wizards who break totalities into little bits of chemistry and physics and then know the essence of the thing itself, thereby gaining the power to build it anew from basic constituents - shades of Hollywood's Frankenstein myth

(in Carnes 1996: 32).

The second 'big lie' Gould cites involves the stereotype of science and history:

> Man must not go where God (or Nature's laws) did not intend - technology transgressing boundaries of its legitimate operations. In other words they should not have created the dinosaurs and therefore must pay the price. Ian Malcolm (Jeff Goldblum) who 'plays the role of eco-conscience' chides the Capitalist entrepreneur John Hammond: 'The lack of humility before nature that's being displayed here staggers me ... dinosaurs had their shot and nature selected them for extinction

(ibid.: 32).

While such criticism remains valid, Hollywood films regularly end up simplifying 'nature' as well as 'history' and 'science', since it is driven by the need to promote a strong narrative which usually demands a form of linearity that promotes 'simple' cause and effect connections.

The isolation of ecological effects framed within an ethical discourse on the genetic manipulation of nature nonetheless remains the core back-story of the film. The use of technology to render nature accurate and believable becomes one of the greatest, all-time challenges to human ingenuity.

Eric Faden, on the other hand, suggests that Hollywood's contemporary 'assimilation of computer technology relies on control, synchronisation, and visualisation', whereas early computer imagery 'was largely shaped by those who equated technology and science with control and predictability'. In the digital age, cinema's spectacle becomes much more 'controllable' (Faden 1999: 70). Focusing particularly on *Jurassic Park*, which 'paints nature as eternally unpredictable and uncontrollable', ironically 'the film's formal construction suggests the opposite'. Indeed, 'nature' (at least the indexical signifier of nature) 'remains very much controllable, all the way down to the last pixel' (*ibid.*: 72).

At the outset it is somewhat disingenuous to dismiss such special effects, and the Spielbergian effect in particular, as simply reaffirming the ideological status quo by 'controlling' nature and human imagination as Faden suggests. While new technology is most certainly driven by economic imperatives, audiences often find ways to subvert their controlling ideologies, and philosophical and even ecological questions permeate the shiny veneer of many spectacular effects.

In computer-generated culture, 'the computer in-frames the world by making it absolutely available and manageable' (Wright in Robertson *et al.* 1996: 229). CGI (Computer Generated Imagery) helps to produce film exposition of otherwise unfilmable nature, such as the close-up representations in *Twister* discussed earlier, to become more 'normalised' and 'naturalised'. A major difficulty occurs, however, with simulating 'natural objects' like clouds, trees and even crowds, 'like the Lumiere crowds' that seem random but are 'also complex and repetitive'. In fact, a surprising majority of so-called 'invisible' special effects created, like the waves in *Titanic* or the chase sequences in *Terminator 2,* are designed simply to simulate and dramatise events in the actual world and save time and money. Only a small percentage of SXF are truly 'visible' and capable of rendering a conventional sublime sense of awe in audiences,[24] as with the ship in *Titanic*, the storm in *Twister*, the shark in *Jaws*, as well as the dinosaurs in *Jurassic Park*.

Many critics assert that such constructed dinosaurs remain zombies, albeit magnificent simulated bodies, which 'lack their own behaviour, their own will, their own drive for survival' (Kelly 1994: 402). This reading is also affirmed by O'Neill's anthropomorphic discussion, which concludes that the only viable 'nature' represented is 'human nature' (cited in Cohen 1996: 306). Such synthetic nature is unfavourably contrasted with the more problematic yet proactive agency within recent science fiction texts, to be explored in the final chapter, where so-called non-human agents help construct radical post-foundational ethical norms for humans as eco-sapiens.

Faden's final conclusion is that the 'synchronisation between apparatus and emerging technologies often results in the shift from spectacle to a self-effacing, invisible style' which 'produces a model detailing the trajectory from the introduction to the standardisation of such new technology which is very much reductive' (Faden 1999: 77). Vivian Sobchack, however, remains much more optimistic about special effects and confidently affirms that from the making of *Close Encounters of the Third Kind* (1977), special effects in mainstream science fiction 'have been transformed from signs of a rational and objective science and technology to representations of a joyous, and sublime intensity - thematically linking postmodern culture's new "detached", "free-floating", and "liberated" sense of emotional transcendence with the transcendental' (Sobchack 1997: 287-8). Combining special effects and live action, or at least prioritising between the historically accurate and the playful but sublime expression, has become a challenging prerogative for blockbuster texts which extensively use special effects and often contradictory notions of 'realism' (as explained by André Bazin, for example)[25] in the creation of their *mise-en-scène*. Yet all forms ostensibly endorse the goal of capturing a sublime evocation of 'nature', as in the analysis of *Twister* above. Sobchack's utopic assertion, I would contend, effectively negates Faden's reductive reading of special effects and explains how the narrative projection of such texts privilege the pliability rather than the fixity of such (simulated) images, while speaking directly to audiences within an ecological and ethical framework. This can be most clearly illustrated by the first encounter with the simulated dinosaurs in *Jurassic Park*.

After a number of pre-credit scenes away from the site of adventure and necessary for the film's exposition, various experts, including a financial agent, finally reach the island together with Hammond, the primary architect of the park. Music reaches a crescendo as the helicopter approaches sight of land and traverses the majestic shoreline, navigating its way into the inner secrets of the island. To reach the ground the helicopter has to directly descend, which dissects the landscape and effectively draws the audience down into the heart of this exotic environment. The descent is framed by a magnificent waterfall, which is conventionally indexical of a pristine environment as in *Emerald Forest*. Finally reaching *terra firma*, the experts progress in two Disneyesque jeeps conspicuously displaying the *Jurassic Park* logo across their bodywork. Driving through the lush pasture, the vehicles stop to 'enjoy the view'. The choreography of touristic pleasure leading to spectatorial pleasure or *jouissance* within the *mise-en-scène* begins, as the 'experts' get a firsthand, unmediated view of a fully functioning giant vegetarian dinosaur. Its sheer size is emblematic of dinosaurs' mythic potency -unlike the more viciously represented caged and unseen raptor in the opening sequence. Warren Buckland proposes that shots showing the humans and the digital dinosaurs interacting, as in this first encounter, are the 'digital equivalent of the long take and the deep focus shots praised by André Bazin for their spatial density and surplus of realism, as opposed to the synthetic and unrealistic effects created by editing' (Buckland 1999: 185).

Unlike the man-eater raptor, the vegetarian giant dinosaur is no threat as it consumes large quantities of vegetation, even unconsciously performing for its audience by standing up on its hind legs to increase its food gathering range. The expert witnesses brought in for their approbation can do little except regress to the awed wonder of children, who have their rationality and scientific world view knocked out of them, as they literally collapse onto the ground. Kneeling in such a reverent posture, they become hypnotised by the sublime vision as they gaze into the lake and observe herds of dinosaurs roaming about freely, signalling the collapsing of time and space to produce the ultimate (chronotope) nature reserve.

In conjunction with this often excessive use of special effects embedded within a mass appeal blockbusting film, it is surprising that Spielberg has been able to overlay his narrative to include a formal science lesson which effectively frames the spectacle. A history of DNA, dramatised by an animated mini-narrative, forms part of the educational element in the 'scientific park' and is reminiscent of 1950s science fiction texts which similarly allowed provocative and contentious ideas to be expressed through scientific monologues which underpinned the narrative exposition.[26] While such formal stylistic and almost distancing elements are considered acceptable for avant-garde texts, it is more unusual to find them embedded within an unashamedly commercial 1990s text. At the same time, the roller coaster narrative ride and excess of special effects are frequently slowed down by expositional group conversations serving to question the scientific ethos of the endeavour and its ethical and ecological motives. The Jeff Goldblum character as the 'chaos theory' expert in particular serves this function and represents the voice of non-scientific rationalism.[27] Framed by stereotypical 'intellectual' glasses, he embodies the antithesis of the action man, who is usually codified by physical prowess and (re)action capabilities. Instead, Goldblum espouses the powers of intellectual and incisive verbal gymnastics, which are provocatively expressed when he glibly concludes his outright dismissal of the park project early on in the film: 'What you call discovery, I call the rape of the natural world'.

Chaos Theory and Ecology

Chaos theory persuasively demonstrates that there are connections between everything and 'teaches us to accept that there will be periods of turbulence in life, but then a pattern will emerge. It teaches us to accept that we can't always be in control and centred' (Wright in Robertson *et al.* 1996: 227). Sobchack even suggests that chaos theory has become a conceptual metaphor for postmodernism, if not always a complementary one. She interprets chaos in terms of a desire to combine the ability to 'impose scientific order' on the world with a 'desire to transcend its physical limitations' and attain a kind of 'digital freedom by entering a mathematical space of infinite fractal depths' (Sobchack 1990: 229).

'There are only so many plot lines in literature - interaction between (classic Apollonian, Augustan) order and (Dionysian, romantic, irrational, chaotic) disorder which tends to occur in Literature (and film)'. By contrast, exclusive and absolute order and chaos fail to resonate 'with the way nature organises itself or the way human perception sees the world . . . Certain character types designed to embody the dynamic interaction between order and chaos, recur in art' (Hawkins in Robertson *et al.* 1996).[28]

Naturally Goldblum's character exposé of the potency of chaos theory is more in-depth in Crichton's covertly ecological novel.[29] Explaining the theory, Malcolm pontificates:

> We have soothed ourselves into imagining sudden change as something that happens outside the normal order of things. An accident, like a car crash, or beyond our control, like a fatal illness. We do not conceive of sudden, radical, irrational change as built into the very fabric of existence. Yet it is. And chaos theory teaches us . . . that straight linearity, which we have come to take for granted in everything from physics to fiction, simply does not exist. Linearity is an artificial way of viewing the world. Real life isn't a series of interconnected events occurring one after another like beads strung on a necklace. Life is actually a series of encounters in which one event may change those that follow in a wholly unpredictable, even devastating way

> *(Crichton 1991: 172).*

This critique of linearity also serves as a potent critique of 'realism' and the classic Hollywood narrative, to which Spielberg apparently subscribes. The film version, of course, uses a shorthand version of (eco)chaos thinking: 'A butterfly flaps its wings in Peking, the weather in New York is different' - the butterfly effect. Malcolm concludes that in spite of the precaution of ensuring that all the dino-animals are created female, he correctly predicts they will reproduce, adapting an ecological chaos theory/paradigm: 'life will find a way'.[30]

Gregory Bateson's seminal systems theory, which critiques the paradigm of survival of the fittest, defines how 'the unit of survival is organism plus environment'. We are learning by bitter experience that the organism that destroys its environment destroys itself.[31] As he regularly affirms throughout his writings, we must learn to think as nature thinks. This grand ecological theory and position is echoed by Malcolm's devastating critique of modern science when he preaches:

> Thirty thousand years ago, when men were doing cave paintings at Lascaux, they worked twenty hours a week to provide themselves with food and shelter and clothing. The rest of the time they could play, or sleep, or do whatever they wanted. And they lived in a natural world, with clean air, clean water, beautiful trees and sunsets. Think about it . . .

> *(Crichton 1991: 285).*

Crichton continues through the prophetic voice of Malcolm:

> But the earth would survive our folly. Life would survive our folly. Only we . . . think it wouldn't . . . If we are gone tomorrow the earth will not miss us . . . Let's be clear, the planet is not in jeopardy. We are in jeopardy. We haven't got the power to destroy the planet - or to save it. But we might have the power to save ourselves

> *(ibid.: 367).*

However, this potent critique of the western progress myth was not included in the film, which may signal the film adaptation's pedigree as a more light ecological text. In a perceptive essay, 'Paradigms Lost: Chaos, Milton and Jurassic Park', Harriett Hawkins concludes how the intertextual links implicit in the narrative correspond with the chaos theorist Ian Malcolm, who predicts:

> as anyone familiar with Milton's epic or the Book of Genesis could have foreseen - Hammond's Eden inevitably fails to behave as planned. In spite of all precautions, dinosaurs not intended to mate or escape, do both

> *(Hawkins 1995).*

The film's ethical position suggesting that humans should not mess with the natural and intended order of evolutionary progress is surprisingly paradoxical, since the revivified dinosaurs can beat any mammal in the park, including homo sapiens. *Jurassic Park* can easily be compared with the myth of 'Paradise Lost', together with the legends of Faust and Frankenstein. Its creative entrepreneur, John Hammond, also believed he could behave like God and was likewise headed for a fall, unlike the morally sanctioned practice and painstaking legitimate research observed at the beginning of the film. In the novel Hammond is devoured by dinosaurs of his own creation and is thus brought down by the chaos theory that Crichton uses as a metaphor for things as they really are. As in 'Paradise Lost', the God/father-figure survives the rebellions of his own creations.

'In the end, Adam and Eve leave Eden hand in hand as equals in humble knowledge of their mutual frailty and mutual need for each other in the chaotic world', realising they 'must henceforth live in' but remain 'unable to command' (Hawkins 1995). Consequently, ever since the Fall,[32] the image of eternal stability, even universal deep ecological certitude, invariably seems unappealing. Aesthetically, at least, human nature appears to embrace chaos and unpredictability. Conversely, however, the unrelieved portrayal of chaos in itself promotes the desire for order to reassert itself, like the seasons in nature which can be appreciated most clearly through the film's closure.

Jurassic Park and Closure

As the protagonists finally leave the hitherto idyllic island in a helicopter (reminiscent of the guilty flight from Vietnam), after having destroyed the atmosphere and natural environment, ecological messages and ethical positions are 'cognitively' signalled and framed for the audience as well as for the protagonists. The final helicopter's ascent casts shadows on the landscape below, echoing the first visualisation of the helicopter in the film which inadvertently re-buried 'authentic' research by scientists who cared nothing for glamour and celebrity. Screen time is provided for addressing a number of conflicting ecologically framed questions focused on both protagonists and, by extension, screen audiences. Unlike the mechanical bird which first arrives on the island, bringing with it 'the viruses of commerce, law, greed, power and self-deception, which flourish under the culture of Yankee imperialism' (O'Neill in Cohen 1996: 307), by the end of the narrative, as the remaining protagonists ascend out of the ecocidal nightmare, I would suggest colonial residues have been disrupted and more all encompassing ecological questions have come into focus both visually and thematically.

The main protagonist's specialist cognitive experiences have become radicalised by exposure to such an ecological experiment which negates the often forgettable fairground/fairytale ride or pleasurable simulacrum as defined by Baudrillard and embodied within much of the Disney oeuvre. The tool of special effects in the film allows audiences to grapple with evolutionary and interactive nuances of 'nature'. In particular, audiences can observe in the faces of the protagonists what they have learned and internalised as they are silently individuated by the final probing camera. As affirmed by Faden, such intimacy is very rare in SFX-driven films, since they often dramatise background perspectives over and above the foreground. Unlike the innocent gaze of the protagonists at the start of their adventure as they descend into the island, their final ascent registers firsthand experience and ethical knowledge of the primary laws of nature.

Yet Rajani Sudan continues to assert that the film's closure maintains a smug affirmation of patriarchal values with the two children on either side of the stereotypical unwilling parent figure. Now at last he has proved himself to be a worthwhile family man, Sudan affirms, much to the delight and satisfaction of the nurturing figure of Lauren Dern. For such critics the closing scene reinforces an ideological affirmation of conventional family values. Sudan goes further, however, and suggests that it also presents the 'white, middle class, educated American family not as a product of biological reproduction but rather as a successful survivor of competitive natural selection' (1997: 110). Throughout his essay, Sudan traces the marginalisation and otherness of the rest of the characters in the film who 'deserved to be destroyed' like the greedy Nerdy mentioned earlier. He even goes so far as to regard the 'female dinosaurs' as 'unnatural creatures' who proliferate 'like those legendary welfare mothers', and therefore have to be 'reconstituted' or 'destroyed' (*ibid*.: 114). Such an otherwise engaging reading degenerates into a crude ideological jump of the imagination which ignores the textual nuances and cues in the final mise-en-scène.

As the camera oscillates between their enclosed space and the outside ecocidal dystopia, framed by the sublime evocation of nature encapsulated through the same majestic waterfall in the background as the flight ascends, many questions remain foregrounded which are not as ideologically polarised as Sudan suggests. Audiences are at last drawn into close-up portraits of the human protagonists, after being preoccupied with the chase and the exotic otherness of the dinosaurs. This is reminiscent of many reflective moments in action adventure movies. Rather than ideological closure with all the loose ends tied up, which at first sight appears to be the focus of such a sequence, this mega-blockbuster allows a form of aperture to be created with major ecological questions concerning humanity's responsibility to its environment left provocatively unanswered.

This ecological and utopic reading remains at odds with the attitude taken by most critics like John O'Neill who endlessly affirm that major questions are not asked by Hollywood. 'Yankee culture knows no bounds to its pragmatism, and its pragmatism encounters no moral limit other than its own failure of nerve. Our culture does not let Nature speak to us - any more than it allows our science to correct our humanism to delimit our science.' In short, he finally affirms that 'the biototalitarianism of the new science totters upon the sublime of our disappearance as a species in favour of a programme or chip whose animation ends in our death' (1995: 308-9). O'Neill's dismissal of the dialogical role of popular culture to talk to itself and critique its own dominant meta-narrative is in many ways as reductive in its elitist didacticism and as deterministic in its logic as that which it strives to dismiss.

Yet the ultimate question remains whether or not the text promotes a coherent ecological message. Have the protagonists finally come to appreciate (together with the audience) the ecological message(s) encoded in the narrative, such as 'life finds a way'; or 'don't tamper with nature'? More negatively is the 'predatory' and capitalistic scientific enterprise sufficiently demonised and critiqued for audiences to appreciate the range of disparate messages embedded in the text. The final image of real majestic flying birds who metaphorically represent the mechanical human carrier, as they soar into the stratosphere achieving their ultimate life-affirming raison d'être, is at odds with the hyper-real, (SFX) genetically recreated, prehistorical birds within the body of the narrative. In the end, natural flight and mobility are valorised as the ultimate expression of transcendent self actualisation and freedom which will specifically frame the following chapter which focuses on road movies.

There is almost a match-cut with the mechanical helicopter and the 'real' birds as they soar into the light of the sun as the credits roll. 'Going into the light' remains a transcendent liminal stage often used within the Spielberg canon. While this metaphor remains underworked in the film and consequently lacks total conviction and depth, Sharkey's 'journalistic' critical conclusion in *The Independent* is compelling:

> Through the hubris of mankind, and our arrogant belief in our dominance over nature, these monsters have been given a second crack of the evolutionary whip! If they get the upper hand, we're finished. You don't have to be a deep-dyed millennial to recognise a particularly resonant metaphor; the narrative acts as a lightning rod for our fears and anxieties that will accompany us throughout the last years of this millennium

(Sharkey 14 August 1993).

Spielberg effectively avoids the Disney project of promoting a 'teacherly text'; nonetheless his film helps to promote a liberal ecological agenda. While *Jurassic Park* provokes several ecological issues, its sequel helps to clarify and consolidate a number of these debates more clearly and effectively and brings Sharkey's ecological metaphors to the fore.

The Lost World (1997)

Spielberg's sequel to *Jurassic Park* has received much negative criticism. Jonathan Romney described it as the 'closest Spielberg has yet come to making his own

Vietnam film'. It is a story about an 'over confident American military moving heavy firepower into a world that is unfamiliar to it and being outflanked by a far cannier indigenous force'. In the end, as in the original, Hammond makes a presidential style address to the nation, endorsing an ecological position that supports 'a new policy of non-intervention'. Romney correctly insists that it is not a 'political film' but merely uses and co-opts 'Vietnam iconography' in the service of Spielberg's familiar theme of 'benevolent responsibility'. The explicit application is used to underscore the thematic subtext, with Hammond having undergone a philanthropic conversion. We are shown 'saurians romping in blissful coexistence on their island utopia -an image that suggests a kitsch airbrushed painting on the cover of a Christian Science manual' (1998: 24).

Adam Bresnick is even more vitriolic, describing *The Lost World* as engaging with the oldest philanthropy of them all, parenthood. T. Rex is a 'better' parent than homo sapiens, for he never abandons his children even when big-time careers call. Bresnick ends his critique by worrying out loud that 'the scariest part is that millions will subject themselves to such clap-trap, all in the name of kicks and being part of the cinematic culture that rules the world's screens' (Bresnick 1997: 18). The narrative disruption, which initiates the need for a hunting expedition, certainly brings into focus this ideological theme concerning family values, which was also foregrounded in the original, and begins with an attack on an adjacent deserted island that remains symbolic of a utopian paradise for man's pleasure.[33] But here an illicit family picnic is followed by a young girl 'straying from the path' of her parent's supervision, providing an opportunity for 'unnatural' creatures to pounce.

Bresnick raises an important dimension of the text while at the same time endorsing the Marxist's most pessimistic prediction with regard to the pernicious effects of popular culture. Nevertheless, I would assert that the underlying utopian theme continues to tantalise an ever-present mass audience, even if the aesthetic 'performance' in the text is less effective than the original film. The Malcolm character (again played by Jeff Goldblum), who has to 'carry the film', has apparently lost his sharp scientific critical faculties, having been neutered by the scientific establishment. Having been discredited by the Ingen company, he is no longer the mouthpiece of critical chaos theory questioning the actions of greedy capitalists as they try to control the prehistoric beasts. They have apparently successfully undermined his critical faculties and natural instinct to whistle-blow on the ecocidal disorder perpetuated on the original island with its unnatural inhabitants. He appears a broken man, incapable of looking after his own daughter, much less aware of his girlfriend's dangerous expedition. Like a conventional melodramatic protagonist, he is reduced to responding to crises rather than having any predetermined sense of pro-active agency.

Similarly, the two other characters on the expedition sent to find his girlfriend noticeably lack altruistic motives, much less endorse conventional heroic ones. One was in some environmental organisation but unhesitatingly admitted that his primary reason for working there was because 90 percent of the staff was female and monetary reward was now his guiding motivation. The third member of the conventionally 'elite' expeditionary force is represented as an uninspiring cameraman.

The head of the hunting expedition (played by Pete Postlethwaite), however, is not interested in mercenary payment and only wants a crack at hunting the most famous 'hunter' in history - by the 'second most famous hunter', man. Like Ahab (as he is jokingly christened by others) or Quint in *Jaws*, he seeks the ultimate adversary, the great land-based leviathan. Only then can he achieve his destiny and affirm that he is truly 'alive', like all the great nature explorers. As suggested by Faden, these (anti) heroes believe that the human species needs to feel in control of nature, technology and their environment to feel fully alive, especially now that the Darwinian instinct to hunt for food has been all but abolished within the synthetic technological culture of western man.

The documentary cameraman provides spot advertising for Nikon (like the ironic display of dino-merchandise in the Disney-like shop), as he captures images of the majestic dinosaurs. 'The Pulitzer Prize is mine now,' he gloats as the 'money shots' are transfixed onto celluloid for spectatorial pleasure. But these high-tech communication and recording devices always appear to let the humans down, since several human agents unfortunately refuse to rely on natural instinct. As our benevolent and eager palaeontologist tries to observe and record the bonding rituals within the Rex family, an automatic rewind camera almost gets her killed when the 'objectified' (applying Susan Sontag's seminal thesis on nature photography) dinosaurs misinterpret the sound of the camera as a threat to their existence. Malcolm pontificates, through the clearest piece of 'scientific eco-speak', how scientists cannot observe and research a native habitat without affecting it in some way. This perennial ethical dilemma for humans has already been discussed through films like *Medicine Man* and *At Play in the Fields of the Lord*, and will become central to a reading of 'the Prime Directive' of *Star Trek* in Chapter 4.

The key motivating premise of the sequel, as with the original, is that all eco-systems are finely balanced and can easily be put out of synchronicity, even by the sound of a camera. While this benevolent and ecologically responsible intervention group merely wants to observe and scientifically analyse the island's unique species, it is their altruistic intervention which finally causes the eco-system to become dangerously unbalanced and destabilised, rather than the more intrusive, imperialist force of hunters who couldn't care less for the niceties of ecological balance and harmony.

Two contrasting *mise-en-scènes* illustrate this collision of agencies and their accompanying effect on the eco-system. The first is almost a critique, even a parody, of the hunt sequence in *Dances with Wolves* explored in the following chapter. Our heroes' and hence the audiences' focus for identification (using classic narrative conventional analysis of 'shot, reverse shot and opposing looks') are positioned in hiding on the top of a hill overlooking a long grass valley. Iconographically they are positioned like native Americans observing the 'unnatural' cowboys traversing the plain. Both stalked and exoticised, the dinosaurs in this instance extend their control and mark on the landscape as the hunt begins with the counter-invasion force. But instead of remaining distanced from the hunt, the spectators/audience becomes vicariously invited to join in the pleasure of the 'ultimate hunt' of an extinct range of dinosaur species. The camera swoops, dollies and tracks, matching the eye-line of the attackers, unlike the more individualised sublime excess first encountered in the original, when unadulterated awe and pure spectacle dominated the *mise-en-scène*.

The human hunters fulfil what is regarded as an innate hunter ritual, validating a hierarchical power structure with man at the top of the food chain and exhibited throughout hundreds of generations and cultures. But in contrast to *Dances with Wolves*, their hunt loses its mythic, symbolic and, most importantly, ethical validation, since the hunting and subsequent entrapment is solely executed for secular pleasure, serving no 'life giving' scientific purpose. The *modus operandi* of the original *King Kong* myth can no longer be sustained or, more importantly, legitimated within a post-colonial, ecologically sensitive late twentieth century western culture. Spielberg positions himself and the audience with his normative critical observers, who both metaphorically and literally maintain the high moral ground, serving both to critique the hunt while at the same time validating, if not legitimating, this form of kinetic excitement.

The cries of the otherwise long extinct creatures as they are unceremoniously captured is counterpointed and contrasted with the later reversal of this hunting motif. In the original, the opening horrific pre-sequel features a heavily fortified caged dinosaur with the audience only able to see a close-up of an eye and to hear angry animal sounds. The violent reality of hunters becoming victims is most cogently illustrated when the chief hunter is outwitted by the superior raptors and provides a foreshadowing of what is to follow.

Romney draws further correlations with the Vietnam war and how 'one hunter instinctively shoots a small dinosaur to provide it with a rationale, a blood lust, to learn to fear man (read American)' (Romney 1998: 24). There is in some ways a sense of ethical (natural) justification as the 'anonymous' invaders (mercenaries) become literally eaten alive by the unseen forces of the despoiled eco-system. From biographical inferences, Spielberg appears to admire the dinosaurs' purity of purpose in defending their young, compared to humans. In many of his films narrative conflict often begins with a lack of parental protection and support, evoking a quasi-conservative validation which many liberal critics find particularly objectionable.

The direct cause for the transformation of the hunt is a result of the white liberal guilt and the nurturing 'feminine' instincts of the scientists as they attempt to save the life of a young dinosaur almost as compensation for the outdated masculine discourse of the primal hunt. Nature has not learned to distinguish between contradictory motives and instincts within the human animal.

In many ways this climax dramatises its narrative role as a moralistic critique of the Darwinian evolutionary thesis within the framework of man's control over nature rather than as part of nature. Its provocative premise dramatises the hypothesis: what if dinosaurs survived the evolutionary chain and man had to face them in a final battle, who would finally survive?

John Hammond, the entrepreneur behind the theme park island, best symbolises the transformation between the two films, as Malcolm sarcastically asserts through the opening exposition. Four years on and he has become transformed from 'capitalist' to 'naturalist', having apparently learned the ecological lesson of the first outing. Dinosaurs should be allowed to live in their natural utopian environment without man's interference. Nevertheless, he still believes that a scientific expedition can be used to study the creatures in their natural habitat and learn from them. Such apparently altruistic goals are dismissed by the non-individualised board of governors who relieve him of his responsibility. These spectacled (grey) men in suits not only provide the money but endorse the more regressive, non-utopian vision of an 'internal Disneyland' with panoptical control and surveillance right in the heart of an American borderland city, San Diego. They even pontificate on why Americans should not have to travel to a remote island to witness the greatest freak of nature.

Reaffirming the outdated imperialist notion of control and ownership evidenced in *King Kong*, Spielberg demands that this dystopic vision and capitalist venture must backfire. The dominant liberal western discourse no longer accepts old-fashioned zoos, no matter how 'progressive' they are with regard to interactivity and engaging with nature. Consequently this voyeuristic vision must be scuppered at great cost to the modernist coded city; as cars, buildings and other symbols of urban civilisation are destroyed. But as the newly transformed aqua-Leviathan wrecks excessive havoc, its biological instinctive motivation simply involves saving its offspring, like any 'good' protective parent.

Hammond's final coda, which ends the film, is significantly reduced to preaching through the medium of a television screen,[34] rather than cinematic dreaming. At last the benevolent philanthropic 'naturalist' pleads for acceptance. 'Leave them alone, they do not want us humans to bother them', he implores. He ends with the continuing mantra 'life will find a way', which becomes as over-codified and potentially meaningless as the Star Wars tag line 'may the force be with you'. The contradictory instinctual human animal enjoys both vicarious hunting and bloodlust together with more altruistic nurturing and caring manifestations within humanity. The command to respect and, even more problematic, to 'ignore' the exotic unmanned island where such exciting creatures exist does not seem possible for a human species which has historically embodied and endorsed both scientific and natural exploration and conquest.

Even the mimetic potency of special effects and the conviction of the Spielbergian magnetism remain finally shallow, reduced to preaching on a television screen. The generic framework of conventional science fiction together with its endorsement of special effects, rather than the more obvious 'nature' genre, is, I will argue in the final two chapters, more effective in promoting and representing deep ecology. But before these can be addressed, we turn to westerns and road movies, which effectively explore the close correlation between human agency and the struggle to find ontological meaning through travel, thereby affirming their coexistence with and in nature and landscape.

Notes

1. In an earlier version of this chapter a case study comparison was made between Peter Weir and Spielberg as contrasting eco-auteurs. But owing to space and the Hollywood focus of the book, this had to be dropped. In particular, Weir's use of landscape, both in his homeland Australia and in America, alongside his endorsement of ecological agents, plays a major role in, for example, *Witness* (1985) and *Mosquito Coast* (1986).

2. However, it must be recognised at the outset that while the aim of linking ecology and romanticism 'looks appropriate', it can 'easily oversimplify both' (Pite in Bate 1996: 357).

3. But, as William Cronon affirms, Turner's frontier achieved its end: 'by erasing its true (narrative) subject . . . The heroic encounter between pioneers and "free land" could only become plausible by obscuring the conquest that traded on people's freedom for another's. By making Indians the foil for its story of progress, the frontier plot made their conquest seem natural, commonsensical, inevitable. But to say this is only to affirm the narrative's power . . . in its ability to turn ordinary people into heroes and to present a conflict ridden invasion as an epic

march towards Enlightened democratic nationhood, it perfectly fulfilled the ideological needs of its late 19th century movement' (Cronon 1992: 1352).

4. Not surprisingly, the biblical name for a garden in Hebrew is 'Eden' and signifies 'a place of delight', which validates an ambiguous dichotomy between what can broadly be delineated as ecological forces (rural/nature) and apparently oppositional evolutionary forces (urban/culture) in western society.

5. The 1994 version directed by Ron Hardy appears to lack any 'real' political/historical context, unlike the post-war original. Instead, kitsch sunsets and petty rivalries between farmers frame a 'rites of passage' narrative of a misplaced boy 'becoming a man' by learning to kill his pet deer.

6. This motif is echoed in many popular cultural texts - most notably *The Deer Hunter* (1978).

7. Wilderness, Leopold argues, was not just fun, but maintained the opportunity for successive generations of Americans to acquire the characteristics of pioneers and to acquaint themselves first hand with the conditions that shaped their culture. While nineteenth-century Romantics and Transcendentalists sensed the unity of the natural world and related it to the presence or reflection of divinity, they often 'regressed' into sentimentality and spiritualism; ecologism, on the other hand, promoted a more (pseudo-) scientific critique of nature and man's abuse of wilderness (Nash 1982: 189B94).

8. Denis Duclos suggests that the reason Boorman's career never really took off (his only two relative successes were *Excalibur* (1981) and *The Emerald Forest* (1985)) is because 'he is too frank in affirming the heroic and apocalyptic meaning of a theme that is central in Nordic literature and simultaneously in approaching the dangerous zone of extreme right-wing fantasy' (Duclos 1998: 36).

9. This is an ecological issue which causes no small amount of controversy, even in the affluent West, with more and more roads being built through the forests and other areas of 'natural beauty'. Consequently, such films do not simply appeal to (historical) colonial guilt but to contemporary eco-problems in the West's own backyard.

10. Both texts represent a totalitarian environment, where the forces of oppression constantly thwart the creative individual who is attempting to produce medical relief or happiness for society. While Robin Williams, as teacher and poet, attempts to instil a sense of aesthetic magic in his students in an otherwise cold and even repressive educational environment of his boarding school, Connery also shuns western materialism in his quest for a universal cure for cancer. The romantic poetry explored in *Dead Poets Society* emphasises this egalitarian, liberal humanist attitude towards nature. It must be questioned, however, whether the truly revolutionary project initiated by the Romantic poets became primarily nostalgic in the new medium of the twentieth century.

11. The anthropologist critic Kay Milton provides a more problematic critique of these commonsense eco-utopic assumptions implicit in such films by affirming that one of the clearest messages that anthropologists can give to environmentalists is that 'human beings have no "natural" propensity for living sustainable with their environment'. Milton continues that so-called 'primitive ecological wisdom is a myth' and 'dams built by humans are as "natural" as ones built by beavers' (Milton 1996: 222). This apparent apologist rationale for human intervention in nature appears to scupper the primary oppositions between nature and culture, particularly in such overtly light eco-texts, by effectively breaking the idealistic illusion of the harmonious evocation of nature on which many Hollywood nature films are constructed.

12. Shamanism is a worldwide practice in which the spiritual interrelationship of the earth with other worlds forms an interwoven fabric of physical and psychic being, affecting all forms of life, both seen and unseen.

13. Nevertheless his prognosis regarding inherent risks to society has achieved consensus within critical discourse. Slavoj Zizek, in *The Sublime Object of Ideology*, questions what he sees as the 'fundamentalist' attitude of 'New Left politics' which (as interpreted by Timothy Morton) since the late 1960s has advocated women's rights, civil rights and ecology along with traditional left politics but 'which succeeded in ghettoising its area of concern' and even toyed with 'extreme right-wing forms of expression'. Nevertheless, even Zizek in 'Tarrying with the Negative' has qualified his opinions, suggesting that ecology's impact will 'sap' our 'unconscious belief in the big Other of power, since events like Chernobyl have rendered "obsolete" notions such as national sovereignty' (cited in Bate 1996: 429).

14. Incidentally the author has subsequently become an ecological campaigner for the protection of sharks and remains somewhat guilty of producing what he considered to have been a negative representation of the species in his best-selling novel.

15. Because of its specialised address, Jungian theory has remained outside the terms of reference of this study. Nevertheless, this form of investigation is certainly fruitful for many of the mythic texts examined.

16. Costner's enemies are scavengers, as in *Mad Max* (1979), who abuse and over-consume scarce fossil fuels, especially oil, with little regard for the future. They are searching for the Holy Grail of dry land, presumably so that they can continue to manipulate the ultimate precious natural resource. Not surprisingly, their crude characterisation remains 'uncivilised' but not the valorised otherness of native Americans. Instead, they remain uncouth in every way, which is even evidenced inter-textually by their ship's name, the *Exxon Valdez*, calling to mind a notorious contemporary pollution disaster. Costner becomes embroiled in their mercenary quest and as a consequence has to protect a (proto)typical family from their common enemy. He remains, however, a true outsider, who is later confirmed in his pre-human powers to swim underwater by acquiring the physical attributes of a fish, including gills and webbed feet.

17. Other, much inferior, 'nature' movies include *Dante's Peak* (1997), which focuses on the 'second most popular place to live in America - for towns under 20,000'. Playing off well-established conventions of the genre - more tightly exposed in films like *Jaws* - nobody wants to be a whistle-blower, until it is too late.

18. Unlike *Jaws* in the 1970s, *Twister* privileges 'natural' special effects over character. The cardboard cutout protagonists are merely a pretext, which helps to over-determine the exposition of dramatic raw nature at its most sublime. The elemental 'cinema of attractions' has turned full circle from its primitive roots at the beginning of cinema's short history and has again become central to its popular appeal. Moments of sublime visual exposition help resonate with the power and majesty of nature. Such representation of nature could be as potentially progressive as, for example, Reggio's much lauded eco-documentaries, while not having the aesthetic panache or purity of his masterpieces *Koyaanisqatsi* (1983) and *Powaqqatsi* (1988). More commercial image-making can also have 'its own life form unanthromorphised, unrelated to human beings' (MacDonald 1993: 140).

19. Torben K. Grodal, in a psychological evaluation of cinema, is particularly scathing when he suggests that Spielberg often embeds his remakes of 'naive' action films in 'pastiche' forms in order to enable the adult viewer to overcome a blend of 'childish' fascination and adult rejection of the emotions encoded in the fictional pattern. Whereas more ambitious 'realist' directors would try to put 'layers of random events and items on top of the narrative pattern', and thus simulate a 'real-world' situation while also having to accept a 'decrease in sequential directedness' (Grodal 1997: 229).

20. Hammond, played by Richard Attenborough, the grand old man of British film, is much more positively conceived than in the book, where he is a 'misguided idealist, guilty of thinking instead of feeling, not a greedy capitalist' (cited in *The Independent* 18 July 1993).

21. Donna Haraway has argued that the narrative of race and evolution has come to be placed increasingly upon the figure of the anthropoid ape. *King Kong* takes this 'a stage further by creating the perfect ethnographic monster. Stuck in the past, doomed to die, Kong is pure simulacrum' (Ront 1996: 188).

22. The hauntingly memorable 'dawn of creation' effects with the lighting, jungle and foliage designed for the primeval island in Merion C. Cooper's original film version of *King Kong* (which was acknowledged as a major cinematic precedent for *Jurassic Park*. The overall influence is made explicit when Ian Malcolm, approaching the giant gates that guard the park, quips, 'What have they got in there? King Kong?') (Freer 2001: 208).

23. Gould begins his critique by clarifying that the word 'raptor' does not mean 'bird of prey' as the palaeontologist Alan Grant initially states. (In fact, 'raptor' comes from the Latin rapere, meaning to seize or to take by force. Later zoologists borrowed the word as a technical name for large carnivorous birds.) Making a classic semiotic explication, he concludes that the

representation 'is not the reality, though audiences can view only through representation and there's the rub'. Such an observation helps to provide an example of the primary conflict between historians as forensic scientists and that of cultural theorists who must implicitly appreciate the potency of representational forms.

24. Sean Cubitt, in an introduction to a special summer issue of *Screen* that focuses on special effects, speaks of how 'the beautiful is ephemeral but the sublime points towards eternity'. Beauty 'alludes to loss -ecological frailty . . . (whereas) the sublime however, from the early films of Méliès and Phalke, points towards a time beyond the mundane, a post-modern time' (Cubitt 1999). Warren Buckland's essay 'Between Science Fact and Science Fiction' ostensibly seeks to prove what can be regarded as an obvious observation that *Jurassic Park* functions within a 'possible world' -the model extension of the actual world (Buckland 1999: 177). He goes on to pontificate that the film goes 'beyond spectacle' by 'employing special effects to articulate a possible world' (*ibid.*: 178).

25. Bazin suggests that there are three types of realism in the cinema - ontological, psychological and dramatic - which demand as little camera trickery and intervention as possible.
1) Ontological realism restores to the object and the decor their existential density, the weight of their presence.
2) Psychological realism brings the spectator back to the real condition of perception, a perception which is never completely determined.
3) Dramatic realism refuses to separate the actors from the decor, the foreground from the background (cited in Buckland 1999: 186).
For Bazin, all three types of realism are achieved via the long take and deep focus because these techniques maintain spatial unity.

26. In Ian Freer's highly informative journalistic study of Spielberg's canon, he affirms that it was Spielberg himself who came up with the way of presenting the 'technical gobbledegook surrounding DNA extraction and cloning' and make it 'believable' (Freer 2001: 210).

27. This role is coincidentally repeated in *Independence Day*. His character even extends his affirmative 'green' credentials by literally cycling into his workstation in a television studio. His opening dialogue helps to chastise a colleague for not using well-marked recycling bins for waste. Later, when the stakes gets much bigger, he helps save the world by relaying a virus to the aliens about to destroy human life, thereby avoiding a descent into nuclear retaliation.

28. 'Chaos theory originally grew out of attempts to make computer models of weather in the 1960s. Weather is a big complicated system, namely the earth's atmosphere as it interacts with the land and the sun. The behaviour of this big complicated system almost defied understanding . . . Scientists learned . . . weather prediction is absolutely impossibe' (Crichton 1991: 75). Yet, incidentally, this remained the uncontested goal in *Twister*, discussed earlier.

29. Joe Sartelle in an essay on *Jurassic Park* suggests that 'the role of Malcolm's chaos theory in the

novel is to serve as a mediating term between capitalism and nature: it reinterprets social forces as natural forces' (Sartelle 1993: 3).

30. Gleich, however, believes that chaos theory could undermine ecology's most enduring assumptions, which are based on a simple sense of equilibrium. Traditional models are betrayed by their linear bias. Nature, he demands, 'is more complicated. All simple deterministic systems could breed complexity . . . systems too complex for traditional mathematics could yet obey simple laws . . . the task of all (scientists and even cultural analysts) is to understand complexity itself' (Gleick 1987: 307-315).

31. As was convincingly expressed in the 'Cybernetic Explanation' in Steps to an *Ecology of Mind* (Bateson 1973).

32. John O'Neill, in an unsubtle critique of the film, 'Dinosaurs-R-Us: The (Un)Natural History of *Jurassic Park*', affirms how the film is 'actually a repetition of the biblical story of "man's" nability to repeat the Divine creative act. This time the agents are Science and Commerce, or Knowledge and Greed, and what is violated by their monstrous desire to clone Nature is fuzzy logic, or the law that any total system must generate chaos' (cited in Cohen 1996: 293). While one must agree with his overall argument - like the way critical theorists misconstrue the primary pleasure of popular culture -O'Neill appears to miss out on its sophistication. By dismissing the movie 'in JP, America can celebrate its emptiness as depth' (*ibid*.:297), he refuses to see, much less appreciate its 'excessive potency'.

33. It was a similar island (Galapagos) which was 'naturally' controlled as a result of its distance from the mainland that Darwin in 1835 described as paradise. Furthermore, he conceptualised from this place a coherent view of natural selection while his crew described the same vision of nature as hell, observing the unusual volcanic landscape and strange lizards, etc. (see television documentary Wild Island, Channel 4, 28 July 1997).

34. Spielberg has always shown revulsion towards television as a medium for its insubstantiality and often its mediocrity, as is most clearly evoked in *Poltergeist* (1982), which he did not direct but in which his influence was pervasive.

3 WESTERNS, LANDSCAPE AND ROAD MOVIES

Prologue

Following on from the overview of 'nature' films which explicitly foreground ecological issues, this related chapter deals specifically with a few seminal westerns and a number of thematically linked road movies. Beginning with *The Searchers* and *Dances with Wolves*, the analysis of these films helps to focus attention on the growing preoccupation with native Americans as a source of ecological agency. Movement and travel, in particular, remain a central preoccupation of American culture. The western and, by extension, the road movie, provide an essential site for ecological exploration, since these generic structures demand spatial and philosophical exploration of the human species and their role on the planet. In particular, landscape and the uses and abuses of it provide the feeding ground for much narrative construction. While it must be accepted that there is little overt reference to the politics of ecology, issues like 'man's' legitimacy to own and control the landscape, coupled with an innate urge to explore the human psyche, which involves appropriation of the natural world, remain prevalent and constitute important covert evidence of the genre's ecological antecedents.

From the 'adolescent' narcissism of *Easy Rider*, which endorses the 1960s countercultural belief in questioning preconceived notions regarding nature, to the feminist evocation of rebellion in *Thelma and Louise* and the more 'mature' expression of liberal agency in *Grand Canyon*, closure and sublime spectacle are foregrounded to help promote deep ecological expressions of 'oneness with nature'. These therapeutically fulfil a deep desire within contemporary western culture. The characteristics of tourism and travel/pilgrimage will be used to foreground the potency of such sublime spectacle that punctuates the closure of these road movies. Such travel/pilgrimage becomes most elegiac, however, in *The Straight Story*, which is not just predicated around extended moments of closure but permeates the whole film.

American Indian Otherness and Ecological Agency

Drawing on social anthropological concepts developed by Mary Douglas (1966), outsiders can be defined as those groups who do not fit dominant models of society and are therefore seen as polluting (Sibley 1995: 120). The American Indian 'other', in spite of remaining firmly in the background within the dominant

Hollywood genres, has nonetheless become a primary focus for progressive ecological values. Instead of polluting the dominant culture, these representational agents came to be seen, particularly by white liberal Americans, as saviours who present a more natural relationship with the environment.

Gerry Mander suggests in *In the Absence of the Sacred* that westerners fear, hate and revere native Indians because they are what must be repressed in order 'for us to function as we do' (Mander 1992: 214). The native American has come to embody and symbolise a progressive form of ecological agency. This is crudely reflected in Mander's list of binary opposites which characterises dominant 'white' or 'technological' people, as he calls them, as embodying all that is socially deficient and ecologically suspect.[1] The myth of the 'noble savage' Indian who lived 'at one with nature' became appropriated by the ecology movement as an antidote to the enormous threat of industrial pollution.

To foreground these debates through representations in Hollywood, it is fruitful to trace some of the many cross connections between the primary American genre of the western and the more recent genre of the road movie. As a genre, the western is based around the opening up of the American frontier and is thematically preoccupied with the general ideological and symbolic transformation of the 'desert' into the 'garden' in a tension between 'eastern' and 'western' values, often dramatised by legal struggles over property and possession. The western narrative embodied travel through landscape in an attempt to create a new American template for civilisation. But while the western heroes rode their horses and wagons and later used railways to traverse the 'barren' inhospitable landscape, road movies often emulated and sometimes reversed this imperialist linear movement.

John Ford embodies this western ideal. In his extensive use of Monument Valley he recognised in nature the true romantic spirit of adventure. Out there, men could 'be themselves' and act out their true masculine selves. This remains a central thematic trope in many of his films, within the constraints of what can be described as 'feminine' social values. These values tend to be defined negatively, as the need to curb individual freedom and encourage settlement within a prescribed quotient of laws and controls, which are continually being imposed. Ford particularly focused on proud male behaviour and how it reflected the ever-present revenge narrative. Outsiders like John Wayne were needed to protect the newly-developing communities from selfish greed and sometimes downright evil, which was forever lurking in the background. But the hero's unwillingness to submit to societal norms meant he was compelled to journey back into the wilderness/desert where he could again become a free agent within nature.

Alongside human agency, the desert in the typical (Fordian) western is also rarely devoid of ideological significance or empty of meaning. Romantics, as discussed earlier, have always looked to landscape to gain inspiration for 'political' utopias. The western incorporated this aspiration in particular by addressing key political/ethical questions regarding what constitutes society and how it should be protected. This is achieved by foregrounding a few iconic, elemental symbols like the sheriff's badge to dramatise the 'need' for law and order, the *mise-en-scène* of the saloon to dramatise the play between libidinal desire and stoic dignity, maybe even a hanging tree to symbolise the ultimate deterrent and, quite often, a barber shop to wash away the (symbolic) 'impurity' of outside nature. Western iconography, as found in Nathaniel Hawthorne's symbolic red letter motif in the *Scarlet Letter*, metaphorically serves as an elemental morality tale involving social and ethical behaviour, which dramatises the polarity between individual needs and public requirements for controlled social conduct.

The primary question that must be addressed is how westerns expose and explore explicitly ecological issues. The audience is certainly positioned to engage and identify with the freedom and excitement of traversing large, environmentally pure spaces. Often in westerns, as the camera draws back, revealing the mediated point-of-view, the audience becomes aware that it is sharing its privileged vantage point of a magnificent landscape with the 'savage' Indians (which is reminiscent of the hunter in a nature documentary), who pose a lethal threat to the lone outsider. The beauty and innocence of the landscape, as it is first presented to the spectator, becomes subsumed by a secret knowledge which cannot be shared with the central protagonist. Consequently the landscape becomes transformed into a site of danger and terror.

This division between the so-called primitive otherness of the native and the white westerner can be appreciated on reading *The Savage Mind* (1966) by Claude Levi-Strauss, who attacks the common notion that modern civilisation is necessarily more cultivated than 'primitive' societies. Modern life is not a sophisticated version of a simple life; it is an altogether different life, based on an entirely separate understanding of the world. Indeed, according to Levi-Strauss, 'savage' peoples with their highly elaborate knowledge of terrain, flora, kingship and ritual, may live a more complex life than so-called advanced civilisations. Such natives consequently can represent and embody a more positive ecological understanding and awareness of the earth's environment.

Whether such polarised representation questions the dramatic evocation of beauty and the romantic nature of this alien territory or simply validates it is difficult to resolve. In many respects westerns have similar trajectories to the nature documentary with various flora and fauna particularised and individuated, only to dramatise in graphic detail the unresolvable and ever-present threat these organisms face in the eternal survival struggle. Each organism is both threatened by and in turn threatens other organisms in a continuous natural cycle within the food chain, leaving this representational eco-system dramatised for human empathy and pleasure. But the western male hero in particular considers himself at the apex of all other species and is often unwilling to accept his symbiotic relationship with all other life forms, including racially othered humans. Consequently, while nature documentaries are constructed as overtly eco-narratives, many fictional westerns can also be read and de-constructed as fictional nature stories, exploring the interrelationship between humans and other sentient beings. In particular, as outlined by Mander earlier, westerns dramatise conflicts between different tribes and pigment types of the same human species, who have often oppositional ethics and values regarding the primary eco-system.

While the American Indians are more usually represented as the hunted prey, such natives might more accurately be appreciated as the 'natural' owners of such a landscape. Being the first to inhabit the landscape and, more importantly, having helped to built up a complementary rapport with the eco-system, they, at least mythically, in spite of contradictory evidence, created a balance and harmony between humans and landscape. Consequently, the Hollywood native representational man/woman has remained symbolically more ecologically harmonious within the landscape compared with the white colonial cowboy hero. Contemporary ecologists believe the new settlers destroyed this balance, with their symbols of progress, like the train, cutting through an unspoilt landscape[2] or the even more destructive western notion of property ownership, which allowed land to be fenced off and protected.

It would of course be an exaggeration to read pre-1960 westerns as castigating the alien landscape and its Indians with their 'irrational' wish to keep the desert 'pure'. Nevertheless, 'oppositional readings' of most early westerns are difficult to find, much less those which eulogise the 'lost innocence' of native Americans and the need for a predominantly white audience to be 'at one with nature'. In the crudest terms, institutionalised racism legitimised such misrepresentation. The American Indian conception of homeland, which evoked a harmonious relationship with nature, was seldom validated and was more often marginalised or dismissed within the dominant white culture. They were continually stereotyped as the 'savage' or, at best, exotic 'red devils' that must be defeated before the forces of civilisation could be fully activated. All too often they were further misrepresented as like the ubiquitous herd of buffalo: dangerous, and even stupid, when charging *en masse*, as they circled around the enclosed wagons.

Consequently, while the filmic American Indians were pejoratively represented as either skulking behind natural protection, just waiting to pounce, or otherwise circling around wagon trains on their horses, the colonising cowboy seemed to traverse landscape in a straight line, unafraid and ready to face all obstacles head on. This concentration of linear motion and progress, and not accepting the necessity to negotiate the natural terrain of the landscape, also reverberates throughout the road movie genre. Landscape is frequently reduced to a space which must be traversed in the shortest distance and time possible.

Desire for more sophisticated images of the other (as the native American and other marginalised categories began to be called within academic circles) became more prevalent from 1960s onwards. In 1960 the Oklahoma state legislature passed a resolution condemning network TV for the treatment of indigenous people, claiming many TV programmes continued to stereotype them as bloodthirsty, marauders and murderers (McDonald 1985: 126).

Many attribute this apparent transformation to America's failure in the long-running Vietnam war, where the enemy was also represented as uncivilised wimps who had no real weaponry, an essential precondition of western virility. The American army with its massive and extensive bombardments was unable to defeat this elusive enemy, which in turn subverted the western imperialist myth that asserted that if you had a gun and if you could shoot faster than your opponent, then this would win the day. Many veterans of the war spoke of the disparity between such western myths that they grew up with and the awful (un)reality of the war. In the real political mess of Vietnam, as numerous 'grunts' witnessed, native enemies could not easily be defeated, aided as they were by a dense forest eco-system, which also conspired against the imperialist intruders.

The Searchers

Such a humiliating defeat was having a profound effect on the normally jingoistic Hollywood fraternity and was allegorically evidenced by John Ford in his seminal film The Searchers (1956), which explored the often contradictory nature of 'man' and his capacity to sink to the depths of primitivism. This theme became a dominant trope in future war films, most notably in Coppola's Vietnam masterpiece Apocalypse Now (1979), which adapted Conrad's novel Heart of Darkness to explore the subconscious disease of corruption within all colonialists' souls. This preoccupation was succinctly dramatised in filmic terms through The Searchers, most especially when Ethan Edwards (John Wayne) is forced to realise that he is no better than his 'savage' enemy, Scarface. Such a revelation was most traumatic for a character who was otherwise the quintessential embodiment of the western hero. After the forced servitude and enslavement of his niece within the American tribal Indian culture, the hero sets out on a long quest to reclaim her back for his own people. But when he finally succeeds in capturing her, he almost kills her himself, claiming she was 'tainted' by the Indian 'primitives'.3

Ethan Edwards becomes the mirror image of Scarface, having already 'scalped' to take revenge on his enemy. A dominant fear concerning Indians centres on the corrosive infiltration of the 'purity' of the American gene pool. Fortunately, Ethan can finally stand away from the brink and reclaim his common humanity, by reaccepting his niece back into the family. In the end, however, the film avoids the dilemma of choosing between the so-called 'civilised' and the 'primitive' nature of native Americans. In any case, audiences could not accept John Wayne, the icon of the ultra-moral western genre, descending to cold-blooded murder of his own flesh and blood.

At last the western genre radically confronted the awesome potency of the outsider or other in western culture. Ford concludes his narrative with Edwards who must again accept his outsider's nature/agency and renounce 'civilisation' and the communal comforts he helped to create and ride back into the wilderness. He becomes no different than the Indian he has spent so long fighting, with the roles of hunter and predator radically reversed. The enemy is no longer simply projected onto the wilderness but also becomes potentially embedded within 'western' (human) nature. Only by making this dramatic shift could the western myth begin to address the radical potentiality of wilderness and ecological discourses. The guilt of the protagonist's white imperialist agency has finally become othered, aided by his long, vengeful quest which forced him to endure a wide range of climate changes over a long period of time. While ostensibly being driven by revenge, like all individuals' mythic quests, he becomes ethically changed by the journey, which is transformed into a pilgrimage, visually codified by the use of the changes of the seasons on the landscape.

Finally, in the closing sequence, he can ride back into the wilderness having become at one with himself and secure in his newfound, almost 'native', endorsement of his environment. The camera and audience's point of view remain positioned on the side of the settled community, framed inside the log cabin, which dovetails with the opening sequence of the film as Ethan enters the story. Now, however, as the audience witnesses his final departure, Ethan must again be reconstituted as an outsider. Having achieved his goal, he can ride away from social responsibility with his head held high. Framed from behind with a majestic open landscape and skyscape before him, he can continue his adventures within an environment which endorses his roving spirit. At last he can fully coexist in nature rather than being psychologically driven by the destructive human emotion of revenge.

The Last of the Mohicans
While a small minority of Hollywood films, like *Little Big Man* (1970), attempt to face up to inherent difficulties of representing the other, a vast majority remain much more circumspect. In particular, to (re)present a progressive ecological other

without continually feeding off regressive stereotypes remains a difficult balancing act, as dramatised, for example, in *The Last of the Mohicans* (1992).[4]

Richard Schickel asks a typical rhetorical question about the recent explosion in conventional classic narrative films: 'Anyone around here heard of postmodernism?' while evocatively exploring the success of Mann's film in his review for *Time* magazine in September 1992:

> From its first images of a deer hunt to its last shots of a hero and heroine gazing westward towards mist-shrouded mountains, the film's sensuous evocations of an Arcadian Wilderness, of the land that was ours . . . draws us into a remote realm, just as the need to penetrate the majesty and mystery of that landscape draws its characters irresistibly onto fates variously ennobling and tragic.

The poignancy of these images involves looking into a world now almost entirely lost. Perhaps it derives as well 'from the memories that stir of movie glories past, when sweeping historical spectacle spread across the screen in a confidently romantic spirit, now also largely lost to us, was a cinematic commonplace' (Schickel cited in R. T. Jameson 1994: 323-4).

This revivified myth of the 'pure' native Indian can be summed up in the final shot of The Last of the Mohicans, as the last surviving Mohican, Chingachgook, looks over the majestic unspoilt landscape. He alone now holds the conscience of his people, which symbolises a harmony with nature. While this mythic harmony is long lost, it remains tantalisingly present in this closing sequence as the camera focuses on his personal grief. However, his evocative representation is severely questioned by the historian Patrick Brantlinger, who regards such films as merely recycling 'the imperialist racism they might otherwise be anatomising and resisting'. Along with 'denial, forgetting or trivialization, sentimental racism is the main way that white America has interpreted its genocidal conflict with native Americans, both then and now' (Brantlinger 1998: 21-5). Taking on board this proposition, such texts can be recognised as 'white' morality tales, which endorse neo-liberal myths of the 1990s, designed to expunge colonist guilt for its predominantly white audiences, with the native Indian at last acquiring the status of hero.

Nevertheless, I would suggest such contemporary nature films are framed within a 'both-and' postmodernist sensibility rather than an 'either-or' modernist one and, if only as a by-product, help to construct a more potentially progressive model of native American representation together with a more fruitful ecological role-model for the future. While such texts appear unwilling to question white agency to the extent that *The Searchers* did, nonetheless they begin to display the issues and certainly foreground nature for ecological exploration. This unashamed romantic and nostalgic preoccupation with the age of ecological innocence remains a potent one for an audience at the end of the twentieth century, unable to attain any real sense of ownership or responsibility for the planet which they have inherited. Instead of the background simulacrum of otherwise synthetic space being created for action adventures, hyper-real space and dramatic landscape is consciously foregrounded as in *Dances with Wolves* and used to evoke a revisionist exposition of 'primitive' nature.

Dances with Wolves

It was not until the 'liberal' 1970s and 1980s and the hugely successful *Dances with Wolves*, which Costner found extremely difficult to fund, that the representations of native Indian culture became both popular and apparently 'progressive'.[5] The director himself affirmed that the film was not made to manipulate audience feelings or just to set the record straight. Rather, he accepted that it was a romantic look at the historical past, when expansion in the name of progress brought American society very little and, in fact, cost it very deeply (cited in Blake 1990).

It is little wonder that such liberal writers and film-makers were motivated to represent a more ecologically progressive culture from a sympathetic point of view - evoking if not reiterating the famous 1970s 'Crying Indian' advertising campaign, designed to encourage white American society to feel guilty about their inadequate stewardship of the land as bequeathed to them by native Americans. Nevertheless, even this so-called progressive text ends up restating an extremely simplistic categorisation of an otherwise alien culture, distinguishing only between 'good' Indians and 'bad' ones. The 'noble savage' is most clearly equated with the Sioux tribe in *Dances with Wolves* or the Cheyenne in *Little Big Man*, while the Pawnee are represented as evil in both films. This strategy has the capacity of addressing 'white historical fear and guilt within the same narrative, providing a way in which a fiction can remain simultaneously true to contradictory emotional responses to history' (Lewis 1995: 202).

This universalising polarisation into moral categories by white film-makers avoids the dilemma of engaging with the actual historical and particularised socio-political context of a complex culture, where concepts like 'good/evil' can be recognised as behavioural effects which simply endorse or negate white perceptions. 'Evil' natives can be distinguished by the visual signifier of easily decoded 'aggressive' war paint. Consequently, audiences expect 'Indians' to kill and massacre; it's in their nature! 'Good' native Indians on the other hand, like similar natives in *Emerald Forest* discussed in the previous chapter, are coded as romanticised, ecologically progressive examples of a benevolent people who must present an alternative and progressive ethical role model for human behaviour.

But at least Costner's hugely successful native American film helped bring many of these debates into contemporary focus. The frontier myth, represented by the Indian hunt in particular, has become America's most enduring vision of the archetypal story, 'the initiation of the boy into manhood and of his heroic rise out of the collective (regressive) unconscious' (Rushing *et al*. 1995: 54). In *Dances with Wolves*, the powerful evocation of a lost authenticity[6] is clearly situated in a (mythic) 'West', before the arrival of the white man, a period traditionally ignored by western film. John Dunbar takes the role of 'proto-ethnographer' rather than that of 'settler':

> His writings become symbols of his 'authenticity', distinguishing him from other white men. But the film also attempts to 'demythologise' the classic Western, whether by inventing conventions or by presenting what really happened . . . reversing traditional structuring antinomy; civilization versus savagery

(Collins 1995: 151).

Jim Collins concludes that *Dances with Wolves* marks a:

> move back in time away from the corrupt sophistication of the media cultures towards a lost authenticity . . . and as a site of successful narcissistic projection . . . in which the original genre text takes on a quasi-sacred function as the guarantee of authenticity; the fetishising of 'belief' rather than irony as the only way to resolve conflict

(ibid.: 152).

The powerful opening scene of this quest to find the frontier before it disappears for good is dramatised by the purification of white agency through a self-sacrificing, Christ-like rite-of-passage performed by the seriously wounded soldier. Tempted by heroic sacrifice, rather than have his leg cut off by the 'butcher' surgeon, Dunbar is redeemed as he rides invincibly in slow motion through a barrage of bullets (even his white horse survives!). Myth rather than historical reality is at work from the start, with such heroic effort causing an end to the stalemate of the two civil war armies impotently facing each other. Later he gets his life's wish, a commission in the furthest outpost, from an officer who is not in control of his bodily functions and is strangely jealous of the newly-decorated soldier's focused quest. The officer's immediate suicide while Dunbar is still in window-shot foreshadows the horror and pain yet to be experienced on the journey to follow.

In spite of his very crude travelling companion who litters the landscape with waste products, the ensuing and extended *mise-en-scène(s)* evokes for the first time the expanse of raw nature and dramatises a landscape that is worth fighting for. This is represented by the camera and sound-track harmonising with the majestic landscape, framing the protagonists as they traverse the frontier from close-up to mid-shot and long-shot. Dunbar's point-of-view forever changes as he glances across the plane of vision. Landscape is being reviewed and witnessed but not always from the protagonist's point of view, which helps to reaffirm an unmediated perspective of sublime excess, rather than a controlling or conquering vision which validates Costner's heroic struggles at the start of the film. His extreme physical pain and earlier suffering is vindicated as he journeys onward and becomes assimilated by the American frontier and the *jouissance* gained from his vision of wilderness embodies the filmic 'Garden of Eden'.

In American discourse in particular, wilderness stands for what nature is before it was despoiled by human beings.[7] It is, according to the historian William Cronon, 'a place of freedom in which we can recover the true self we have lost to the corrupting influences of our artificial lives. Most of all, it is the ultimate landscape of authenticity' (Cronon 1995: 80). But, as N.K. Hayley affirms in a special volume on eco-criticism in New Literary History, this view of nature requires that humans be absent from it, which leads to the paradox:

> If we allow ourselves to believe that nature, to be true, must also be wild, then our very presence in nature represents its fall. The place where we are is the place where nature is not. As a result, wilderness loses its power to authenticate our lives as soon as we try to take advantage of its redemptive potential

(Hayley 1999: 675).

Together with a historical form of amnesia,[8] Americans also desire the nostalgic touristic pleasures of luxuriating within a landscape of spatial excess. As a continent and an enormous land mass, the nation state of America often triggers images of the Garden of Eden, especially among European immigrants who make up a large percentage of the film-making fraternity as well as the audience. Hollywood frequently exploits this awesome and sublime version of an open continent.[9]

This primitive lust for 'purity' continues to transcend so called postmodernist fractured meta-narratives and can in many ways be regarded as evoking a holistic ecological consciousness. The spatial irrationality of the opening exposition of the civil war in *Dances with Wolves* serves to privilege but less effectively critique white American society's historical preoccupation with individual heroism and self-destruction. While native Americans (re)present a purer expression of nature as seen later in their 'unspoilt' habitat, untainted by the baggage of colonialist wars, nonetheless they also become victims.

While issue can be taken with this evocation of the Sioux, there is most certainly, as Robert Baird affirms, an ongoing process in the 'American imagination' which consists of the white discovery of, and the renaming and adaptation into, the tribal society of American Indians (in Bird 1998: 196). A major section of *Dances with Wolves* is therefore devoted to interracial attempts at communication (unlike the more divisive and explicitly racial trajectory of *The Searchers*) and the final acceptance of Dunbar into the native community, which is signified by his acquisition of a native name. Baird also suggests that this interracial meeting occasioned two possible outcomes: 'a metamorphosis of the WASP into something neither white nor red' or 'the annihilation of the Indian' (Bird 1998: 196).[10]

Michael Coyne nonetheless speaks for many critics when he dismisses the film's 'conventional message', which remains at the core of its 'counter cultural idyll'. By sidestepping 'miscegenation by conveniently having a white woman (Mary McDonnell) as a ready-made romantic interest living among the Sioux . . . the film is not so much a repudiation of WASP American [values]' but, like George Bush's 'kinder, gentler society', remains 'a hymn to an attractive, authentic [and ecologically harmonious] culture in which nice young WASP couples may find a home' (Coyne 1997: 188). Consequently, the apparent liberal white transformation in *Dances with Wolves* is not as it seems.

This tension is illustrated in a key scene which is enlarged from the original version of 28 seconds to over two minutes in the 'director's cut'. It is the night scene after the big hunt where Dunbar observes the results of the savagery with severed human bits prominently displayed as trophies. 'I looked at the familiar faces', his authorial and controlling narrative voice affirms, and realised that 'the gap between us was greater than I could ever have imagined'. The illusion of (ecological) harmony between the races is certainly foregrounded and dramatised by Dunbar's shock at such realisation, in spite of all his efforts to bridge the racial divide. The otherwise revisionist trip designed to reconstruct Costner's outsider persona as a progressive ethical agent remains inconclusive at best.

A central preoccupation for the western has always been what wilderness can do to an individual -the potential to reduce him to his essence then restore him, or alternatively, consume him. This preoccupation is most effectively evidenced in another related genre which is concerned with stories that America tells itself. Road movies specifically foreground travel across the continent involving a journey of self-discovery. But unlike the Disney(land) experience which is predicated on control and inauthenticity, the road genre is, hypothetically at least, based on freedom and individuality. The genre tends to favour outlaws over lawmen, 'romanticised outcasts, who find their souls by defying societal restrictions' (Coyne 1997: 191).

A major reason why the western went out of fashion, according to Fred McDonald, was because 'Westerns were for a society which was simpler and understood less' than today's urban sophisticates (cited in Ryan *et al.* 1988: 26). No longer could new generations accept horses as a means of excitement to fulfil their male fantasies. Road movies updated the mode of transport and also became ecologically relevant for the modern world. Nonetheless, even if the generic conventions may have changed, the core narratives and thematic concerns have not. Landscape remain potent, evoking a sense of wonder and adventure in an audience who at least initially understand little and care less for what some feminists regard as the 'pure' eco-values of mother Earth.

As suggested in Chapter 1, the counterculture preoccupation of hippie romanticism both articulates and feeds off the myth of the western: a man and his mount, acting as frontiersmen, wanting to go where no other man has gone before, holding a belief that life must be kept simple. But the ultimate message - that if there is some problem, just move on - can be, and often is, ideologically conservative. It is nevertheless surprising that this genre also helped promote the broad based ecology movement. By beginning to push forward legislation to protect the environment and promote a rediscovery of 'natural' agriculture and food, the counterculture became a culture of alternative values based in nature (Kearney 1988: 322). The seeds of ecological growth and awareness and its corollary, the planet's destruction, have been most clearly articulated within the conventional constraints of this 'philosophical' genre.

Romantic Travel and Road Movies

When Jean Baudrillard equated modern American culture with 'space, speed, cinema and technology' he could just as easily have added the road movie as 'its supreme emblem' (Cohan *et al.* 1997: 1). In many ways, road movies are similar to the trajectory of many westerns, since both build on a physical and mental landscape and 'compose a specific cultural grammar that stands behind the way the journey is organised from start to finish' using 'several alternative destinations' (Eyerman and Lofgren 1995: 67). The romantic movement invented a kind of traveller, usually codified as a wandering male, on the road of endless nostalgic desire. For this romantic traveller the whole world and all space became a vast homeless home, helplessly drawing on fantasies and idealisations which insured the endlessness of (his) desire. The journey became in many ways the object itself, loved as much for deferring what was equally feared and desired.

Critics also suggest that the great interest in travel writing in America was due to the rise of romanticism, 'the largely unexplored conditions of America, the self-consciousness and provincialism of the new nation which stimulated intense interest among American and European travellers' and provided fascinating glimpses of exotic spots which could be purveyed as 'scientific information' (Buell 1975: 190). Most notably, Waldo Emerson and his American form of transcendentalism inspired Thoreau, who went on to write the celebrated 'green' treatise *Walden*. *Wilderness*, in particular, which even as late as 1830 constituted three-quarters of the American landscape, was a space of 'pilgrimage' which romantics and future activists like John Muir believed helped to reveal clearer moral truths concerning human nature. In particular, Muir was instrumental in promoting pressure groups like the Sierra Club to protect the 'spiritual' values of sublime landscapes such as Yosemite National Park (the first example of a protected public park in the world)[11] from an increasing number of pressures.

Classic American novels like *Moby Dick* and *Huckleberry Finn* are also centred around journeys. The hero gives up his place in society and withdraws back to nature. This form of 'nature' becomes a source of inspiration while at the same time the greatest adversary. This ever-present narrative trajectory helps to frame the western, and in contrasting ways, the road movie, by exposing how the heroic agency of otherness is promoted, which in turn helps to dramatise core ecological principles. Only when nature is fully accepted and appreciated and the protagonists become part of nature can they finally meet their destiny. To activate the journey, the automobile remains central to the road movie's potency.

The Myth of the Automobile

With all their speed forward, they may be a step backward in civilisation. It may be that they won't add to the beauty of the world, to the life of men's souls, I'm not sure. But the automobile has come and almost all the outward things are going to be different because of what they bring. I think that men's minds are going to be changed in subtle ways because of automobiles.

It may be that in ten or twenty years from now, if we can see the inward change in men, by that time, I shouldn't be able to defend the gasoline engine, but I would have to agree that automobiles had no business being invented

(spoken by Eugene Morgan in The Magnificent Ambersons (1942); Williams 1982: 1).

Since they were invented, cars have embodied a whole new world, becoming an iconic symbol of modernity. Barthes more specifically articulates how little by little the dynamic of driving 'replaced a very subjective logic of possession and projection. No more fantasies of power, speed and appropriation linked to the object itself, but instead a tactic of potentialities linked to usage: mastery, control and command, an optimalization of the play of possibilities offered by the car as vector and vehicle, and no longer as object of psychological sanctuary' (cited in Foster 1993: 126).

Marx confidently affirmed how technology discloses human nature's mode of dealing with nature, the processes of production which sustain life and thereby also lay bare the mode of formation of social relations and of the mental conceptions that flow from them (Marx 1967: 352 in Harvey 1996: 149). To enable the car to achieve its implicit objective of freedom and mobility, for individuals who could afford such commodified necessities demanded of the new industrialised world, the very face of the landscape had to be moulded to provide a comprehensive road network. The car, like other technological breakthroughs within the mass communication industry of the twentieth century, embodied the new world order, concurrently invoking the enormous potential of mankind while at the same time sowing the seeds of man's possible destruction.

But how can road movies possibly be discussed in the context of ecology when they appear to care little about the public good, particularly with the greenhouse effect hanging over the environment. On a more prosaic level, an eclectic radical moralises, 'Do the public *really* want to see the gasoline guzzling V-8 of their dreams, racing down the highway - a dream they (must) never fulfil!' (Iche 1990: 201). While audiences might wish to answer in the negative, even if this wish is not articulated, the textual potential for foregrounding a fractured ecological message remains compulsive within the road movie genre.

Road movies like westerns are built around notions of freedom and mobility. Most particularly, with the horrors of depression in the 1930s, the movement of the car itself became a symbol of hope. As a distinct genre, however, the road movie did not come to prominence until the late 1960s, forged by the beat writers of the 1950s and legitimised by its countercultural valorisation of existentialist philosophy.[12] Writers like Alan Ginsberg, William Burroughs and Jack Kerouac[13] in the 1950s were extremely important for the development of road narratives, which dramatised all the good things that life has to offer. The road became a ritual of manhood, a way of proving yourself (Eyerman and Lofgren 1995: 54-9).

Easy Rider

This existentialist genre became successfully codified with the 1968 classic *Easy Rider* when the market demanded a youth-oriented genre which apparently catered for a predominately male-addressed audience and endorsed the themes of adventure and exploration, just as the western had done in its heyday for previous generations. Bert Schneider, Rob Rafelson and others explored this 'ride into nature' as a metaphor for the escape from urban oppression into the 'freedom' of self-discovery (Ryan *et al.* 1988: 23). But, as one critic rightly qualifies, this growing endorsement of self-discovery and freedom was continually explored from a male narcissistic point-of-view, resulting in regression to a warm, comforting (maternal) environment in the face of the constraints of modern human existence.

Christopher Lasch, in his classic treatise, astutely contends that the narcissist 'depends on others to validate his self-esteem' and continues that for them 'the world is a mirror', whereas for the rugged individualist or western hero his environment is 'an empty wilderness to be shaped to his own design' (Lasch 1978: 10). 'Nature' is often portrayed as a utopian space for narcissistic self-fulfilment or, alternatively, a site of paranoia or even destruction with regard to everything that curtails male desire.

Yet a core pleasure of road movies, as with westerns before, remains the unexpected nature of travel with a lack of certainty as to future events. This form of travel reinforces the notion of freedom and the ability to traverse cultural and political boundaries which has remained a constant narrative thread in almost all forms of action cinema. Most significantly, by the 1960s, with the enormous growth in the automobile industry, American citizenship in particular embraced car ownership as the overriding requirement for overcoming the restraints of geographical provincialism, thereby delimiting other forms of economic or social marginalisation. This is embodied most clearly within the youth cultural phenomenon of *Easy Rider* and the main character's search for a 'new spiritual place for themselves', which became most appropriate for the 'counter-culture and the modern world' (Cohan *et al.* 1997: 51).

Upon release this relatively cheap, non-mainstream, even experimental film became an essential part of 1960s iconography, embodying the hopes and fears of the time, earning over $60 million worldwide (Hill 1996: 8).[14] Nevertheless the film was full of contradictions, especially with the adolescent idealism of Hopper and Fonda coupled with the self-righteous paranoia of many of the other protagonists. The first copy promotional slogan enticed its audience: 'A man went looking for America, but couldn't find it anywhere'.[15]

Easy Rider is at once a travel poster proclaiming the continued presence of the old West and its historical and mythic associations, and a nightmarish portrait of small towns, cities and the end of the frontier (and the world). 'It is a celebration of the freedom of the road and the beauty of the landscape and a dissertation on the end of the road and the repulsive banalities and industrial blight that disfigure the scenery'. The film certainly invokes 'both affirmative and critical visions of 1960s America, making it more of a measure of its times than either its original or later audiences could imagine' (Hill 1996: 199).

Easy Rider has become the quintessential road movie, which remains a most flexible genre, capable of accommodating a wide range of complex themes. On the one hand, road movies are characterised by the romantic depiction of the speed and machinery of cars and bikes, the seemingly limitless opportunities of modern travel and the celebration of individual identification and improvement. But on the other, the genre also reveals the 'elusiveness of liberty in an over-industrialised world, the homogenisation of experience in a global economy, and the alienation and oppression suffered by many who live in this brave new world' (*ibid*.: 66). In particular, recent critics of the road movie genre frequently decode the genre across the polarising axis of emancipation and emasculation.

The film's narrative begins with a rejection of technology, including an abandonment of the cities built since the West was won, and is heavily influenced by hippie guru Herman Hesse's *Journey to the East*. Fonda wanted Billy and Wyatt's odyssey from LA to Key West to illustrate the rootlessness, loss of spirituality and destruction of nature created by America in the twentieth century. As the journey unfolds, both were to come to realise the material nature of their motives and to yearn for deeper values and goals. The film's west-to-east trajectory demonstrates the end of the frontier, as in *Dances with Wolves*,[16] alongside the hopes it held for individual freedom and national progress.[17]

Easy Rider's cinematography of the American landscape also indulges in picturesque road montages - referred to as 'travelogue' sections by its original reviewers - which allow spectators to 'experience the vastness of America's physical beauty' (Brode in Cohan *et al*. 1997: 20). The film further magnifies such cinematic strategies by emphasising the protagonist experience of the landscape via the use of travelling point-of-view shots as explored in nature films, discussed in the previous chapter.

Critique of 1960s (Neo-)Idealism

Lasch contends that 'the belief that society has no future, while it rests on a certain realism about the dangers ahead, also incorporates a narcissistic inability to identify with posterity or to feel oneself part of a historical stream'. He continues to discuss how the 'ideology of personal growth, superficially optimistic, radiates a profound despair and resignation. It is the faith of those without faith' (Lasch 1978 : 51). This critique of the 'idealism' of counterculturalism is made even more explicit when he concludes how (all) 'new age movements seek to restore the illusion of symbiosis, a feeling of absolute oneness with the world' (*ibid*.: 246). As our young (innocent) protagonists lay dead on a 'barren' roadway - killed by the forces of rural backwoodsmen, the audience is encouraged to question the meaning of their death and what their journey into nature has meant. Alternatively, one could argue that there is none, since nature's animism has not offered up the answers, only alienation and isolation.

One of the ways counterculturalists sought to fight oppression was through the deep strain of the communitarian movement which Martin Buber in *Paths to Utopia* (1960) described as 'resistance to mass or collective loneliness' (cited in

Roszak 1970: 14). But as suggested in a later chapter on science fiction, there remains an inherent contradiction in such a movement. While 'community' claims to be about tolerance and acceptance, giving the impression of embracing diversity, in reality it 'seeks to deny difference and reject challenge to established norms of behaviour and belief' (Cloke and Little 1997: 277). All of this is at odds with the so-called 'ideal' of rural community '(the warm, tight-knit and accepting community being a central focus of contemporary constructions of rurality), and the recognition of difference' (*ibid.*: 277). This tension continues beneath the surface through the 1970s and 1980s, as can be seen through feminist debates around *Thelma and Louise*, to be discussed later. Furthermore, it could be argued that by the 1990s and the post-materialist liberal agency of *Grand Canyon*, many of the lessons and difficulties raised by Lasch and others alongside more pervasive difficulties connected with the nationalist and frontier discourse became more assimilated while displaying a new 'maturity'.

Easy Rider ends with both Wyatt and the flag lying bloodied and burning, the significance of which has been endlessly deconstructed by critics of all persuasions. Wyatt and Billy are blown off their motorcycles by shotgun toting Southern 'red necks'. But as Wyatt's motorcycle explodes in flames, an aerial shot places the wreckage within the context of a landscape vista and clinches the tragic proportions of the assassination. Roger McGuinn's version of Bob Dylan's 'It's Alright Ma (I'm only Bleeding)' also liberalises the apocalyptic dimension of the final act (Cohan *et al.* 1997: 193). This dramatic use of violence and closure is, of course, a common trope in Hollywood and is most clearly echoed in the ending of *Thelma and Louise*.

Films made during the late 1960s helped create what Todd Gitlin has referred to as an 'edgy apocalyptic popular culture' bred by catastrophic political violence (cited in Cohan *et al.*1997: 197).[18] In one sense, the Left movement got side-tracked from dealing directly with political issues by media images that displaced activism through spectacles of violence offering a negative vision of the potential of the counterculture and its strategies of surviving within a repressive society. From Gitlin's point of view, apocalyptic imagery in the media polarised the political struggle so monumentally that effective, radical political action seemed hopeless (*ibid.*: 198).

In *Easy Rider*, the road represents the illusion of freedom. Billy and Wyatt's lack of responsibility for the land and their violent deaths on the road mark the end of a bad trip. The movement from west to east reverses the pattern of American development as documented by the imperialistic western genre. Their journey has been cut short with a romanticised landscape conspiring in their demise as the camera pulls back to reveal an anonymous 'road to nowhere'.

Postmodernity -The Road to Nowhere!

Michael Atkenson concludes in his survey of road movies in *Sight and Sound* that the American genre in particular is 'too cool to address seriously socio-political issues. Instead, road movies express the fury and suffering at the extremities of civilised life and give their restless protagonists the false hope of a one-way ticket to nowhere' (Atkenson 1994: 16). But as the American Indian mystic M.N. Chattergee puts it, 'if you don't know where you're going, any road will get you there. The journey's the thing' (*ibid.*: 16).

The postmodern condition[19] appears at odds with the formalist device of attempting a linear road narrative which can be exemplified by the oeuvre of Wenders or, more specifically, David Byrne's rendition of 'We're on the road to nowhere' as a young girl is framed along an endless road in his directorial debut *True Stories* (1986). Byrne's homage to middle America and his eulogy on 'mediocrity' at the same time explores, through a didactic history lesson, the colonising imperialism embedded in modern American society as prehistoric dinosaurs and later native Americans were wiped out to make way for the current proliferation of computer technology and shopping malls. Such movement echoes Norman Denzin's important assessment of the postmodernist condition which

> is everywhere and nowhere. It has no zero point, no fixed essence. It contains all the traces of everything that has come before. Its dominating logic is that of a hybrid, never pure, always compromising, not 'either-or', but 'both and' . . . Its logic of use and utility can turn anything from the past into a commodity that is sold, or used to sell a commodity in the present

> *(Denzin 1991: 151).*

Unlike western heroes who had a biography and a past to anchor themselves in and even the counterculturalist hippie movement in the 1960s, which had a bourgeoisie culture to react against, the postmodernist creative aesthetic often appears to be locked into the dilemma of philosophical relativism which lacks the controlling solidity of time and space to anchor meaning, truth and identity. Popular culture as expressed by critics like Iain Chambers is not appropriated through the 'apparatus of contemplation' but, as Walter Benjamin once put it, through 'distracted reception'. Consequently (postmodern) road movies must end up by circulating with no final resolution found, which nonetheless can produce greater openness and engagement for mass audiences. The broadly linear cause/effect narrative structure which dominated Hollywood up to the 1960s was, at last, slowly breaking up.

Denzin remains pessimistic, however, when he suggests that popular ideological scripts fight such postmodernist 'relativism' by providing a political structure which keeps ancient narratives alive.

> These myths are many and include the nuclear family, heroes with white hats or horses riding into frontiers which remain to be conquered, or into cities (nation states) which need to be saved; a rugged individualist who overcomes enormous handicaps on their way to finding wealth, happiness and personal fulfilment. In short Capitalism needs and uses anything and everything to perpetuate its hegemonic control over popular culture
>
> *(ibid.).*

Fredric Jameson also concurs that postmodernity reflects a crisis of American power which can be linked to the countercultural movement of the 1960s. Nick Heffernan perceptively affirms that the counterculture both protested against this expansion of power and yet was necessary to it 'in that its assault on prevailing bourgeois values and distinction further cleared the way for the radically levelling effect of commodity exchange' (in Murray 1995: 285B7). Dean MacCannell in his seminal *Empty Meeting Grounds: The Tourist Papers* goes even further with these connections by postulating that postmodernity as a periodising discourse did not exist until the end of the Vietnam war. He suggests a central problem for postmodernity involves the creating of 'ersatz communities', which become postmodern only when they develop 'consciousness of themselves as models and learn to profit from their image' (*ibid.*: 81). Such a critical position encouraged a greater questioning of outmoded modernist discourses including the role and function of nature and landscape on human agency.

As Heffernan contends, if postmodernism is the substitute for the 1960s and a compensation for their political failure, some 'new kind of ideological hegemony' is required to counteract the faltering of American global economic and military supremacy since the mid-1960s (in Murray 1995: 287).[20] Jameson in particular explains how 'culture' provides an imaginary or symbolic resolution of the historically specific contradictions of late capitalist societies and holds onto the emancipatory project of modernity. He speaks of the need for a 'new social system' which can be formulated through culture.

Given its bleak and fatalistic ending, it is intriguing that many viewers and critics recall *Easy Rider* as an artefact of 1960s idealism rather than as a harbinger of the increasingly cynical tone of decades to come. Lee Hill concludes that *Easy Rider* remains explicitly focused around the contradictions that lie behind so much of the ambition underpinning the American dream. 'Its visual splendour does not obscure its tragic argument: the idealism of the 1960s, like the money in Wyatt's gas tank, was too easily acquired and taken for granted, until it was squandered and violently destroyed' (Hill 1996: 55). Consequently, while *Easy Rider* shifted the consciousness of the baby-boomers, it did not necessarily signal, much less promote, a direct political shift.

Whether *Thelma and Louise*, the highly successful road movie directed by Ridley Scott, reverses or at least problematises any of these generic difficulties within a framework of ecological expression is a focus for the discussion that follows. In particular feminist discourses are framed by critics who rail against expressions of narcissistic male ego-mania in *Easy Rider*, whose agents become obsessively evoked within countercultural representation rather than more conventional forms of eco-consciousness. Nonetheless, some critics, such as Roger Horricks in *Male Myths and Icons,* argue that such texts promote the possibility of a 'utopian restitution being made by men'. As already highlighted in the discussion about westerns, the same argument can be applied to road movies: 'men live in the sensuous landscape of Eden, and are permitted a kind of homoerotic ecstasy of death and love' (Horrocks 1995: 173).

But male filmic protagonists often find it almost impossible to achieve nurturing and (holistic) solace in nature. Continuously driven by the urge to move on, they often miss the signs of their coexistence with and in nature. White male agency as outlined through *The Searchers, Dances with Wolves* and elsewhere in this study, has to overcome enormous cultural and ideological baggage, whereas the native outsider (or nurturing female), appears less constrained and more in tune with the ecological forces of nature. At least this is how the burgeoning feminist academic industry often, if unconsciously, portrays this gender dichotomy and reconstitutes 'nature' alongside an endorsement of female agency. Consequently, an apparently more progressive if also flawed utopian evocation of human agency can be explored within the cult role-reversal 'feminist' road movie *Thelma and Louise*.

Eco-feminism: A Contradictory Discourse
(A Case Study of *Thelma and Louise*)

> Eco-feminism . . . values motherhood and the raising and parenting of children and the maintaining of comfortable habitats and cohesive communities as the most high-ly productive work of society . . .
>
> *(Henderson cited in Dobson 1995: 188).*

Initially, *Thelma and Louise* was regarded as a feminist reworking of a male genre with women taking the place of the male buddies, together with an interrogation of male myths about female sexuality, especially since cars (or bikes) and guns are traditional symbols of power and bound up with images of the masculine (see

Tasker 1993). Consequently the film spawned a huge debate involving the empowering potency of the 'women with guns' phenomenon. Critics speak of its 'exhilarating fantasy', while at the same time provoking an ideological counter-reaction, 'if only it were so simple'. But at least its an 'upbeat celebration of women's potential' together with its provocative 'signifiers of (woman's) pleasures', which accurately serve to locate the 'discourse in the postfeminist universe of the 1990s' (Macdonald 1995: 159-60). This at least questions the dominant hegemony of patriarchy while remaining lumbered with often restrictive, or even faulty, co-relations with nature.

Andrew Dobson affirms that at one extreme within eco-feminist debate there is the so-called 'feminine principle', which ascribes values 'uniquely' characteristic of women, namely a caring and nurturing nature that in turn promotes a direct correlation with deep ecological principles. The two protagonists in *Thelma and Louise* apparently have to renounce these proto-ecological qualities to achieve independence from patriarchal dominance. The protagonists move from the supposedly female space of domesticity and home to the freedom of 'male' space that is the great outdoors. At the outset Geena Davis is a shy childlike woman, playing the role of a meek housewife to husband Darryl's macho self-centredness. Louise (Susan Sarandon) is a waitress, capable and in control, balancing the demands of customers and workmates. Textually this reading is affirmed by comparing the neatness of Louise's apartment with Thelma's inability to decide anything as she packs almost everything she owns for the trip.

Feminist reviews, like the one in the July issue of Sight and Sound by Manohla Dargis, suggest that the film embodies classic western archetypes 'with a twist'. 'What begins as a woman's retreat from masculinity - a weekend slumber party - ends up an adventure of girlfriends, guns and guts . . . Women look to each other to survive'. Her perceptive conclusion, however, is that this issue is resolved not via 'woman as nature, but women in nature' (Dargis 1991: 18). The director in a interview in *Sight and Sound* asserts that he tried to make the heartlands look as exotic as possible but disagreed with a strictly feminist reading of the film. 'Its not about rape, its about choices and freedom.' The only solution is to make your choice which in this case 'is to take your life'. This strange evocation of suicide appears at odds with critics' endorsement of the film's 'will to pleasure, not power' and how 'tired scenarios and cliched landscapes are reinvented and resuscitated with fresh perspectives' (*ibid.*: 18).

Various (post)feminists, however, have reacted to this apparently myopic gender appreciation by positing what Dobson calls 'deconstructive feminism', which involves looking at the implicit dualism that informs the oppositional gender discourse explored above. Amy Taubin wonders in her interview with the director why the two protagonists were not allowed to live in the end or why audiences were not allowed to look at their bloodied bodies and realise (our) complicity in their death. As the director asserts, the film has a broader agenda, albeit a commercial one, rather than the exclusive affirmation of feminist principles. This is probably a major reason why the film remains so popular and timeless, addressing both the feminist cultural transcendence over landscape together with a particular incursion into the perennial war of the sexes.

Thelma and Louise follows the path of many of its predecessors, taking the off-road instead of the interstate highway and travelling the side roads from Arkansas through Oklahoma and New Mexico, which is a traditional route for gangsters and western heroes. The road and its destination become a metaphor for life itself. As many critics affirm, while the American dream is essentially about success and security, about 'making it', the road is about escape and freedom and a questioning attitude to such dominant social values.

While male protagonists often use the road to flee from the clutches of castrating females, female protagonists, on the other hand, cannot simply escape from patriarchal pressures because of the gendered assumptions of the genre (Roberts in Cohan *et al.* 1997: 62). *Thelma and Louise* - vividly shot by Adrian Biddle (*Aliens*) and edited by Thom Noble (*Witness*) - refuses the western trope of the final shoot-out, choosing instead a bittersweet and highly contested freedom from patriarchy through the suicidal acceleration into the natural abyss. Many critics suggest that the main protagonists must import masculinist concepts of gender identity to their roles. It cannot be over-emphasised that normally neither 'the road' nor 'the West' as locations of adventure have been spaces for feminist debate in an attempt to (re)construct a progressive form of female agency, with women more usually represented as passive and submissive.

Patricia Mellencamp contrasts the director, Ridley Scott, and his 'feminist' aesthetic to John Ford's classic western style and sets the tone for much feminist criticism of the film.

> *The film's aerial shots are not like John Ford's Monument Valley, conquering the land, triumphant over space. Thelma and Louise almost become part of the land, neither conquered nor conquering . . . In the end, death allows them to 'keep on going'. In a series of extreme close-ups, they are smiling, without fear, looking at each other, laughing. They hold hands and kiss, the Polaroid they took at the beginning flies away, the car is held in a freeze frame over the canyon. In the end Thelma and Louise defy gravity, gaining mastery of themselves, becoming triumphant over death. The ending is courageous, profound, and sublime*

> *(in Jayamanne et al. 1995: 40).*

Such affirmation of woman's difference can, however, lead to the polarising position which remains 'essentialist, reductive and representative of an ideological/theoretical justification of patriarchy' (Sargisson 1994: 85).

Nevertheless, leaving aside Mellencamp's eulogy, many critics found it difficult to come to any form of feminist consensus regarding the film. Within a broadly socio-historical context, the film takes on its particular meaning in relation to women's changing social status and gender roles in the political economy of America after the Second World War. For most critics it generally represents the social reality of white, post-war baby boomers. Thelma is unhappily married and Louise is single, like a lot of women in America. In particular, some critics were totally dismayed at the film's transformation into a buddy movie and its apparent appropriation of patriarchal agendas, especially within its evocative closure. What encouraged so many women critics to take this film so personally? 'The answer must lie in the film's openness to the fantasmatic scenarios one can bring to it' (Willis in Collins 1993: 122).[21]

In spite of cogent criticism, these potent protagonists came to symbolise escape for a whole generation of (post)feminist critics, who were not given the 'heroic fantasy' of *Easy Rider* and its heroic ilk during the counter-revolutionary period of the 1960s. Yet like their alter-egos in *Easy Rider*, a price has to be paid for such heroic freedom and their 'adolescent pose' conveys the stereotypical romantic fantasy of the tragic situation. The two female protagonists kiss and hold hands in a symbolic 'suicide love pact' before driving off over the sublime precipice.[22]

Craig Owens, in 'The Discourse of Others', remarks on how 'in order to speak, to represent herself, a woman assumes a masculine position; perhaps, he argues, this is why femininity is frequently associated with masquerade, with false representation, with simulation and seduction' (cited in Foster 1983: 59). As in Ridley Scott's other big box office success with Sigourney Weaver, *Alien* (1979), 'the only conceivable fate for a woman with the right stuff is to be driven off a precipice into oblivion' (*ibid.*).

The inability or even unwillingness of many critics to appreciate the often contradictory and excessive 'pleasure(s)' of the text, effectively misses the 'transgressive' utopian nature of the film as defined by Sargisson and others in Chapter 1. *Thelma and Louise* certainly offers numerous contradictory pleasures, including a somewhat 'adolescent' agency and exposition of a feminist eco-utopian space. This is most clearly affirmed by Yvonne Tasker, who suggests that the film is a fantasy which works through a drama about 'limits and transgressions', together with an exploration of a new type of space. 'Thelma and Louise operates within a different set of terms, which we might think of as - utopia' (Tasker 1993: 154).

Third Space and Closure

Gillian Rose in *Feminism and Geography* affirms:

> I want to explore the possibility of a space which does not replicate the exclusions of the same and the other . . . feminism through its awareness of the politics of the everyday, has always had a very keen awareness of the intersection of Space and Power

(Rose 1993: 137).

Michel Foucault's notion of 'heterotopia' (other spaces) focuses on the space 'in which we live, which draws us out of ourselves, in which the erosion of our lives, our times and our history occurs'. He asks why has time 'been treated as richness, fecundity, life, dialectic, while in contrast space has been typically seen as 'dead, fixed and immobile' (cited in Soja 1996: 14).[23] This evolution of 'third space' is most particularly evidenced in the ending of *Thelma and Louise*. Probably the true potency of the closing image has remained undervalued, which is why critics especially find it hard to understand, being unwilling or unable to assess utopic moments in film which often swamp narrative causalities embedded in it.

The frozen image of the car, framed at the centre of the *mise-en-scène* displaying a romanticised image of a sublime natural precipice, is reminiscent of the famous match-cut in Kubrick's classic science fiction film *2001*, when a bone, fashioned as an evolutionary, technological symbol of violence for our prehistorical ancestors, is hurdled up into space and becomes transformed into an advanced spaceship touring the galaxy. This counterpointing of temporal continuity, while critical of the human and technological evolutionary process, is majestically visualised as the ship floats within the stars to the glorious romantic music of Strauss. Similarly, audiences have become transfixed with the ending of *Thelma and Louise*, as evidenced through many of the critical readings cited above. It is not inconceivable, I would argue, to read the 'unnatural' image of the scene as producing an equally potent metaphorical match-cut which reflects audience desires, hopes and fears particularly framed within an ecological discourse.

As the American open-top convertible is frozen in mid-air, with its two romanticised heroines at last 'controlling' or at least 'negotiating' their co-equal destiny, the audience is allowed space and time to appreciate the protagonists' significance within an iconographically potent sublime landscape. Metaphorically and spatially they are at last in nature, as Dargis suggests; at one with the natural eco-system as opposed to surrendering to the forces of patriarchal law and order. Their journey has allegorically become transformed into a 'pilgrimage', having secured utopic meaning for their lives. Time and narrative processes do not matter anymore as they become frozen and immortalised in space.[24]

The automobile, a conventional symbol of pleasure and escape, becomes a primary constituent in the aesthetic make-up of the still image, recording and solidifying the majesty of one of the great sublime natural spectacles of planet Earth. Rather than demonstrating the consequences of such movement, which would result in a wreck, a pollutant on the natural landscape like the motorcycles in *Easy Rider*, the static image becomes a potent, albeit unsubtle icon and symbol of romantic human endeavour in the struggle against oppression. 'Nature', at least metaphorically, has been appropriated to validate this struggle and provide a more universal meaning above and beyond the specifics of gender power politics.

Thus pure representation of idyllic nature and the creation of a 'third space' also provides a powerful link which feeds off the roots of American transcendentalism, using the metaphoric potency of the sublime as a motor for the primary utopian impulse which needs an awesome natural eco-space for its fulfilment. Postmodern spectators have at least potentially acquired the semiotic discursive capabilities of both embracing and constructively decoding therapeutic natural signifiers such as the Grand Canyon.

Harvey typifies an ideological critical consensus which positions space (and time) as being defined by the forces of capitalism. Within ideological power structures many factors clearly influence the human experience of space, especially ethnicity and gender. Massey also correctly pinpoints how 'different social groups have varying experiences of space' (Massey 1994: 61-2). Major influential cross-disciplinary critics including Durkheim, Levi-Strauss (1963), Hall (1966), Bourdieu (1977) and others all affirm 'different societies produce qualitatively different conceptions of space and time' (Harvey 1996: 210). Nevertheless, recent geographical and cultural exploration of spatial metaphors has tried not to become transfixed by the polarising negativity of such ideological discourse. Edward Soja, in a passionate evocation of a 'third space', attempts to anchor the postmodernity project while eulogising Henri Lefebvre as the founding father in the study of spatiality. Such space also provides a forum for ecological expression, particularly when applied to excessive spatial closures of *Thelma and Louise* and other films in this study.

While a reading of both *Easy Rider* and *Thelma and Louise* evokes a romanticised 'adolescent' exploration of the application of space and landscape to provide a powerful metaphor for motivational, even transformational, praxis, Grand Canyon presents a more 'mature' self-referential exposition of this phenomenon. By implicating both gender and race (even class) and framed within a deep form of ecological expression and understanding, *Grand Canyon* calls on contrasting evocations of space and place.

Grand Canyon: (An Evocation of a Liminal Eco-space)[25]

The closure of *Grand Canyon*, like the over-determined closures in *Easy Rider* and *Thelma and Louise*, becomes the primary focus for discussion in this chapter. I will explore how such closure promotes a 'utopian eco-spatial diegetic' as expressed by its upwardly mobile (white,) liberal, guilt-ridden and ecologically aware protagonists.

> Lawrence Kasdan's Grand Canyon (1991) which he also scripted with his wife -in which a white motorist (Kevin Kline) strays from the LA freeway, gets lost in an area strikingly similar to where the major riots occurred in LA -faces certain attack by a gang of black males and is rescued from the terrifying predicament by the 'good black' tow truck driver Danny Glover. After many complications, misunderstandings and earnest efforts to bridge racial chasms, and even class, the main characters celebrate a new-found communality as they gaze at the wonder of nature, like tourists, from the rim of the Grand Canyon

> *(Nichols 1994: 32).*

A primary fantasy element within film narrative is its ability to use time-space compression, which can allow agency to be acted upon and effect social, spatial and political change within the parameters of filmic conventions. A lot can happen in two hours of filmic time. From the beginning of the film, major structural and racial problems are exposed within the spatial parameters of LA. In the end, such fissures, while not resolved, are nonetheless subsumed within an all-embracing eco-narrative.

The film opens with establishing shots of contrasting basketball games. One involves Glover in a friendly, non-spectator driven game, whereas the other is driven for spectatorial pleasure by professional black players performing, within a predetermined and controlled space, for a large audience made up mainly of white folk. Kline's voyeuristic attention is split between the game and the visual pursuit of beautiful women walking around the stadium. As in Hitchcock's *Rear Window* (1954), his male gaze spells trouble.

Kline exhibits a strong if secret desire to shun conformity, to overcome feelings of being shackled by white middle class 'professional' values. His trouble becomes predictable when he refuses to go with the orderly flow of traffic and accept his predetermined white coordinates within his defined city-space. He tries to break out of this predetermined 'cognitive mapping' (Harvey 1992: xiv) within this hyperspace and risk the 'chaos' of the urban jungle. The literary convention of fate and predetermination, together with Kline's subconscious will to master his environment, exposes him to 'real' danger that his director friend only talked about and siulates in his pulp flick adventures.

This acceptance of 'risk' is narratively linked with notions of 'space'. Harvey contends that

> within each capitalist epoch, space is organised in such a way as best to facilitate the growth of production, the reproduction of labour, power and the maximisation of profit . . . It is through the reorganisation of time/space that capitalism is able to overcome its periods of crisis and lay the foundations for a new period of accumulation

(cited in Urry 1995: 22).

One critic goes further to argue that the whole settlement pattern of America should be understood as one vast venture in real estate speculation. 'Old places have to be devalued, destroyed and redeveloped while new places are created' (Veblen cited in Harvey 1992: 6). Architecturally-designed model flat complexes become ghettos as real estate prices control the life cycles of whole populations. American city development can, according to Mike Davis (1992), be crudely traced through the continuous movement of middle-class whites out of the inner cities and into the suburbs as blacks and Hispanic under-classes take their places. In some areas this is followed by the gentrification and re-appropriation of inner-city space.

White Humanist Anomie

The human needs addressed in *Grand Canyon* include the urge to exercise control over the environment and behaviour in the light of a breakdown in perceived social norms of humanity. Anthony Giddens affirms that human agents have a basic desire for some degree of predictability in social life. They have a need for what he calls 'ontological security' or confidence and trust that the natural and social worlds are as they appear to be (cited in Haralambos *et al.* 1990: 817). *Grand Canyon* clearly dramatises this predominantly white ontological (in)security dilemma through the narrative trajectory of its protagonists. Giddens, and other theorists who seek 'optimistic' answers for societal problems, are often criticised for putting too much emphasis on the ability of agents to transform structures simply by changing their behaviour, recalling the 'voluntarist versus determinist' debate cited in Chapter 1. Structuralist features of society cannot just be changed at will, at least not on a time scale that actors involved might wish (Haralambos *et al.* 1990: 818). Nonetheless, filmic time/space compression can complete this wish-fulfilling fantasy.

Space has become the new metaphor for the same old historical processes and ideological struggles, with 'the local apparently equated with place and the global with space' (Grossberg in Chambers *et al.* 1996: 174).[26] Henri Lefebvre (1991) explains how 'social relations which are concrete abstractions, have no real existence save in and through space. Their underpinning is spatial.'

> Place presents itself to us as a condition of human experience. As agents in the world we are always 'in place', much as we are always 'in culture'. For this reason our relation to place and culture become elements in the construction of our individual and collective identities
>
> *(Entrikin 1991: 1).*

J. Nicholas Entrikin, however, suggests that twentieth-century scientists generally considered 'place' to be of relatively minor significance, primarily owing to the modern human ability to control and manipulate the environment, except, of course, for the dispossessed minority. But with the steep rise of risk - particularly ecological - in modern society, which cannot, as Ulrich Beck suggests, be controlled within a global capitalist system, place and environment are acquiring newfound meaning both practically and within abstract grand theory.

Critical consensus of Grand Canyon is effectively represented by Toby Young writing in *The Guardian,* who regards the film as a 'guilt-ridden parable of our conservative age'. The film was hailed as capturing the 1990s zeitgeist. 'After yesterday's rioting (sparked by the police beating of Rodney King, captured on an amateur video tape) it had the added authority of being prophetic' (1 May 1992).[27] In general, most critics were worried about its 'soft-centred' liberal agenda. The paradox of *Grand Canyon*, argued the *Economist*'s US columnist Lexington, was that 'for all its well-intentioned liberalism, it nevertheless has become a keynote film for the Bush electoral campaign -the fear of crime, the emphasis on "family values" and the belief in the power of individual do-gooding can make a difference: (Bush's "thousand points of light")'.

In the confrontational nightmare at the start of the film - a central focus of identification for the majority film audience - the danger is averted by the black saviour, analogous to the plebeian forest worker who controls and contains the metaphorical forest. Glover serves to maintain the engine of travel and spatial mobility in this urban environment.

The threat to white spaces such as Hollywood is a threat to the very core of white civilisation, in particular the American dream. The adolescent gangster, however, who wants to rob Kline rationalises that the gun gives him respect, as he asks his fellow black man for his reasons for intervening in the situation. 'Are you asking me a favour as a sign of respect or because I've got the gun'. Glover replies eventually. 'If you hadn't the gun, we wouldn't be having this conversation.' The gangster laughs, his spatial knowledge affirmed. 'I knew it; no gun, no respect' - thereby validating the gangster's power over the ghetto space.[28]

However, Glover, as the audience later finds out, has a much larger, all-encompassing ecological appreciation of space which provides him with a self-contained heroic mind set. Like the old western hero or the revisionist native American outsider, he does not have to own or control space to feel powerful or to co-opt a sense of identity from it. Instead he represents and embodies a form of 'stewardship' (a favourite Green Party notion) over his environment, unlike the 'adolescent' protagonists in Easy Rider and Thelma and Louise who remain ego-centric and preoccupied with redefining a new self-identity. The journey of knowledge for most of the characters in the film is to come to appreciate this eco-spatial inclusivity and stewardship initially embodied in Glover, which serves to position and even negate all their personal problems. Speaking directly for the majority law-abiding audience, Glover pontificates: 'That dude is supposed to wait with his car, without you ripping him off.' Recalling the Green Party political slogan -'think globally act locally' - he affirms the symbiotic relationship and interconnectivity between space and place. Here he endorses the (abstract) liberal conception of 'place' above and beyond the power nexus of ownership and control which is both liberating and a necessary precondition for place/space harmony within a deep ecological context.

This desire for an abstract form of spatial utopianism can be appreciated by understanding the social values and world view of the dominant group. They have long learned the anti-materialist message that acquisitiveness and greed do not bring happiness but have also apparently out-used the American nationalistic egalitarian meta-narrative of 'equality, truth and justice', which has little efficacy for them in their post-industrial and post-colonial world. The rhetoric of these constitutionally inscribed humanist values have effected little change over the traditional social ills of poverty and racism. At least metaphorically, like Kevin Costner in *Dances with Wolves*, they crave a progressive philosophy of agency which would overcome their feelings of national and global impotence and attempt to find it in utopic and ecological narratives.

In *Grand Canyon* the black outsider embodies a holistic form of eco-knowledge and only by experiencing themselves 'experientially, experimentally and existentially' (applied from cultural tourism) can such agents help produce an ecological and inclusive evocation of the sublime abyss of nature and allow them to appreciate their true function and holistic identity. The protagonists in *Easy Rider* and *Thelma and Louise* also attempted with varying degrees of success to experience life and nature in this way.

Nevertheless, while MacCannell and others argue that all tourists embody a quest for authenticity and even the sacred, others like Baudrillard contend that (all) cultures are 'staged' and are in a certain sense 'unauthentic'. Closure in *Grand Canyon* helps to combine all three levels of the experience of the tourist gaze, with the express aim of promoting a more satisfactory engagement with space/place. In fact, it could be argued that cinema in general, and such spectacle in particular, offers its immobilised spectator access to a virtual utopia while encouraging a more direct connection between the viewer and his cosmos.

In their eternal quest for a memorable if disposable quote, film reviews often find it difficult to endorse texts which call for ontological, or even spiritual, readings. Toby Young of *The Guardian* affirms that what makes this post-60s melodrama particularly attractive to 'conservatives' is its religious content. The film, he concludes, stops 'just short of endorsing theism', citing Kline's screen wife: 'What if there are miracles, Mac . . . what if we're so unused to miracles we don't recognise them when they happen?' Taking a purely cynical but commonly held view, feel-good movies like *Grand Canyon* help to produce a pleasant sense of being concerned without costing audiences anything more than the price of admission. Ecological historians could cite this phenomenon as suggesting, even validating, a shallow form of ecological inclusivity which avoids having to deal with root causes and issues, while at the same time appeasing middle-class guilt and anomie.

Paul Coates nevertheless affirms that Kasdan rescues rather banal material through what he calls a 'formal operation' which 'redeems and restores meaning to it' by representing it as an 'exploded dream'. The film's richness and mystery come from 'the persistence of narrative coincidences that are now inexplicable and seem to point to something beyond themselves'. *Grand Canyon* is not necessarily self-referential but is rather 'a source of miracles' (cited in Seidman 1994: 192). This exploded dream comes to full realisation in the final journey and evocation of an otherwise liminal eco-space, where the landscape evokes a form of 'sublime transcendence' at the majestic *Grand Canyon*.[29] As in *Easy Rider* and *Thelma and Louise*, the narrative meaning and power of the film finally depends on interpretations of the closing sequence at the real but also symbolic canyon.

Cynthia Freeland confirms that the concept of the sublime has been little used in film and seems to denote only an 'antique or even a debased aesthetic concept'. Her essay 'The Sublime in Cinema' concentrates exclusively on art films, particularly *Aguirre, The Wrath of God* (1977) and *Children of Paradise* (1944) that appear more acceptable within the academy and probably reflect an inherent prejudice against the potentiality of more mainstream popular texts. Nevertheless, she cogently affirms that the sublime depends on a tension between our highest sense-making faculty, imagination, and our highest human faculty, reason. Kant speaks of the sublime as involving a kind of 'outrage of the imagination' (in

Plantinga and Smith 1999: 65-70).[30] Looking out into the canyon, the protagonists, and by extension the filmic spectators, similarly begin to appreciate their own lack of true knowledge and understanding. Paradoxically, it is this ignorance which draws them closer together as a 'symbiotic' community.

This exploration of 'scenographic' space, as defined by Bordwell, encourages modifications by camera movement and allows a 'kinetic depth effect' within the audience (Bordwell in Burnett 1991: 232). This effect is certainly achieved in *Grand Canyon*, as the camera majestically moves across the extensive vista, continuously framing the 'look' of the protagonists. Anne Friedberg asserts that motion pictures have constructed 'a virtual, mobilised gaze by means of which the spectator would travel through an imaginary spatial and temporal "elsewhere and elsewhen"' (Friedberg 1993: 2).

The impression that many critics remain unconvinced with this 'positive' interpretation does not always take into account the conventional hermeneutics of the filmic textual analysis and is frequently predicated on a cynical, regressive reading. It could be argued that the audience perception of such excessive spectacle need not necessarily be tied down to vicarious identification with the protagonists but remain free floating and embodying most effectively Deleuze's assertion that film's soul craves thought. This can be demonstrated using traditional analytical tools of identification, through analysing camera point-of-view(s), outlined in earlier chapters and referred to above. The audience is induced in this closing sequence into a state of pro-active looking, by the excessively choreographed spectacle, above and beyond the confines of the narrative.[31] Such spatial excess affords the audience a place to engage with and connect with their universal ecological selves in a less confined and conventional way than, for example, in the closure of *Jurassic Park* discussed in the previous chapter.

Nevertheless, in a review in *Wide Angle*, one critic affirms that such representation of 'beautiful space' merely serves as background:

> Despite the ability to fill the screen with gorgeous geography, all is background, not foreground; all is context, not content. On the screen we read human faces better than we read the face of the land. The emotional and experiential power of geographic authenticity is rarely tapped or unleashed

(Nietschmann 1993: 5).

Drawing on Turner's (1969) notion of liminality and transitional place, I would strongly suggest that such closure also encourages a less reductive even utopian experience. The protagonists standing at the precipice (of civilisation) are situated between the naive adolescent spatial parameters explored in earlier examples and a more potentially 'mature' evocation of a series of energised eco-spatial relations. Nevertheless, this stage of liminality framed against the 'spectacle' provided at the Grand Canyon opens up the possibility of a 'third space'. It also maintains at least creative dissonance between the earnest community of agents participating in the spectacle, which impact on their interrelationships as they look into the precipice, with 'raw nature' at its most elemental and sublime. The film's closure self-consciously focuses on the grandness and natural beauty of the landscape and provides a potent signifier for audiences to engage with their own fantasies of a utopian ecological environment, above and beyond the narrative specificity of the text.[32]

This eco-utopian reading incorporates this trajectory. Instead of classical closure, audiences are presented with an 'excess of signification' that allows for the metaphysical engagement with spatial identity which is posited as coexisting with more contemporary psychological and temporal identity. As the protagonists construct a tableaux standing at the edge, staring into the abyss of spatial continuity, they can overcome their anomie, their feelings of impotence, and acquire a newfound communality with each other having been enriched by their co-presence with and in landscape. They have (potentially at least) acquired the ability to co-opt their preconceived notions of place and identity towards endorsing an eco-utopian sensibility.

As this utopian reading demonstrates, film theorists can learn a lot from the way 'geographers represent place as the location of direct experience, a sensuous swirl of emotion and perception and myths, which rational analysis can only ignore or destroy' (Rose 1993: 71). *Grand Canyon* helps to demonstrate how spaces need not necessarily be represented as static but instead become an active process aiding human agency. The evocation of landscape as codified by the Grand Canyon is not seen as a static tourist attraction but a means for a dialogue between ethnic groups. The tourist site in Grand Canyon can become the motor, the philosophical or psychological 'black box' for audiences and protagonists to express their hopes, fears, desires and utopian dreams rather than simply remaining subsumed within a uni-directional romantic gaze.

In particular, John Urry's articulation of a variety of tourist gazes (romantic, collective, spectatorial, environmental, anthropological)[33] is most effectively applied to nature filmic spectacle. Urry's categories of tourist gaze(s) involve transforming the 'romantic gaze' into a 'collective one' while at the same time transforming the spectatorial gaze into an environmental one, alongside maintaining all the attributes of human nature's unique subjectivity. Appropriating traditional models of identity ranging from romanticism and especially applying notions of spatiality, many fractured agents seek to explore a new way of engaging with their (white) anomie. Within a particular utopic narrative teleology, the canyon serves to 'heal' racial problems as they focus on the majesty of spatial representations of landscape, evoking also the wish fulfilling fantasy of the white liberal protagonists to achieve oneness with the cosmos as they look into the void.

Herbert Marcuse, a champion of ecology, believed that not only did the degradation of nature affect the prospects of human survival but it also diminished human self identity and worth. He argued for a new relationship between humanity and nature where 'the objective world would no longer be experienced in the context of aggressive acquisition, competition and defensive possession, and furthermore nature would become an environment in which human beings would be free to develop the specifically creative and aesthetic human faculties' (Marcuse 1972: 64). Such 60s countercultural abstract ideals became transformed through more 'mature' filmic reality at the end of the twentieth century.

Because the final look is choreographed by an inter-generational as well as a mixed racial group, the symmetry with nature is more equivocal and ecologically balanced than a conventional representational evocation of nature. The *mise-en-scène* dramatises how these eco-sapiens are not dominating or surveying the landscape as spectatorial tourists but are evoked as spatially insignificant, while finally transforming the ritual of their journey into a 'pilgrimage'.[34] Unlike the violent and terminal closures of *Easy Rider* and *Thelma and Louise*, the chronotope of space and time is more therapeutically collapsed in *Grand Canyon*, allowing audiences to oscillate between the pro-filmic agents and the clear focus of the *mise-en-scène*, which reflects directly back on their status as human beings in nature. Ostensibly the observing and communing protagonists looking out into the canyon help provoke a symbiotic discourse between the fractured interiority of human place and the holistic chaos of eco-space. A mythic symmetry is being evoked which is often lacking within more conventional hierarchical romantic discourse.

Unlike the conventional closure of the big close-up kiss, or the haloed sculptural light on a beautiful human face, contemporary audiences are more often exposed to the cinematic energy, even entropy, of raw nature. Such a pro-active filmic aesthetic can be read as Hollywood's move outwards towards a more provocative evocation of non-human agency, which is most essential to homo sapiens' communal happiness and fulfilment. This fantasy closure provides audiences with a potent sublime metaphor and at least the illusion of becoming active agents within an eco-spatial diegetic. Nevertheless, this form of spectacle and engagement, for all its therapeutic potency, remains confined to 'moments' of excessive evocation of nature which are firmly cued only through closure within the majority of road movies.

Coda: The Straight Story (2000)

William Cronon suggests that there is a range of narrative questions ecological historians should address, including:

-What do people care most about in the world they inhabit?
-How do they use and assign meaning to the world?
-How does the earth respond to their actions and desires?
-What sort of communities do people, plants and animals create together?
-How do people struggle with each other for control of the earth, its creatures and its meanings?

And on a grander scale B

-What is the mutual fate of humanity and the earth?

(Cronon 1992: 58).

Such grand, all-inclusive questions are addressed in varying degrees in the films discussed in this chapter and throughout the book but are most allegorically encapsulated in this evocatively simple road movie which concludes this chapter. In particular, the film draws upon America's national physical beauty alongside the magnetic appeal of movement through the landscape. More time/space is given over to 'pure' nature in *The Straight Story* than is allowed in most Hollywood film; furthermore, it is evocatively foregrounded rather than contained within the background. Throughout the film's relatively short journey the camera frames the central protagonist within the rich agrarian corn belt, coalescing the visual aesthetic of a western and a road movie.

The director, David Lynch as auteur, is more usually associated with surreal, quirky tales from the cult *Eraserhead* (1976) to the TV phenomenon *Twin Peaks* (1989). Yet he became fascinated by this true story of an elderly man who needs to make peace with his brother after many years of separation. To achieve his quest, Alvin Straight (Richard Farnworth) insists on carrying out his 'pilgrimage' on a miniature 1966 John Deere tractor because his eyesight is so poor he cannot drive a conventional automobile. Unlike the other protagonists addressed in this and other chapters, Alvin has already learned to appreciate the power of 'nature' and his own symbiotic (but not insignificant) place in the cosmos. His real power as an agent of transformation is his ability to radiate a (mature) form of humility alongside human stubbornness on his journey of discovery. The narrative journey constantly privileges the changing moods of landscape and skyscape as captured by the evocative cinematography of Freddy Francis and the music of Angelo Badalamenti.[35]

The film echoes the aesthetic purity of Thoreau's *Walden and Civil Disobedience* (1886), which has become a primary marker in the growth of an ecological sensibility and permeates much nature representation on film. In Thoreau's writings there is a profound sense of trust in nature as a means of balancing man's empty materialistic urges, which also tempers Alvin's quest.

> I went to the woods because I wished to live deliberately; to find only the essential facts of life and see if I could not learn what it had to teach, and not, when I came to die, discover that I had not lived

(Thoreau cited in Smith 1999: 49).

A formalist textual reading of the film reveals its similarities to a classical musical piece, which is reflected in the movement/scene index cited in the DVD version[36] The opening credits showing a close-up of static stars framed within the clear night sky is a recurring motif throughout the film, as evidenced by the video's cover design. Such gazing resonates with the urge, particularly explored in later chapters on science fiction, to look beyond the ethereal to find a new source of human nourishment and engagement within the cosmos.

The subsequent setting of the scene by a slow pan over cornfields is reminiscent of *Reggio's Koyaanisqatsi* (1983) and *Powaqqatsi* (1988), which most explicitly foreground nature as the centre of engagement. As the camera pans slowly across the *mise-en-scène*, a thud comes from inside the house which is not heard by the overweight, sun-worshipping neighbour who has gone into her house to get a snack. The whitewashed surface of the side of Alvin's house transcribes images and shadows of the fields and sky outside onto its surface.

The unseen shock of our chief protagonist falling to the ground is unlike the stylish (but stagy) heart attack of the father at the opening of *Blue Velvet* (1986), with the dog drinking from the water hose, oblivious of his owner convulsing on the ground. Instead of the picket fence, suburban life style exposed at the start of Blue Velvet, this more understated opening focuses on the unfussy windowsills and whitewashed blue-collar home while drawing attention to and underscoring the stoic immobility endured by the main protagonist inside.

The film audience knows something uncomfortable has happened inside the house but remains impotent even in satisfying its curiosity. Instead we must wait and endure the passing of time as light changes on the whitewashed walls and a crony from the nearby bar comes over to investigate. The old man is found lying on the ground, unable to get up but also unwilling to cry out for help, which at first appears symptomatic of a 'death wish'. But, as we later find out, he stubbornly wants to rely on nobody and to become mobile only at a pace he can take responsibility for. In any case, he knows his daughter will eventually turn up. Clock time has much less telescoped significance for him. One of the benefits of old age, he later affirms, is the wisdom to distinguish 'the chaff from the pure nourishing corn'.[37]

From the start, external nature is consciously foregrounded with human agency kept almost hidden in the background. The old man who will become the initiator of the journey does not need instant visualisation and identification. Unlike most Hollywood heroes, he does not demand attention and almost wants to 'blend with nature' like his plain and simple house. This practical evocation of stoical patience is very different from the escapist fantasy and excessive energy and desire for mobility which remains dominant within youth fixated popular culture and is exemplified in earlier journeys explored in this chapter.[38]

Alvin, typical of many elderly folk, does not want to go to see the doctor to confirm his future life expectancy or endure the indignities of being asked to disrobe while observing the instruments of scientific examination. His doctor tells him that if he does not 'make changes' quickly there will be 'serious consequences'. Alvin fully appreciates that old age is regarded as a 'disease' whose 'cure' reflects the ultimate taboo of death, which is seldom accepted much less represented within Hollywood film.

These inevitable biological consequences are rebelliously ignored, an attitude which is not just the preserve of the young. When we next see him he is lighting up a cigar and telling his daughter what she wants to hear. The illusion of normality must be maintained at all costs. Later, while failing to cut his lawn owing to defective machinery, he enjoys with his daughter the spectacle of a night storm. Such *jouissance* is interrupted by a ringing phone,[39] which is eventually answered by Rose. The bad news that Alvin's brother has had a stroke becomes the *raison d'être* for the film's narrative. This current familial crisis is dramatised by the house being bathed in a protective blue sheen of storm-light which almost envelops the *mise-en-scène*.

The seasonal storm is echoed in the subsequent night scene which is aurally signified by the muffled sound of a grain factory elevator harvesting the corn,[40] providing a backdrop and punctuating sound effect as father and daughter observe the stars. Helped by such tranquillity, Alvin quietly announces that he has to make the journey to see his brother in spite of all the logical impediments raised by his daughter earlier. Rather than attempt to justify his motives, he entreats her to 'look at the sky, Rosie? The sky is so full of stars tonight.' Contemplation, engagement and communality are all encouraged and foregrounded by the ontological pleasure and security of looking into the stars which, as with several other films discussed in this book, builds up to the final act of communion at the film's closure.

To frame and activate more intense ecological contemplation, the opening sequence of Alvin's spatial journey choreographs the symbolic relationship between his latent immobility and his psychological journey to find meaning from and in the cosmos. The scene tracks through a close-up of a continuous yellow road marking sign followed by a pan over the unconventional rig with its green cover as it slowly traverses the marked road space and up onto the horizon and finally directly up to the sky above - a framing shot which is held for what seems like an inordinately long period - and then back again to the road and the rig, demonstrating how the vehicle has barely moved. This continuing evocation of the 'tortoise and hare' allegory by drawing attention to other speedy vehicles upsetting his revere counterpoints Alvin's lack of mobility and becomes strangely infectious throughout the journey. Particularly because road movies embody and endorse movement and progression, such apparent lack of movement embodied within his determined agency in many ways promotes a 'deeper' appreciation of nature.

Like the Odyssey, Alvin's first outing is a false start, getting him no farther than the Grotto (with its religious connotations), as predicted by his acquaintances in the town. He has to hitch a lift from a busload of OAP tourists who have the landscape navigated for them. Alvin cannot accept such passive travel that efficiently consumes and appropriates rather than experientially engages with nature.

Owing to his lack of sensual awareness, especially his poor sight, Alvin's stoical spirit has to work even harder to commune with his environment. Hence his journey cannot allow randomness and inconsequentiality. This is a luxury appropriated by the younger traveller within popular film culture. Each incident on the road, therefore, has added significance both allegorically and thematically, which serves to extend Alvin's ability to reconcile memory and identity.

Just to present a flavour of these incidents, I will focus on the first involving a young pregnant girl, hitch-hiking to get away from responsibility and her family. She arrives at Alvin's night camp unable to fulfil her adolescent desire of movement to escape her lot. At first she exposes her youthful honesty and impetuosity by dismissing his rig as a heap of junk, at which he gently scolds her to 'eat your dinner missy'. Their meeting allows Alvin to articulate the power of blood ties, particularly those between mothers and their children, like his daughter Rosie, who is considered 'a bit simple'. He tells how she had four kids and one night someone else was watching the children when a fire started and one boy got badly burned. The state decided that she was not suitable and so they took away her children. 'Not a day goes by but she does'ent pine for those kids.'[41] This piece of dramatic exposition is reinforced by a match-cut of Rose's face back home looking out into the night sky and also contextualises her close observation of a child chasing a ball in an earlier scene. Alvin affirms that a family is like a bunch of sticks tied together: alone they can be broken but together they are invincible.

Critics may suggest that such evocation of family and blood ties equate with a right-wing, conservative agenda which *de facto* serves to marginalise outsiders and 'others', as in *Thelma and Louise*. But the old man, while affirming his moral point of view, speaks from a position of knowledge and personal experience rather than abstract ideology or censure and therefore succeeds in influencing the pregnant young girl. As a sign of her endorsement she leaves a bunch of twigs tied together for Alvin to find when he gets up alone in the morning. In spite of his failing eyesight, this unambiguous signal is telegraphed to him and to the audience.

The most ecologically friendly and helpful couple he meets, Danny Riordan and his nurturing and supportive wife, allow him to camp in their yard and even offer to drive him the rest of his journey. The couple speak of their enjoyment at crossing the river, especially when the trees are in colour. Such classic natural beauty is certainly foregrounded in many shots throughout the film but our hero perceives beyond such 'chocolate box beauty'. Alvin describes his hosts as 'kind' people talking to a 'stubborn' man. His journey is most certainly now affirmed as a pilgrimage where stoic behaviour as part of a Waspish ethic affirms that hardship must be endured to achieve the full benefit of the trip. Watching Alvin head off early the following morning, Danny appears envious of his pilgrimage. One could suggest his witnessing helps to give him sustenance for his own metaphorical future journey. Audiences are encouraged to accept the rationale of such motivation, not as a form of selfish egotism but as a necessary form of self-exploration.

Space is no longer an obstacle as Alvin finally crosses the Mississippi over a man-made bridge, which is attested by David Nye to be evidence of a form of 'technological sublime'. Watching the symmetrical steel supports framing the space while observing the moving water below, audiences are transported by the human prowess of man's ability to traverse landscape in all its forms. Even Alvin's lowly mode of transport becomes imbued with the heroic grandeur of an epic adventure, as in the ultimate Quixotic story and primal road narrative.

Alvin's last night in the wilderness is spent in a graveyard - with its heightened symbolism - where he is welcomed by a priest who tells him that he is in good company with the remains of French trappers making up one of the oldest cemeteries in the southwest. Death is no longer the enemy but instead becomes an essential part of the life cycle. Nonetheless, Alvin's will to act continues as he strives to fulfil his quest and reconcile himself with his Baptist brother. His primary justification for his close bond with his brother centres on memories of extreme cold and almost nine months of winter, which is finally revealed to the priest. 'We talked about the stars and whether anyone else was out in space.' He concluded that they 'pretty much talked each other into growing up'. While he can survey the stars alone or with his daughter, he yearns for his soul-brother to commune in this essentially spiritual exercise.

After a slight delay Alvin reaches his destination and faces the possibility of rejection alone. The first glimpse of the house where his brother lives is reminiscent of Thoreau's *Walden*, set apart within 'wild nature' and dominated by an untrammeled habitat with a prominent porch to observe the delights of raw nature. He shouts out, 'Lloyd' and the suspense is allayed when a frail Harry Dean Stanton appears on the porch with the aid of a walker (intertextually, his unshaven gaunt image is reminiscent of his character in *Paris Texas* (1984), still wandering the desert looking for a meaning to life). After a short silence he asks, 'Did you ride that thing all the way out to see me?' Alvin nods and as the (melo)dramatic tension rises, Alvin is ushered into a seat beside his brother. Lloyd does not need to articulate his appreciation at their newfound communion, which is metaphorically conveyed through the final mise-en-scène. Time is elided as night falls and both brothers look up into the stars and become again at one with the cosmos. However, the stars are most clearly not static as before; a three-dimensional effect is created by their combined experienced vision. They appear to be travelling, in spite of their current immobility, at the speed of light through space and effectively communing with the cosmos.

Tim Kreider and Bob Content's review in *Film Quarterly* remains most critical of such a utopic reading.

> But the stars are not an ambiguous image of serenity, of making peace with the past and coming to rest as Alvin's hopes to do. There's no divine grace or forgiveness in evidence for him, not even the vision of maternal tenderness granted the suffocating Merick (*Elephant Man*) looking up to the stars . . . Alvin's endlessly expanding starscape could just as easily signify vast emptiness and indifference, or the absurdity of human striving in the face of unsurpassable sublimity, or the profound gulf between human yearning and any answering assurance.

> *(Kreider and Content 2000: 32).*

Such a pessimistic reading ignores much of the visual and aural cues reiterated throughout the narrative. Nonetheless, such a questioning interpretation of Alvin's psyche is certainly interesting, even if it results in an inability to endorse this utopic exposition. This final image recuperates Harvey's 'time-space compression' concept as a critique of global capitalism, which here serves as a final metaphor for the transcendent ecological connectivity between all nature and the cosmos.

Old age has found an appropriate signifier for the ultimate journey, which evokes a spiritual pilgrimage rather than a sensory shallow touristic exercise in traversing empty landscape. Like all the great epics, Alvin as prototypical hero has now put his life in order in preparation for his final journey 'back to nature'. Instead of the postmodern road to nowhere, the 'road' leads to an ultimate sublime affirmation of human consciousness as part of the global life cycle. The road movie reaches its apotheosis as an ecological pilgrimage.

However, a majority audience require 'lighter' and more therapeutic and representationally younger agents to take them on this ontological and ecological journey. Science fiction above all other genres fulfils many of these requirements and is the focus of the final chapters in this study.

Notes

1.

Technological Peoples	Native Peoples
Private property as primary	no private ownership/no inheritance
Goods for resale	goods produced for use value
Currency system	barter system
Nature seen as resource	nature viewed as 'being'
Hierarchical political system	non hierarchical
Concept of 'state'	identity as 'nation'
Revere the young	revere the old
High impact technology	low-impact technology
Saving and acquiring	sharing and giving

(Mander 1992: 215-19)

2. For example it is common knowledge that the white settlers massacred the roaming buffalo, not for food, as the Indians did, but simply to colonise the land and force it into submission and fulfil (civilised) eastern economic expectations about the production of profitable cash crops. Official American policy as referred to by the historian William Cronon was designed specifically to starve the Indians by taking away their food source. Nature became an adversary which had to be curbed, even violated, to accord with white man's greedy desires (Cronon 1992). However, revisionist historians like Cronon go on to assert that the arrival of the horse, which came to the Americas in the seventeenth century - like the car for the twentieth century - transformed the native American culture from a rooted people to a nomadic one. They could now follow and hunt the buffalo wherever they roamed and slaughter them at will. Within a generation the Great Plains became the centre of a huge rise in population which in turn decimated the bison population. Later, of course, the species was all but finished off and almost brought to extinction by white settlers and professional hunters.

3. Linda Williams makes an interesting comparison with *Thelma and Louise* and the similar revenge stories of the protagonists which 'grip us because of their mythic excess'. While such excess and alienation is linked with the masculine in *Thelma and Louise*, it is a strange form of

feminine which grips *The Searchers*. 'Both films have mature heroes (Louise and Ethan) who have mysterious, guilty pasts about which they do not speak.' Haunted by an unlawful desire for his brother's wife, Ethan 'shares a measure of guilt with the savages who have raped and abducted her. Though victim of the Indian's violence, Ethan shares it as well. Louise too has a clouded past ...' (in Henderson and Martin 1999: 544).

4. A range of simplistic oppositions can be decoded for a Hollywood audience from the publicity still of Daniel Day Lewis as Hawkeye in the film. He poses bare-chested with a gun standing upright in his clenched fist. As he looks intently at his audience, his straight black 'Indian' hair is romantically counterpointed against the wooded landscape in the background. The caption reads, 'The synthesis of European and Native cultures'.

5. Yet some critics, for example Buscombe *et al.* (1998), suggest that sympathy for Indians has been the rule rather than the exception throughout the history of the western.

6. Jim Collins cogently argues that films like *Thelma and Louise*, *Blade Runner* and *Dances with Wolves* 'all depend not on hybridisation but on an "ethnographic" rewriting of the classic genre film that serves as their inspiration, all attempting, using one strategy or another, to recover a lost "purity", which apparently pre-existed in the golden age of film genre' (Collins 1995: 131).

7. Writers like Jack London, for example, make one believe in the power of 'nature', especially dramatised within 'wilderness'. The author's message is that wilderness must triumph: you either join it and live by its ways, or you succumb. Exposure to 'America' and its capricious elements place supreme demands on the individual, which become an important and ennobling message for a nascent democracy that nurtured the rights and related resourcefulness of each individual.

8. Lewis, in *The American Adam* also reflects on how revisionist Americans wished to be 'emancipated from history and undefiled from the usual inheritances of family and race' (Lewis 1995: 1) as ironically expressed in the highly contentious film *Forrest Gump*.

9. Yet Albert Boime, in 'The Magisterial Gaze', speaks of the unresolvable contradictions inherent in the 'taming of the frontier' and embodied in westerns in particular:
'On the one hand, their conditions of success depended on the raising of the wilderness and the cultivation of a splendid civilization, while with each inch of cultivated soil a little piece of their innocence disappeared. There was no way not to glorify the material development as progress, and there was no way to avoid condemning its results. The realization of the American dream implied the total corruption of the dreamer' (cited in McDonald 1999: 15).

10. The latter resolution was found most frequently in popular culture from the 'penny dreadfuls' onwards. However, the metamorphosis of 'white into red' developed rapidly in the 1950s through the sympathetic western and cogently signalled in *The Searchers*, discussed earlier, with the redemptive myth reaching its peak in *Dances with Wolves* (Bird 1998: 196).

11. The creation of national parks can be seen as symptomatic of guilt, which accompanies the impulse to destroy nature. The human species destroys nature on an unprecedented scale, and then in response to such wrongs, we create parks, which re-stage the nature/society opposition but are entirely framed by society. Great parks are the 'good deeds' of industrial civilisation and quietly affirm the power to stage, situate, limit and control nature. One character in Alan Rudolf's *Equinox* (1992), whose narrative coincidentally also culminates (like *Grand Canyon*, to be discussed later) in the protagonist seeking solace by 'looking' into the sublime landscape, humorously speaks of a desire to go on a pilgrimage to this quintessential sublime site 'before it disappears'.

12. The French New Wave critics also helped to glorify the western and later the road movie as embodying the existential imperative of human nature and its struggles to find new meaning within an inhospitable landscape and outdated bourgeois social structure.

13. Kerouac's celebrated novel *On the Road* (1958) captured 'the great sense of relief that marked post-war American society and culture, a need to make up for time lost at war, a need to consume, as quickly as possible, all the good things that life had to offer' (Eyerman and Lofgren 1995: 58).

14. Budgeted for $375,000, Hopper's directorial debut made over $50 million worldwide during its original release and won the 1969 Cannes Film Festival award for best film by a new director.

15. Baudrillard found the same emptiness when he visited 'America', only an endless chain of signifiers, signifying nothing. 'What is new about America is the clash of the first level (primitive and wild) and the 'third kind (the absolute simulacrum). There is no second level . . . The Cinema and TV are America's reality' (1989: 104).
As Norman Denzin affirms in an essay on Baudrillard's 'America'; movement, and travel or 'speed is simply the rite that initiates us into emptiness' (Denzin 1991: 6).

16. Modernity remains a stigma associated with civilisation, which in this case is the South, whereas in *Dances with Wolves* it is the native Indians and the dominant culture's treatment of them and their lands. The image of the West assures the viewing audience of the enduring presence of the historical past and the ideals of patriotism through what amounts to a transcendental view of America as an 'idyllic wonderland' which is 'untouched by human hands' (Stich cited in Cohan *et al.* 1997: 192). While the West is idealised, the South remains demonised.

17. Yet *Easy Rider* is not simply a counter-nationalist film. On the contrary, it vividly crystallises the tensions between nationalism as a process evolving through time and nationalism as a thing already realised, a thing to be preserved from the assaults of history. According to Homi K. Bhabha, the film's
highways and landscapes are positioned between two extremes: the affirmative patriotism of Americana in the mass media and the raucously critical demystification of Pop Art, between the

romantic, nostalgic yearnings of the former and the violent, apocalyptic mood of the latter (cited in Hill 1996: 184).

18. Gitlin goes on to describe *Easy Rider* as a 'lyric on behalf of paranoia, saying to the counter-culture: yes, you'd better fear those ignorant Southern fascist hard-hats'. The counter-culture became 'transfixed by the image of their demons as they watched this cautionary tale' (*ibid.*: 197).

19. While Jameson perceives postmodernism as a generalised condition of late capitalism, other critics' talk of the ambivalence of the 60s countercultural movement especially with regard to incorporation and resistance. Consequently, such a countercultural movement can be regarded as a utopian prefiguration. Where Jameson perceives aimless pastiche, others critics find anxious ambivalence. Reed speaks of 'a gesture towards utopian redemption of culture . . . that knows itself to be a failed gesture' (but) 'does not wholly succumb to the immense forces of incorporation Jameson elaborates' (Reed 1992: 157).

20. It might appear to some that the post 9/11 'war on terrorism' has afforded American imperialism a renewed sense of ideological hegemony long lost since the trauma of Vietnam.

21. The film represents 'a detour - a trip projected across the space between two images -the snapshot Louise takes at the beginning of the trip and the final still that permanently suspends the women in their thunderbird'. *Thelma and Louise* suggests that audiences need to 'reconceptualize feminine desires and to shift our framework so that it can accommodate not only need or want but also demand. At the same time we need to acknowledge the conflicts and contradictions that inhabit our fantasies' (Willis in Collins 1993: 128).

22. The meaning of this pact, especially if read as a 'lesbian subtext', veers between 'subjection to a hetro-phallic law and the ecstasy of the abyss - [but] they chose the latter with very little hesitation' (Griggers cited in Collins 1993: 133). Ann Friedberg, however, is less reductive in her reading, believing cinema also allows women to 'experience "flanerie" in the form of a mobilised virtual gaze', which is greatly extended within the potentially 'transgressive' form of the road movie (cited in Cohan *et al.* 1997: 356).

23. Bakhtin's notion of chronotope remains an engaging concept in this area of study. It makes clear that there is an intrinsic connectedness of temporal and spatial relationships. Spatial analysis and theories emanating from geographers and social science disciplines in particular provide a central focus point towards investigating the expression of utopian ecology embedded especially within postmodern culture. This spatial diegetic emanates from the roots of the romantic sublime but more recently has begun to permeate within a postmodernist sensibility, especially when married to human agents as characterised in *Grand Canyon*.

24. Like a long line of classic mythic western heroes, this static mise-en-scène produces iconic over-determination (as in the final slow-motion shoot-out in *Bonnie and Clyde*) as they transcend the

diegetic narrative limitations of their spatial trajectory and become a frozen signifier for the spectatorial pleasure of the (female-addressed) audience. The forces of violence and self-destruction are finally transformed into a simulacrum, which for some readers becomes a metaphor for a 'progressive' feminist discourse at the liminal edge of transformation.

25. Simon Schama in *Landscape and Memory* (1995) speaks of similar natural phenomena such as Yosemite and their 'spiritual potential'. However, in order to keep (them) pure we have to occupy (them). Such magnificent sites serve less as a recipe for (ecological) action than an invitation to reflection.

26. Initially place/space can be distinguished by affirming the commonsense notion that place embodies the concrete, micro level of human engagement. 'Place', said Heidegger, 'is the locale of the truth of being' and 'dwelling is the capacity to achieve a spiritual unity between humans and things' (cited in Harvey 1992: 11).

27. White guilt remains an ever-present spectre, especially within the post-industrial environment of the West. 'No matter how hard we try to forget, modern civilization was built on the graves of our savage ancestors, and repression of the pleasures they took from one another, from the animals and the earth. I suspect our collective guilt and denial of responsibility for the destruction of (so called 'savages') pleasure can be found infused in every distinctively modern cultural form' (MacCannell 1992: 24).

28. David Chaney speaks of how the 'Professional classes' can best 'control social space'. In an unusual analogy, he constructs a case that 'professional robbers' in Reservoir Dogs can 'transform a place into their space for the duration of their business' (Chaney 1994: 177). Such a parody exposes a prevailing wish for such control but in this film - as I would suspect within the mind set of a majority of white liberals in LA, such control has been forfeited to black hoods - at least in such places as the inner city ghetto.

29. The sheer size of the canyon is, of course, difficult to comprehend. Its depth is so terrifying that many pull back in fear after the first glimpse. It measures 280 miles long and up to 18 miles wide - representing two billion years of geology in 15,000 feet of tilted-up stone carved down by the Colorado River. Buffalo Bill after a visit wrote in the visitor's book: 'It was too sublime for expression, too wonderful to behold without awe, and beyond all power of mortal description' (cited in Nye 1994: 42).

30. As explored in Chapter 1, it was Kant most particularly who associated the sublime of the North American landscape with a certain kind of primitive mentality and native wildness that could be differentiated from 'thicker' cultures of the European Enlightenment. Kant reckoned in 'Observations on the Feeling of the Beautiful and the Sublime' that 'among all savages there is no nation that displays so sublime a mental character as those in North America' (1960: 111 cited in Pease 1994 : 229).

Kantian liberal politics rests on two basic myths:

1) On the analogy that beauty is the moral good - the idea of harmony serves as an ideological basis for the social contract.

2) On the analogy that the sublime threatens the individual and society with annihilation which is the ideological basis for obedience (see Kroker and Cook 1991: 165).

Kant defines the sublime as an 'object (of nature), the representation of which determines the mind to regard the excavation of nature beyond our reach as equivalent to a presentation of ideas' (cited in Zizek 1992: 202). 'It is precisely nature in its most chaotic, boundless, terrifying dimension which is best qualified to awaken in us the feeling of the sublime' (*ibid*.: 203). But, as Nye effectively argues in *American Technological Sublime*, 'rather than the result of solitary communion with nature', the sublime becomes an experience organised for crowds of tourists as in Disney(land) and in cultural artefacts like Hollywood film which end up 'transforming the individual experience of immensity and awe into a belief in national greatness' (Nye 1994: 43).

31. Narrative film theory speaks of 'suture', which connotes the idea that the subject is stitched together by (film) language; but as Allen asserts, it also suggests that, as in surgery, a wound or hole is covered over that always leaves a scar. This 'space' can of course suggest progression towards a form of transgression.

For Outard, the shot/reverse shot presupposes a role for the spectator in comprehending it that provides a model or analogue for the dialectic of the subject's relationship to language as it is described by Lacan. Outard posits a 'mythical' moment in the spectator's encounter with the first image of the shot/reverse shot sequence when he does not see the image as an image but experiences it as a fluid, fantasmatic reality and recognises the frame in a manner that is only fleeting and unstable. (This corresponds to Lacan's idea of fantasy of engulfment and awareness of frame - like the mirror metaphor) (see Allen 1995: 34).

32. K. Von Maltzahn concludes his *Nature as Landscape* by asserting that 'we must commit ourselves to the cultural sublimation of our desires and the enhancement rather than disfigurement of our fellow human beings and natural beings and our common dwelling place, the earth' (Maltzahn 1994: 129).

33. Urry constructs five forms of tourist gaze:

Romantic - solitary, sustained immersion gaze involving vision, awe, aura.

Collective - communal activity, series of shared encounters gazing at the familiar.

Spectatorial - communal activity, series of brief encounters glancing at and collecting different signs.

Environmental - collective organisation, sustained and didactic scanning to survey and inspect.

Anthropological - solitary, sustained immersion scanning and active interpretation (Urry 1995: 191).

34. In 1993 Zygmunt Bauman, in *Postmodern Ethics*, dismissed the metaphor of 'postmodern nomads' as a way of understanding 'modern pilgrims' (tourists). Unlike pilgrims, nomads do not have a final destination which plots in advance their itinerary. 'Nomads, therefore, are a flawed

metaphor for men and women cast in the postmodern condition. Vagabonds or vagrants offer more apposite a metaphor . . . What keeps him on the move is disillusionment' (Bauman 1993: 240).

Later, in an essay 'From Pilgrim to Tourist', he asserts that 'In modern society, pilgrim is no longer a choice of the mode of life, less still is it a heroic or saintly choice . . . Pilgrimage is what one does of necessity, to avoid being lost in a desert; to invest the walking with a purpose while wandering the land with no destination. Being a pilgrim, one can do more than walk - one can walk to . . .' (in S. Hall 1996: 21). What better way to appreciate the philosophical core of the road movie than in this play between 'disillusionment' and goal-seeking motivation?

35. Martha Nochimson in *Film Sense* describes the film as a 'mellow picaresque story' while affirming that Lynch's art is all about the 'will to lose one's will'. In the 'sublime panoramic and aerial shots of the farm belt', Lynch celebrates the 'bounty of the fruitful, material American earth as the context for his tribute to the endurance of humanity, even in the heart of a desperately isolated and rigidly self-righteous patriarch' (Nochimson 2000: 2).

36. Music, which has not been textually discussed, yet remains central in appreciating this and many other films, punctuates and underpins this nature exposition. The foregrounding of nature in all its forms from bright sunlight to dramatic storms drives the whole narrative and does not act merely as a mood enhancing signifier. The same music idiom running through the film punctuates and underpins the centrality of this evocative nature film.

37. The humour of the situation is dramatised with the fat sun-worshipping lady becoming shocked by his immobility and asking 'what is the number of 911' to get help, together with his daughter's (played by Sissy Spacek with a mental problem) consternation and instinctive reaction: 'What have you done with dad?' -both of which responses disgust his gruff old friend who asks if Alvin is 'nuts'!

38. According to the estimations of Edwin Jahiel (who, incidentally, suggested that Lynch 'pulled a Cocteau'), the trip would take five weeks and cover 254 miles at an average speed of 5 miles per hour (cited in www.prairienet.org/ejahiel). The director held his nerve throughout the film by dramatising the apparent lack of movement while keeping the narrative both simple and concentrated.

39. The only other time this form of electronic communication is consciously used is when Alvin needs to get more money on his travels. Otherwise he needs the isolation and natural acuity of being mobile-phone-less.

40. Some ecologically astute audiences may suggest the representation of genetically modified corn - which equates with the majority of American farm production - raises the prospect of 'pure/impure' nature.

41. In a provocative and auteurist reading of the film in *Film Quarterly* (Fall 2000), Tim Sreider and

Rob Content suggest that there is more hidden than is suggested by my reading. Taking a later incident, which I ignore, that foregrounds a fire brigade's practice of putting out a house fire as Alvin careers out of control down a hill, the reviewers affirm that this signals Alvin's culpability in his grandchild's injury. It was he who was the babysitter, which caused Rosie's children to be taken away from her. While this may be inferred, it does not take away from his striving for forgiveness even redemption.

4 CONSPIRACY THRILLERS AND SCIENCE FICTION: 1950s TO 1990s

Prologue

The roots of science fiction and its potential to expose several ecological fears within western society can be seen most explicitly in American 1950s B-movies. The post-war period legitimised an expansionist mass production engine fuelled by an unheard-of growth in conspicuous consumption. This encouraged western culture to present and maintain, if only superficially, a sense of progressive evolution within an overall plan that was premised on 'improving' society through the conquest of nature. At the same time, the break-up of post-war certainties augmented by the cultural effects of the atom bomb in particular helped to spark a critical ecological representation which initiated a radical reappraisal of this otherwise unquestioned form of progress.

Yet the predominant interpretation of 1950s B-movies, particularly in the light of the Cold War, has continued to be centred on anti-Communist paranoia or fears of an enforced Fordist/McCarthy-style conformity. A newly-constituted ecological interpretation, I will argue, repositions these strictly ideological readings alongside a more modernist discourse of rational control and technological mastery. The chapter will begin this historical reappraisal by examining the naturalisation of American human conformity, which ostensibly validated social and cultural Fordism as it came to be known. Close analysis of conventional exposure of the red paranoia of 1950s America through the seminal *Invasion of the Body Snatchers* (1956) will be compared to the psychologically obsessed agency in *The Incredible Shrinking Man* (1956) and framed within nascent ecological preoccupations embedded within 1950s science fiction.

These thematic representations and preoccupations continued with the 1970s resurgence of science fiction through a more reflective form of eco-paranoia, which will be illustrated through readings of *Soylent Green* (1973) and *Logan's Run* (1976). While cult 1950s narratives like *The Incredible Shrinking Man* posited a nascent redemptive belief in eco-spiritual harmony, more contemporary 1970s science fiction conspiracy films helped create a more reflexive and overt exposé of major ecological issues.

Central to this preoccupation with representation of self and human agency is the feeling of 'loss and the desire for unity that is born of (such) loss' (Campbell in

Glotfelty 1996: 134-5). Ecologists often highlight this experience of lost unity, even separation, from the rest of the natural world and a desire to regain it as central to the core meaning of human nature. Such 'desire' often goes 'beyond the human' (*ibid.*) and serves as a philosophical bedrock for a form of deep ecological affirmation above and beyond the ideological mapping of human nature which is predicated on more recognisable notions of race, class and gender differences.

As Colin MacCabe suggested, there has been 'no new attempt to theorise the relations between politics and film' since the 1970s. In its place there is what he describes as 'a load of local ideological readings, fuelled by identity politics which rarely engage with film as form and history' (MacCabe 1999: 124). This preoccupation with 'local issues' and 'identity politics' has resulted in cultural theorists often playing safe and avoiding the risk of addressing the 'big picture' involving human ontology within which ecological debates must have a central position. What it means to be an 'eco-human' is, of course, more difficult to discuss, much less textually analyse, than the more manageable and definable aspect of gender and identity politics which is more clearly coded and delineated, at least in representational terms.

A key metaphorical breakthrough that solidified a deep holistic approach to planet Earth occurred with the scientific actualisation of space travel and the ability to (re)present the whole planet for the first time using the perceptual tools of photography. This paradigm shift is innocently signalled within the closure of *The Incredible Shrinking Man* and contrasted with a more contemporary example, *Contact* (1998). Yet this apparently linear, even historical, evolution of ecological representations is far from deterministic, as is clear from a psychological interpretation of ecological agency explored in *Contact*.

1960s countercultural idealism, explored in the previous chapter, has also had a profound impact on the science fiction genre. Gene Roddenberry's cult television series Star Trek and subsequent spin-off films like *First Contact* (1996) will be investigated to articulate variations in representations through the creation of memorable and engaging non-human life forms like Spock and Data, together with pernicious enemies like the Borg, which help to articulate radical ecological expressions. 1970s examples of science fiction like *Soylent Green* and *Logan's Run* help to illustrate the transformation towards a more eco-centric evocation of agency together with a more complex engagement with controversial ecological issues, particularly population control.

Hollywood cinema in general is good at portraying effects but finds it difficult to show causes which might address underpinning ecological problems. Causality is primarily a motivational agent of character and plot, propelling the narrative to a final resolution. However, following the growth in scientific knowledge and ecological awareness, science fiction texts began to appropriate a form of diegetic realism through applying conventions of docu-drama within the overall fictional style. For instance, in the eco-conspiracy film *Endangered Species* (1982), journalistic evidence of animals being killed by chemical testing alongside other forms of ecological causality is built into the formal structure of the fictional reality of the film. Finally, the chapter will conclude with a reflective, if sometimes cynical, expression of ecological risk management in *Safe* (1994) - interesting because it effectively splinters the pervasive myth of individualised human self-hood and productive human agency.

Roots of 1950s Science Fiction

Of all the conventional Hollywood genres, science fiction appears to be the most amenable to ecological and social questions - both formally and within a historical context. This is especially true since the genre has always 'bracketed off a special kind of space' where 'technology and humanity interact, as each helps to measure and evaluate the other' (Telotte 1995: 195). This section begins by exploring how 1950s science fiction B-movies present a potentially universal 'green' message embedded within a more recognisable and well-documented 'red' agenda directly connected to the Cold War fear of the bomb. The 1950s Hollywood science fiction B-movie initiated this cultural process of charting the expression of ecological issues, particularly focusing on planetary ecological misuse and how to cope with such effects through the device of applying 'what-if global conspiracy' formats to the various narratives. While it would appear at the outset that fear of nuclear energy, together with the misuse of pesticides, were simple narrative devices as in the Pandora's Box myth, nonetheless such exposure consolidated the use of ecological expression in Hollywood film.

> Few things reveal so s harply as science fiction the wishes, hopes, fears, inner stresses and tensions of an era, or define its limitations with such exactness

(Gold cited in Feuer 1990: 15) .

By its very nature, science fiction film, in some way or other, calls into question the world we live in and accept as absolute. While many of the ideas that run through these films are often fanciful, nevertheless, even if distorted and sometimes obtuse, they represent attempts to think in a genuinely speculative way about the future(s) that awaits us.

Yet, for many critics, the dominant task of film history continues to involve analysing the circumstances under which the cinema was appropriated as an instrument of ideology with a clear political imperative. McCarthyism represented a concerted ideological attack on the political establishment and used the mass media to scare the public into becoming suspicious of a left-wing conspiracy to undermine the American body politic. This was allegorically represented through science fiction as exposing the threats to free speech which threatened America in the 1950s, especially with the so-called 'social realist' film losing its institutional support.[1] The 'red menace' became a major dilemma for many left-wing artists in Hollywood who found it difficult to comment about society through their art and were encouraged to expose each other as traitors to their newfound homeland of America. Academic critics affirmed that these science fiction films covertly addressed these historical tensions, reflecting the hysterical fears of a Communist take-over by the 'enemy within' which swept across America in the 1950s. What is less appreciated, however, is that for the first time these films also helped construct a universal, if nascent, eco-consciousness through the growing understanding and fear of (non)natural forces and their resulting threats to human nature.

The representation of nature, both human and non-human, becomes central to this revisionist appreciation of 1950s science fiction film, which concentrates on the pervasive but often undetectable alien forces menacing the human world. The alien other, in particular, serves a representational function beyond the specific hermeneutics of American Cold War politics and signals the beginning of a new ontological threat, which focused on the real possibility of the extermination of all life forms on the planet as a consequence of the dropping of the first atom bomb. Homo sapiens (at least Americans to start with) had the scientific power to exterminate all life forms on the planet. This newfound potency encouraged the growth of critical ecological discourses expressed in films like *Them* (1954), *The Thing from Another World* (1951) and *Invasion of the Body Snatchers* (1956), which will be discussed in detail later.

Scientific Exploration: Nuclear Catastrophe

Before World War Two, scientific exploration was considered largely benevolent, promoting a utopian meta-narrative which underpinned the values of western civilisation. Opinion leaders continually used the image of science, technology and progress to legitimise political decisions and governmental policies. Even President Truman, speaking about the 1945 atom bomb, spoke of harnessing the basic power of the universe and the force from which the sun draws its power. As a counterweight, however, the much-maligned science fiction B-movies of the period often subverted this scientific endorsement, exposing the potentially harmful ecological effects of nuclear development in particular and undercutting its hegemonic consensus in general.

1950s science fiction most specifically addresses these nuclear fears:

In the post Hiroshima world, science fiction made emotional sense. The fears that science fiction had treated in the past were too real and the genre flourished as a means of simultaneously highlighting and banishing these fears as film after film depicted the awful consequences of the misapplication of technology and man's inability, after much destruction, to regain control of his destiny

(Hardy 1995: xiv).

Such critics affirm that the 1950s was a decade in which anxiety, paranoia and complacency became entwined. On the threshold of space, 'man' had discovered and used a force so frightening that it could mean the extinction of the human species. The world, only so recently saved for democracy was, once again, and in spite of Truman's endorsement, divided by fears around nuclear power. The New York *Times*, in an editorial a day after Hiroshima, asserted that human beings faced the prospect either of destruction on a scale which dwarfed anything thus far reported or, alternatively, a golden era of social change which would satisfy the most romantic utopian. While Hiroshima unleashed the possibility of man's annihilation at the hands of his own technology and even the promise of reducing him to the status of robot, life in the 1950s was unthinkable without the support of that same technology.

Peter Biskind affirms that where science causes problems, it often solves them too. For example, in *It Came from Beneath the Waves* (1955), a giant octopus spawned by nuclear testing is finally destroyed by an atomic torpedo. While so-called 'conservative films questioned science', Biskind concludes, 'they by no means rejected it wholesale. Science was fine, so long as it was under control, subordinated to traditional values' (Biskind 1983: 105).[2] As long as the issue was framed as a choice between 'atoms of war and atoms of peace', it is hard to see who could be against the development of nuclear power. Such powers became 'an incontestable symbol of technological progress' (Gamson 1992: 52) but many 1950s B-movies like *Them* dramatised the dark side of this uncontested optimistic assessment.

Them

In *Them* (1954), directed by Gordon Douglas, a child (Descher) is discovered wandering in the desert in a state of deep shock by two policemen. Nearby they find a wrecked trailer and a single track in the sand from which they hear a chilling cry on the horizon. Back in town, Deake, the policeman, hears the cry again, steps out of a building and is never seen again. An FBI agent, Arness, investigates and discovers that atomic tests in the desert have produced a giant species of ant. Eventually a resolution is found when the ants are destroyed in the sewers to which they have escaped. The potential ecological side-effects of nuclear fusion are of course exaggerated for dramatic effect but are nonetheless explored from within a 'teen-flick' horror B-movie format.

Yet many critics read *Them* as primarily reinforcing racist ideas through an anti-Communist tract, with the ants codified as communists.[3]Alternatively, Vivian Sobchack suggests that such creature films of the 1950s are about the preservation of social order. 'What is called for is teamwork, co-operation, and organisation' (Sobchack 1997: 44). Cohan suggests that *Them*

> does not mean to raise doubts about the achievements of science in unleashing the bomb any more than the postwar biblicals mean to question the existence of God in the wake of Auschwitz. Rather than evoke intellectual or moral interrogation by its audience, *Them* takes pains to differentiate one social order, that of the ants, from another, that of the human community which the monsters threaten
>
> *(Cohan 1997: 131).*

All of these readings assume that 'ants' must anthromorphically articulate some direct attribute of human society. A deep ecological reading, however, promotes a more holistic, less partisan position, focusing on the consequences of the big ecological picture rather than simply abstracting an ideological fit, which reduces inanimate nature to effective surrogates for race, class or even gender debates.

A more accurate contextual reading can be appreciated by looking at Spencer R. Weart's exploration of the 'images' of nuclear fear and the success of the *Godzilla* series - the 400-foot prehistoric reptile that stamped Tokyo flat (reflecting 'firsthand' experiences of the bomb) - and similar 'bomb fears' in America. In *Them*, as already indicated, killer ants the size of buses crawled out of the desert near the Trinity test site, 'a fantastic mutilation', as the film's scientists explained, 'probably caused by lingering radiation from the first atom bomb'. Contemporary moviegoers, Weart argues, 'found that plausible enough to put them into a cold sweat. After the army exterminated the creatures, an official in the film worried that if such horrors followed the first test, what would come from all the bombs that exploded since' (Weart 1988: 192).[4] This reading begins to articulate contemporary global ecological fears and debates embedded within such texts, yet often ignored by film critics preoccupied with more 'local' identity debates.

Similarly, *The Beast from 20,000 Fathoms* (1953), directed by Eugene Lourie, begins with a dinosaur which is awoken in the North Pole as a result of scientific nuclear experimentation. While there is no intrinsic critique of such experimentation, its consequences are explored using the monster motif. The narrative helps to evoke the awesome power contained within nuclear energy and how such force cannot be controlled through ordinary (i.e. non-scientific) means.

However - and ultimately affirming the paradox implicit in 1950s culture - while a nuclear explosion caused the terrible monster to come alive in the first place, a radioactive isotope is also required to destroy the terror in the end.[5]

Peter Biskind in his study of 1950s B-movies also signals the possibility of a supra-ecological reading by proposing that many of these cultural artefacts remain preoccupied with 'nature' defined as 'the *Other*' and it is this 'othering' tendency which 'threatens to disrupt and destroy culture'. Biskind adds that science also exists in order to control nature but if it resists this control, 'nature becomes monstrous' (cited in Jancovich 1996: 17).[6] While analysis of 1950s B-movies, which explicitly use fears of nuclear power together with other radiation scares to feed various types of eco-paranoia, is relatively straightforward, other films, which appear less preoccupied with nature, require more careful investigation. For instance, the classic *Invasion of the Body Snatchers*, which focuses particularly on an alien threat, remains ostensibly preoccupied with a specific form of right/left ideological paranoia and appears resistant to the more overt ecological paranoia cited above. Nonetheless, the film's primary trajectory remains focused on human identity together with the implications for a progressive expression of ecological identity as opposed to those emanating from anti-human life forms.

Invasion of the Body Snatchers

1950s America was steeped in representations of conformity aided by post-war economic expansion, with the 'pod people' in *Invasion of the Body Snatchers* serving as an effective metaphor for the McCarthy show trials. McCarthyism promoted mob rule and the diminution of human individuality. [7] For many critics, the 'pod people' came to reflect non-individualised simpletons who accept losing their personality and selves for the good of the system, not unlike the Communist system or the Borg in *Star Trek*, to be discussed later. Political debates can more easily be engaged with when displaced through representation of societies that are non-terrestrial.

The Cold War, which was much like any other war with regard to how the mass media functions, essentially served to polarise public opinion. The slogan demanded of every citizen affirmed 'You must be either with us or against us'. Freedom of expression has not got the same cosy liberal meaning during such periods as compared to peace time when the mass media, not to mind audience/public manipulation, is not as strategically important to the body politic. The takeover of 'normal' middle American town-folk by alien pod people while they sleep represents the eternal struggle to uphold sacred liberal notions of humanity, which must be defended by right-minded individuals. Kevin McCarthy sums up the mood when he says to Dana Wynter in the film, 'All of us harden our hearts, only when we have to fight to stay human do we know how precious life is - like for you and me.'

Mark Jancovich, however, promotes a gender reading by asserting that for most intellectuals in the period 'conformity meant emasculation'. In the novel from which the film is adapted, Jancovich asserts, 'Humanity is associated with irrationality and with feelings and emotions.' Miles, the main protagonist, proposes how 'it is creativity, hope and most especially desire which are essentially human'. For Miles, the greatest proof that the pods are different from humans is that 'the former lack a sense of sexuality and sexual difference' (Jancovich 1996: 65-6).

A more universal and persuasive ecological reading can most clearly be signalled in the scene that provides firsthand witnessing by the chief protagonists of the ultimate corruption of the sanctity of nature. The *mise-en-scène* in the greenhouse, where the four 'right-minded' protagonists and friends first discover the truth of the alien invasion, graphically illustrates Biskind's 'other' through the perversion of nature, which is beginning to swallow up the small rural community. Normally a habitat for controlled nurturing growth, protected from the harsh elements, the community is overtaken by a harvest of 'unnatural pods' that are designed to take over the human race. The doctor and chief protagonist offers a conventional scientific explanation, citing 'atomic radiation of plant life' and 'some form of mutation' as a probable cause of such awesome unnatural growth.

A later scene, which shows the main protagonist spying on the early morning scene in the small town square from a first floor window, affirms the pervasive implications of such unnatural proliferation. Again the overall effect is unnerving in that it subverts the naturalness of an ostensibly bustling street market *mise-en-scène*. The perversion of the nurturing and stewardship role and function of conventional farming agents, as they disseminate seed to aid the destruction of the human species, must rank as one of the most anti-ecological tropes in filmic history (which incidentally is comically perverted by the bug-alien farmer in *Men in Black* discussed in Chapter 1). The coldness and utilitarian functionalism of these non-human creatures becomes a perversion of communal rural values, while at the same time dramatising the anti-human attributes of these pernicious aliens who simply need to assimilate to survive. Life is simple for the pod people (either read as Communist or, alternatively, as those who expose others during the 'red scare' in America), whose only instinct is to survive. They have no other emotion such as love, hate or ambition but silently and single-mindedly conspire to acquire seed to infiltrate and procreate throughout the country. 'Ordinary' people become mere functional tools of a totalitarian nightmare. Their representation is evocative and similar to the continuing threat implicit in many science fiction characterisations of aliens, where non-sentient beings regard the ecological imperative of life as totally reductive, with no need for love or emotions, only the crude Darwinian instinct to survive. Such agents do not conform to any form of symbiotic harmony within a nurturing holistic eco-system or offer any addition to the evolutionary gene pool but instead treat all 'natural' organisms as either food or, alternatively, a host victim to help take over the much sought after planetary biosphere.

The normative liberal-humanist values of the chief protagonist serve to counter the dystopic world view embodied in the aliens and help to promote the view that what ultimately elevates true human existence is a holistic, emotional engagement with the world and all its sentient life forces. This conventional deep ecological principle is foreshadowed, for example, by a nurturing empathy for a dog almost killed on the road which symbolises Dana Wynter's human(e) credentials. But this unquestioning affirmation of these ethical values, as well as the ontological opposition between aliens (who in every other way replicate human form and consciousness) and humans, is most dramatically and horrifically illustrated later. Only when the doctor kisses his beloved, after leaving her for a short time alone in a cave, does he realise that finally she too has been 'taken over'. The over determined shot/reverse shot, revealing horror through an extreme close-up of the doctor's eyes together with his shocked facial expression, has fascinated audiences and film-makers ever since. Only when human agents perceive what they could lose and 'have to fight to stay human' can they then begin to appreciate the full horror of their predicament.

The Incredible Shrinking Man

This preoccupation with ontological notions of human nature is more personally and psychologically addressed within *The Incredible Shrinking Man* while avoiding references to contemporary 'local' ideologies, except for gender politics. Unlike *Invasion of the Body Snatchers*, which never questions the hero's ethical or scientific justification in the face of a pervasive anti-natural force, the 'shrinking man' must learn to face up to his transformation and reappraise his relations with nature and his environment. The narrative becomes a microcosmic example of one man's search for identity within the radically changed environment of his erstwhile controlled domestic habitat.

The Incredible Shrinking Man, directed by Jack Arnold, provides in many ways a striking example of eco-spiritualism. Scott Carey, the main protagonist, begins a process of diminution after exposure to an odd combination of insecticides and radioactive materials. The film first holds to an objective, eye-level schema that emphasises the banality of Scott's suburban existence. As in *Invasion of the Body Snatchers*, the deadpan banality emphasises the horror of the transformation by grounding it in the experiential familiarity of the everyday. As the shrinking continues for Scott, the style changes.

The disjunction of cinematic space is unsettling, literally dislocating . . . Once he falls into the basement the camera changes radically . . . Objects are transformed here in the paraspace: pins become swords, matchboxes offer shelter from the storm, pencils serve as life rafts, spiders turn into hellish monsters. Commodities become objects.

Sobchack concludes, 'we as viewers, are forced . . . to constantly re-evaluate our responses to the ordinary and normal, to the animate and inanimate' (in Bukatman 1994: 160-1).

On a more prosaic level, audiences immediately connect with the use of special effects to create this diminutive world view. Yet these 'primitive' special effects, addressed in particular to a newly-created teenage audience, are often dismissed as cheap spectacle. This appears at odds with the literary antecedents of 1950s science fiction films, which tended to be more narrative and content driven than the contemporary SFX filmic variety. Peter Biskind dismissively suggests that the 'visual blandness' of such films was appropriate to the mood of conformity while providing an ironic counterpoint to their alarming premises. It was science fiction more than any other genre that caught the hysteria behind the 'picture window' (Biskind 1983: 103).

For the literary academic critic, however, less emphasis is given to the function of these special effects and their qualities as spectacle (Doherty in Feuer 1990: 148) than to the literary back-story. In spite of rather than because of their - pedigree, almost fifty years later they have become legitimate sources for popular cultural excavation.

The Incredible Shrinking Man is most frequently read as a parable on emasculation using psychoanalytic (especially Freudian) terminology. Mark Jancovich's analysis of the source book for the film suggests that Cary 'fears losing his feelings of superiority and significance as a man and becoming subordinate to others' power and authority' (Jancovich 1996: 161). Jancovich goes so far as to assert that the 'film not only provides a critique of the values of maturity, but overtly flaunts the "sensible" and the "realistic" in favour of a world of childlike imagination and awe' (*ibid*.: 170). At the same time, through 'the sympathetic handling of the monstrous outsider', the film also questions 'what it means to be human, and so establish the right to be different' (*ibid*.: 89-90).

The film most clearly projects and dramatically simulates a microcosmic environment, so that Scott (who becomes emblematic of homo sapiens) can begin to reappraise his (im)potency over his environment. The causal-effect narration, which initiated the reduction process, is explicitly ecological, involving exposure to a lethal pesticide (mysteriously appearing in a dark cloud) while on a boat at sea.

Also his resultant physical shrinkage is most certainly emblematic of the loss of male potency symbolised by his marriage ring falling off his finger. Nevertheless, I would suggest, the transformation that follows promotes a radical ecological appreciation of self and agency together with the more obvious gender exposé.

J. P. Telotte accurately sums up its continuing appeal by analysing how the film (re)presents a basic metaphor which explores 'how to cope with a world and a self that no longer has a common or consistent measure' (Telotte 1995: 188-9). Such overt fracturing of the coherence of human nature, much less masculinity, together with the disintegration of an environment which places human nature at the controlling epicentre, also suggests the splintering of a modernist sensibility and produces a philosophical challenge to a coherent understanding of human nature. Nevertheless, the transcendent finale reaffirms a holistic meta-narrative and helps, Telotte concludes, to 'locate a hope'; a sense not simply 'that we are in the process of creating our replacements, assisting in our extinction, but that we are also reframing and reaffirming our humanity' (Telotte 1995: 188-9).

This is most clearly articulated through the ending of the book, which is faithfully visualised by the equally provocative closure of the film adaptation. As Scott is finally liberated from his basement prison, a new 'eco-human' agency is created. Gazing in awe and in empathy with the stars and the heavens, he achieves an extremely holistic epiphany by unconditionally accepting, in spite of his diminutive status, that he is part of the cosmos. This 'eco-spiritual' conversion is confirmed by his final filmic voice-over speech, which culminates with an affirmation: 'To God there is no zero, I still exist.'

Throwing away the ego-centred preoccupation of man's power over nature which was never questioned in *Invasion of the Body Snatchers*, the 'Shrinking Man' takes on a new rejuvenated self-hood once he accepts his co-equal existence and status with the rest of life. Sobchack supports this ecological reading:

> What creates the terrifying wonder and pessimism in these films is not primarily the giant ant or spider, nor the creature, nor the alien invader ... Rather what evokes awe and terror is the terrain of Earth itself ... we are forced to a pessimistic view of the worth of technological progress and of man's ability to control his destiny

(*Sobchack 1997: 112-13*).

Nevertheless, Sobchack appears to dismiss the film's ending, describing it as 'gratuitous' yet 'metaphysically upbeat' and concludes that 'visually the whole film moves us pessimistically and existentially away from the supposed security of human relationships, the comforts and connotations of "home", into a vast, unstable, and non-anthropomorphic universe' (*ibid*.: 135-6).

But, surprisingly, this apparent disorientation serves to promote a more holistic vision of ecological values. For example, Manuel Castells picks up on this positive reading and even endorses its utopic affirmation of a 'non-anthropomorphic universe'. Castells suggests that the holistic notion of integration between humans and nature as presented by deep ecology writers does not refer to 'a naive worshipping of pristine natural landscapes, but to the fundamental consideration that the relevant unit of experience is not each individual, or for that matter, historically existing human communities' (Castells 1997: 125). To merge ourselves with our cosmological self we need first to change the notion of time, to feel 'glacial time' running through our lives, to sense the energy of stars flowing in our blood and to assume 'the rivers of our thoughts endlessly merging in the boundless oceans of multiformed living matter' (*ibid*.: 126).

Scott Cary has certainly abandoned his own desire to assert 'masculine dominance and rationality upon the world'. He even comes 'to recognise the value of alien worlds and forms of existence, and revels in the new sensations and experiences which they offer' (Jancovich 1996: 163). Jancovich succinctly confirms this eco-spiritual interpretation of the film's closure as opposed to the novel's ending:

> Carey comes to accept a universe without hierarchies in which he does not need to assert his dominance and independence. He comes to see existence as a 'gigantic circle' in which 'the infinite and the infinitesimal' meet. Instead of the novel's endless layers of existence each with its own value, the film suggests that the cosmic and microcosmic meet. As Carey disappears into nothingness, he attains cosmic stature and is finally at one with existence. If God is invoked at this moment, he is not a patriarch who exists independently from creation, but is the cosmic universe itself. In this way, the film values innocence over knowledge, the undeveloped over the developed, and immaturity over maturity. While Carey is not a child at the end, he rejects the values of adult masculinity and maturity in favour of a blissful union with creation

(*ibid.: 194*).

This rejection of the values of adult masculinity is posited as central if a new utopian ecological sensibility is to be born and developed. This transformation is provocative and romantic but remains framed within a modernist notion of agency, which valorises the transcendent harmony that can be achieved if protagonists align themselves with the power of nature. This utopic closure will later be contrasted with Contact (1999) where the female protagonist, instead of rejecting gender identity, uses her 'transcendent' experience in space to become reconnected with the comfort-blanket memory of her father which helps to overcome her psychological incompleteness and motivates her scientific career. This inability to move beyond the psychologically driven clutches of her childhood memories helps to highlight an emerging weakness within conventional ego-centric (rather than ecological) agency, which is most fully exposed in the final reading in this chapter.

Like many of the 'sublime' endings analysed in this study, space and time become frozen in the filmic diegetic, with Carey serving as a cipher for audience understanding and appreciation of his newfound ethical and philosophical standpoint. Scott Bukatman succinctly suggests that the sublime 'indicates a crisis in the subject' by disrupting the customary 'relationship between subject and external reality. It threatens human thought, habitual signifying systems and finally human prowess' (in Kuhn 1999: 265). Such sublime moments become enriched by affording the filmic space and time to make meaning ecologically significant. A nascent ecological 'learning space' is provided for audiences to oscillate between identification with this diminutive human agent and his awe-struck inclusive speech and identification through the expansive nature of the stars as the camera pans across the heavens. But such awe is tempered by a form of childish innocence and ignorance with Scott, unable to return the look from beyond the pull of the earth's gravity. With the evolution of space travel as a scientific possibility, such innocent fantasy could become more dialogical, allowing for a more reflective form of non-anthropomorphic expression.

Planet Earth: A Defining Eco-Metaphor

A primal visual metaphor which helped promote a new holistic vision of earth became physically possible when space travel allowed cameras to represent the planet for the first time as a separate and *total* eco-system. This unique evocation of 'our' planet is comparable to other revolutionary visual metaphors of scientific freedom. Instead of Galileo looking up at the stars and imagining man's role in space travel, human exploration became a more active process of investigation capable of seeing for the first time the macro eco-system to which all sentient beings belong.

Symbiotic human expression began to reach maturity with the merging of an innocent sublime connection with the planet and the cosmos discussed above, together with the scientifically validated visual image of our spherical planet as a holistic eco-system. 'When we see the earth from space through the brilliance of science,' the Prince of Wales, a promoter of ecological values, asserts in a BBC documentary, 'it confirms an age-old instinct in man, which we have been made to feel almost ashamed to admit , that we are part of nature' (23 May 1990).[8] As several ecological critics conclude, 'We need ecology to discover what a biotic community means as an organisational mode.' Only planet Earth as an ecology has a range of 'eco-systems which generate a spontaneous order that envelops and produces the richness, beauty, integrity and dynamic stability of (its) component parts' (Attfield and Belsey 1994: 22-6).

Marshall McLuhan went even further by connecting this planetary evocation of nature to the birth of ecology and observed:

> When Sputnik (1957) went around the planet, the planet became programmable content, and thus became an art form. Ecology was born, and Nature was obsolesced
>
> *(cited in McKibben 1990: 80).*

Bill McKibben in his best-seller *The End of Nature* coincidentally reiterates McLuhan's idea and further suggests that there is 'no such thing as nature anymore'. We have 'killed off nature - that world entirely independent of us which was here before we arrived and which encircled and supported our human society' (McKibben 1990: 86-9).

Human nature could finally be scientifically visually codified and recognised as part of a planetary eco-system. Some idealistically suggest that this realisation will become as revolutionary, in its intellectual effects, as previous revolutions which continue to promote 'outdated' concepts, especially endless material growth and destructive nationalism. This form of 'interplanetary ecological holism', clearly signalled in the closure of *The Incredible Shrinking Man*, might eventually teach humans their symbiotic relationship with all other sentient beings, together with the stewardship demands of conservation and protection. Particularly for environmentalists,

> the NASA photographs represented not just a view of the world but a world view, one in which humanity was destined to destroy the earth and itself unless it mended its ecologically unsustainable ways and finds common ground for working and living together on this frail and finite planet. The environmentalists attempted a re-vision(ing) of the earth, appropriating the image from outer space as a means for changing the way people visualised the planet and thus conceptualised their relationship with it
>
> *(Bryant 1995: 44).* [9]

William Bryant, however, regards these 'essentialist' visions and sentiments as 'naive idealism', which may simply be misplaced. Bryant in 'The Re-vision of Planet Earth: Space Flight and Environmentalism in Postmodern America' (re)constructs an oppositional position to this apparently 'progressive vision', which tries to appropriate the beautiful blue photo-image of our planet to endorse continuous exploration and the conquering of nature 'in an evolutionary journey towards an ever more exalted state of humanity' (*ibid*.: 45). An Enlightenment-inspired faith in the 'progress' of humanity, through space exploration, remains at odds with an ideological reading of such travel that endorses the promotion of nationalistic and scientific virility. This contradictory utopic expression of space has continued as an important subtext in science fiction representation.

However, this apparently innocent utopic vision of space travel coupled with the preoccupation with the earth's fragile eco-system soon faced more pervasive opposition, according to Bryant, as spaceship earth became saturated and commodified as a dematerialised image rendering 'space, time and experience depthless' (*ibid*.: 59). Bryant connects such 'regressive' representations with the beginning of postmodernism and its preoccupation with simulacra, surface imagery and relativistic agency.[10] The potent symbol of eco-awareness had, he believes, in many ways been emasculated by the forces of commodity capitalism and concludes that the only way forward to assert our eco-conscience and 'to disrupt this flat veneer' is to embody a 'radical otherness' which is not taken in by such commodification (*ibid*.: 61).

While Bryant's critical objectivity with regards to the commodification of planet Earth iconography in the service of ideological regeneration is convincing, his demands for 'radical otherness' which signal the possibility of separateness from the fickle mire of postmodern simulacrum is somewhat problematic and will be fully explored in the final chapter. The potency of sublime images of the planet, together with natural features like the Grand Canyon, cannot fully be reduced to the technical and mechanical means of their reproduction. Suspect intentions embedded in the construction of such potent images - as with the analysis of special effects and *Jurassic Park* in Chapter 2 - while important, do not necessarily invalidate or negate the positive and productive utopic potentialities within these mythic metaphors as they continue to address and reflect on human consciousness. Conceptual and creative forces are not necessarily crippled by the corruption, or at best impurity, of a range of myth-making representations. This evolving complexity and plurality of meanings embedded in the planet can be appreciated by drawing comparisons between the earth-bound, pre-space travel evocation in *The Incredible Shrinking Man* and the more knowing yet conventional idealistic appreciation of the planet and space travel in *Contact* (1997), which appears surprisingly 'old fashioned' - even endorsing conventional modernist ideals. In particular, the following reading can be framed around its inability to endorse Bryant's critique from a feminist standpoint which finally renders 'space, time and experience depthless' (*ibid*.: 59).

Contact

Contact was co-written by the famous astronomer Carl Sagan, who echoes Leopold's famous 'land ethic' in affirming how

> We have begun to contemplate our origins; we speak for the earth. Our obligation to survive is owed not just to ourselves but also to that cosmos, ancient and vast, from which we spring

(Sagan 1980: 345). [11]

The film charts the story of Ellie Arroway (Jodie Foster), who is orphaned at the age of 9 and grows up obsessed with the possibility of scientifically communicating with distant planets. Like Scott's 'shrinking' man, to achieve her dream she must learn to take a leap of non-scientific faith, to grow to love such cosmic wonder without necessarily having all the answers. Unlike Scott, who is a layman, she joins the SETI (Search for Extra Terrestrial Intelligence) project and devotes her professional life to the ultimate scientific/philosophical quest. Ellie's life quest is finally validated by a 'wild psychedelic ride to the alien system', where the extraterrestrials, in order to commune with her, construct a kind of 'virtual reality landscape based on her own memories' (Davis 1999: 234).

Like its 1950s counterpart, the film is also a paean to faith and optimism in the eternal search for knowledge of the 'Godhead' to reveal the true purpose of human nature. The lack of certainty coupled with the striving for some form of meaning is provocatively asserted by the incantation, 'If there's nobody out there, it's an awful waste of space'. This is enunciated first by her father as they contemplate the stars and the infinite dimensions of space, second by a religious leader (who cannot yet replace her father emotionally or spiritually), and finally by Ellie herself as she becomes capable of affirming this utopic logic.

Psychological readings[12] in particular cite the 'father-daughter' reunion in space as reinforcing regressive patriarchal norms and recreating a 'pristine vision of early paradise where father and daughter can be together again'. According to Jung's 'Symbols of Transformations', in most religions 'it seems that the formative factor which creates the attributes of divinity is the father-imago, while in older religions it is the mother-imago' (cited in White and Wang 1998).

Religious reviewers like Bryan Stone in the *Journal of Religion and Film* (1998) seek to square 'religious' and 'scientific' faith as expressed in *Contact*, which consciously tries not to 'yield to the standard Hollywood convention of trivialising religion by presenting those who embody faith, as misinformed, confused, ineffective, fundamentalist, or fanatic'. In spite of various reservations, Stone lauds the film's courage in exploring spirituality and matters of faith head-on, which is still rare in Hollywood cinema.

Like *Men in Black*, the opening sequence of *Contact* with its seemingly endless zoom-out from galaxies and stars to the hero's eye, counterpointed with the wormhole journey to an alien environment towards the end of the film, evokes and visually reinforces a transcendent connection between humans and the(ir) cosmos. Towards the end of the film, Ellie contemplates a handful of sand that sparks off images of a tropical beach (narratively derived from the rather crude painting of Florida which she created as a child) that becomes her personalised objective correlative for eventual contentment as an eco-sapien. The grains of sand help to recapture her comforting 'vision of an alien world' where her biological father becomes materialised for her benefit.

Somewhat like Sol in *Soylent Green* to be discussed later, she is ritualistically escorted into the spaceship to make her journey into space. Oriental escorts ceremoniously bow before they leave Ellie alone to face her fears. The subsequent exaggeration of confinement - rarely if ever used to dramatise claustrophobia for male astronauts - helps to affirm her heroic yet at the same time stereotypical gender-based role. The emotional narrative trajectory of her character in this film is similar to *The Accused* (1988) and more particularly *Silence of the Lambs* (1990), where the heroine is also driven by a psychological block, which must be resolved before becoming psychologically 'balanced'. The journey to meet her father simultaneously allows her to satisfy a scientific urge to witness alien life and a personal desire to become psychologically whole again after the loss of her parents.

In the end, everything in her transcendent psychological space is represented via 'chocolate box beauty', which is equivalent to the mantra of the hero in *Forest Gump*, the directors' earlier Zeitgeist movie. This visualised sentimentality is strongly contrasted with Ellie's first realisation that astronomy will dominate her life. She recalls to her would-be lover how she remembered observing Venus and being told that its beauty was primarily visible as a result of the various poisonous gasses circulating around its atmosphere, which convinced her of the primacy of the discipline. But apparently because of her psychological impairment she is unable to transcend the restraining carcass of self sufficiently enough to truly feel 'glacial time' as expressed earlier and therefore must remain a faulty protégé and agent for eco-human engagement. Consequently her ecological agency, namely her wish to find holistic harmony, remains fatally compromised.

The pervasive nuclear fears explored initially in the 1950s are countered by spacemen, who give hope in a world where vision of the stars is sometimes obscured by pollution and the ever-present potential of nuclear destruction. This otherwise utopic vision of space-agents is further obscured by a regressive form of gender stereotyping which is avoided in the evocation of masculinity in *The Incredible Shrinking Man*. Nevertheless, sparks of utopian representation, embodying the wish-fulfilling urge for harmony with the eco-cosmos, clearly enunciated by the 'Shrinking Man' has not been lost at the end of the millennium.

The *mise-en-scène* set in the sand in the latter half of *Contact* continues to focus on Ellie kneeling down in a supplicant religious pose, while observing a sublime landscape (similar to the *Grand Canyon*) and hence reminiscent of the closure of *The Incredible Shrinking Man*. However, this apparently utopic vision negates the possibility of Ellie creating Bryant's new form of 'radical otherness'. In particular, Ellie cannot rise to the challenge of social integration, much less any radical form of otherness, remaining trapped within her psychological determinants. Her journey from orphan to mature scientist demonstrates, at best, a faulty sense of transformation and remains a flawed prototype as an ecological agent.

This is most graphically illustrated in a sequence after Ellie has given evidence to another committee on the unrecorded events of 'first contact'. When she leaves the court escorted by Joss, her surrogate-father/lover, it is he who has to speak to the reporters and general public massed outside. She has no public voice but instead privately smiles in approval at her benefactor, a religious visionary who sees beyond the personal and the scientific and eulogises upon her purity of heart and continued faith in herself. Her latent characterisation is incapable of developing like the 'Shrinking Man' who effectively mutates outside of the corpus of egocentric selfish agency.

Since the late 1960s and 1970s, ecological agency and expression became much more contradictory, as can be appreciated by analysing the *Star Trek* phenomenon from the 'countercultural' 1960s into the 'postmodern' 1990s. The *Star Trek* series illustrates how human ecological contradictions and conflicts are best explored using alien life forms as a counterpoint to human forms. In particular the notion of 'otherness' as contradictory is most clearly illustrated by *Star Trek*, which helped create a whole new world view alongside other potential life forms, which were at best sketched out within 1950s B-movies.

Star Trek: First Contact

Space, the final frontier. These are the voyages of the Starship Enterprise. Its continuing (5 year) mission, to explore strange new worlds, to seek out new life and new civilisations, to boldly go where no 'man' has gone before.

This opening mantra of the original *Star Trek* series serves to position the series within the frontier myth conceptualised by the Turner thesis and the Americanisation of the West, which is extended into extraterrestrial conquest. *Star*

Trek served to legitimise this otherwise outdated and politically incorrect myth. Aliens can more easily be accommodated as the other within science fiction culture and concurrently help to reinvigorate these myths, while not having to conform to the particularities of the earth's socio-political systems. Explicit threats to the earth's fragile eco-systems as a consequence of alien life-forces remain a constant thematic preoccupation throughout the series' history.

The central experience of space travel in *Star Trek* is dramatised by encounters between humans and non-humans. This encounter ('first contact') is framed by a liberal egalitarian humanism, which sought to offset the imperialist polarisation between cultures as evidenced throughout the history of the West in particular. Driven by a form of countercultural utopianism, Gene Roddenberry, the creator of the series, invented the key philosophical and narrative device of the 'Prime Directive' because he wanted the (western) Federation to act as a corrective to the 'bloody history of (imperial) exploration' (Richards 1997: 13). This Directive is considered to be the highest moral authority and is defined as the sacred right of every sentient species to live in accordance with its normal evolutionary pattern. This Prime Directive[13] can be contrasted with the more altruistic and less homo-centric notion of an 'Ecological Directive'.

Yet according to Karin Blair, the original television series corresponds with the

> national disgust for the old ethics that demanded destruction of the evil alien in Vietnam and also left America without a viable concept of hero. *Star Trek* responds to the need for such an ideal; the character of Kirk overlaps with the dedicated man of action, the traditional ship's captain, while at the same time adding something new. He is at home with his emotions . . . Within the *Enterprise* we have a new model for a human garden where work, knowledge and change contribute to the civilisation of human nature . . . the trajectory of the *Enterprise* is not towards destruction but creation, it is not a fall but a flight . . . the sought after garden is no longer 'out there' in nature . . . but inside the human mind and its conscious construction. As Gene Roddenberry, the original creator of the series, asserts, we as travellers need . . . to fully experience the trip. We are all aliens and as such 'are part of each other and of everything that is'
>
> *(Roddenberry cited by Blair in Newcombe et al. 1982: 183-97).*

Roddenberry's apparently egotistical evocation of the personal 'trip' is signalled in my reading of *Contact* but I would argue that *Star Trek* helped to move beyond this egotistical fixation by counterbalancing human agency with other forms of sentient beings. The protagonists in the original *Star Trek* series with its international cast and crew always appeared to assert their individuality (and humanity). Nevertheless, they also endorsed the implicit hierarchical power structure under the command of the 'waspish' Captain Kirk. Sitting in his control chair, it is ultimately Kirk who determines the course of action, in spite of apparently paying lip service to a progressive form of consensual leadership.[14]

Furthermore, Captain Kirk and his original crew from the first 1960s television series seldom had any self-doubts that they were ethically correct, whereas Jean Luc Picard (played by Patrick Stewart, an experienced Shakespearean actor) in a later 1980s version *The Next Generation (TNG)* and the rest of his crew are full of ethical and ideological doubts. *TNG* is set 78 years after the original mission which ran for seven series before transmuting into a series of big budget films from 1994 onwards (Fulton 1995: 453). This new series even elevated psychology 'to the status of a hard science by bringing a counsellor to the bridge to join other specialists' (Harrison et al. 1996: 1) and moved a long way away from the cosy liberal individualism of its roots.

In one television episode, which correlated with the back story for *First Contact*, which is discussed later, Picard was captured and made part of the archenemy, the Borg. While his capture helps him understand their tactics, its effects also compromise his objectivity. This is particularly significant for human ethics, as Leslie Felperin suggests in a review in *Sight and Sound:* 'Piece by piece the difference between the Borg, whose drones are dispensable, and the federation fighters who will sacrifice their lives for their own philosophy of self-determination become less distinct' (Felperin 1997: 49). This continuous preoccupation with the opposition between human and non-human nature becomes the focus for an ecological reading of this very influential series, which has remained popular since the 1960s.

Post-Human Othernes
The central embodiments of (post)modernist 'otherness' in Star Trek include Spock in the original and Data in *TNG*. Both characters must continually struggle against human prejudice and the dismissal of their 'exotic' nature. They are quintessential representatives of the other[15] whose lack of human emotion is a cause of alienation (Harrison et al. 1996: 96). While they remain the most logical and overtly rational characters in the series, they also pose the most contradictory, yet pertinent philosophical questions concerning the nature of the universe and the human role within such a system (Richards 1997: 184).

Roddenberry's vision of the United Federation of Planets remains a vision of rational social progress based on a western model - even if overtly racist, as suggested by Daniel Leonard Bernardi in his book *Star Trek and History: Race-ing towards a White Future* (1998). In the mythic future world view of *Star Trek*[16], 'humanity has straightened itself out and created a functioning galactic democracy'

(Richards 1997: 149) which incorporates and validates an ecological balancing system. This utopic world view reaffirms the series' enduring appeal based on its 'humanity and optimism' (Fulton 1995: 440), while at the same time overcoming more conventional divisions between race, class and gender. This apparent negation of 'identity' and 'local' ideological difficulties helps to both expose and dramatise the bigger ontological dilemma implicit in this macro space drama: namely, how can one determine 'human' (or cyborg) value within the multitude of earthly flora and fauna and, by extension, conflicting intergalactic eco-system(s).

A good example that illustrates conflicting attitudes concerning the liberal idea of self-determination and neutrality explicitly embodied in *Star Trek* and the Prime Directive is represented in a sequel, *Star Trek Insurrection* (1998). Picard and his crew discover an idyllic planetary community which lives in harmony with nature, negating any expression of inter-human competition. On investigation, however, they discover that the 600 Ba-Ku who live there have not aged for hundreds of years. Consequently, this ecological Holy Grail of a habitat is eagerly sought after, not least by the otherwise non-interfering and egalitarian Federation forces. Picard and a few of his immediate crew actively rebel against Federation orders to avoid contact with, much less support for, this utopic communitarian society, which has consciously rejected technology owing to its detrimental effects on 'human nature'[17].

The freedom of 'right thinking' individuals to maintain such an environment is, the narrative suggests, worth fighting for. Nonetheless, in the end it remains a Disneyesque place/space to holiday in - not for serious consideration as a long-term alternative lifestyle. Like the altruistic and benevolent tenets of light ecology, human agency - even in futuristic space travel - remains anchored in existing social practices, rather than promoting any radical reversal of living practices that demands a 'deep' ecological conversion. Such tensions can be refracted and articulated most effectively within the upsurge of interest in communitarianism[18] and the interdisciplinary application of systems theory.[19]

There are, of course, conservative and radical inflections of communitarianism [20], which have become highly contentious, but generally its followers object to the idea of the neutral state and believe it should be abandoned for a 'politics of the common good'. In a communitarian society, the common good is concerned with a substantive conception of the good life, which defines the community way of life. 'Whereas Marxist perfectionism ranks ways of life according to a trans-historical account of the human good, communitarianism ranks them according to their conformity with existing practices' (Sandel 1984: 207).[21]

Implicit throughout the *Star Trek* series, from its roots in the 1960s to the more recent variation in *TNG*, is a type of communitarian philosophy that dramatises the idea that without community and citizenship[22] there is no liberation, only the most vulnerable and temporal armistice between an individual and oppression. The often apparent communion between human and alien culture is reminiscent of the communitarian philosophy which affords a necessary bulwark to the selfish individualism underscored by the mythic American dream that over-determines hierarchical individualism at the expense of a form of symbiotic egalitarianism. This dualistic model amounts to the demand to 'be like me or disappear' (Haber 1994: 126). This tension between individualism and community remains ever present, if often buried and unresolved in the later series, especially through narrative closure. But, as Honi Fern Haber persuasively affirms, '[C]ommunity must not mean a shedding of our difference, nor the pathetic pretence that these differences do not exist' (*ibid*.: 113). This paradox becomes most pronounced and often contradictory in encounters with 'Body Snatcher type organisms' called the Borg.

More recent episodes and film spin-offs serve to dramatise a range of permutations implicit within ecological strategies of self-determination, evolving from individualist to totalitarian systems and which address in often diametrically opposed ways the primary ecological directive of organic survival, played out within a range of 'exotic' habitats. Like the 'Body Snatchers', the Borg also promise a 'better quality of life' but demand in return the sacrifice of individuality and emotion, like any totalitarian regime. They promise 'optimisation through effective use of component parts, rather than perfection of individuals through an improved understanding of the transcendent ideal of human nature'. The Borg finally threatens the 'annihilation of difference through assimilation' (Harrison et al. 1996: 108) and embodies the antithesis of the Prime Directive, which is too big a price to pay even for the most fundamentalist, deep ecologists.

Star Trek: The Next Generation prophesied an end to the Cold War by declaring peace between Klingon and human cultures, and offered the cyborg organism, as opposed to the 'Body Snatchers' prototype, as a more progressive model of human subjectivity. While the original series also foregrounded non-humans like Spock, nonetheless their otherness was framed as only an exaggerated aspect of human psychology. Spock's dominant (Vulcan) rationality and logicality had to be tempered with human frailty to become fully acceptable and functional. This helps to offset Bernardi's reading of a racist agenda beneath the stereotyping, since what the othered characters embody is often a powerful antidote to the apparently hegemonic (white) consensus and agency.

The new Borg enemy reflects an even more advanced form of ecological organism, which uses all life forms in its endless quest for continuous adaptability and evolution. Unlike the libertarian notion of citizenship and individuality espoused in earlier series, the Borg symbolically embodies a coherent macro system and its ultimate survival is finally all that matters. There is absolutely no accommodation for ethical or individual needs embedded in the organism, much less any conceptualisation of the other. Data quizzically affirms its anti-human agency when he says to the Borg Queen in *First Contact*: 'Believing oneself to be perfect is often the sign of a delusional mind.'

Not surprisingly, the Borg is conventionally read within a gender paradigm as in the Alien trilogy, as the bitch overweening mother figure, especially since the Queen Borg, played by the actress Alice Krige, typifies the stereotype. But such a potent, post-Darwinian representation also serves as a metaphor for a 'pseudo progressive' organism with no sense of intrinsic individuality or centrifugal control points. Instead this alien other can adapt to new stimuli or environmental dangers much more effectively than any other planetary organism, while, at the same time, remaining resilient to destruction, aided by its hive-matrix type structure. The ultimately (in)destructible cyber-system does not depend on any form of interactive symbiotic environment for survival (like the T1000 cyborg in T2 to be discussed in the final chapter) and therefore can withstand all exterior organisms and forces. The Borg embodies the representational equivalent of scientific 'anti-matter'. Consequently, this dystopic signifier can be described both as an evolutionary nightmare and, at the same time, an antidote to the illusion of human primacy in nature.

Visually the Borg constituents are so creepy, with their cadaverous complexions and complex body piercing paraphernalia, that one can appreciate why death obsessed artists like Damien Hirst cited them as his favourite artistic creation in *Star Trek*. Such a potent expression of the ultimate alien being is also reinforced when counterpointed with human attempts to defeat it. In *First Contact* this is chilling, because it evokes so well the fragility of humanity. For example, the visual vulnerability of Picard walking outside in open space, on the hull of the *Enterprise* tied down with magnetic boots, dramatically reinforces both the spatial inconsequence of man together with the conventional heroic, if precarious, quest to maintain the ever-present deep ecological Prime Directive, which commands humans to coexist as equals with all other sentient beings.

This reaffirmation of the individual within the confines of a holistic form of humanity is both reflected and critiqued by the Borg, since its total unquestioning commitment to the survival of the greater community, like many 1950s B-movie antagonists, is both awe-inspiring and frightening in its implications. Such a phenomenon is analogous to the promotion of the evolutionary paradigm of new systems theory where boundaries become indeterminable. However, the cult critic Kevin Kelly notes that 'eco-systems and other functioning systems, like empires, can be destroyed much faster than they can be created'. Consequently, Kelly intones how humanity must 'listen to the system' and 'see where it wants to go'

(Kelly 1994: 191). This is a long way from the total rejection of alien life forms recommended by the 'Body Snatchers' to all 'right-minded' humans.

But Kevin Robins in a sceptical critique of such apparently radical systems theory contends that this utopian vision of new mass technology proposed by visionaries like Kelly and others are 'all driven by a belief in Transcendence': a faith that, this time around, a new technology will finally 'deliver us from the limitations and the frustrations of this imperfect world'. Utopia, Robins concludes, 'is more than just a pleasure ground. Communications translate directly into communion and community'. We need to dis-illusion ourselves, especially since the 'technological imaginary' continues to be driven by the 'fantasy of rational mastery of humans over nature (even extraterrestrial) and their own nature' (Robins 1996: 86).

However, Robins ultimately goes too far, totally dismissing (post)modern society as 'not an alternative society but an alternative to society' (*ibid*.: 246), an assertion which will be questioned in the final chapter. Critical discussion of 'alternative', if totalising, systems embodied within such populist science fiction texts remains both healthy and fruitful for developing forms of 'cognitive mapping' of possible future(s) and establishing eco-metaphors for evolutionary and symbiotic modes of human consciousness. Gregory Bateson, who was influential in the countercultural movements in the 1960s, forcibly asserts how the species that destroys its environment destroys itself. Representative archetypes like Picard and the Borg provide powerful contrasting prototypes within this primary ecological and evolutionary debate.

The Borg provides a potent metaphor that expresses a form of ecological representation and agency, exemplifying the beautiful symmetry of the system, which, unlike the crew of *Star Trek*, makes few concessions to conventional notions of eco-humanity. A technologically driven belief in a truly sustainable (Borg-like) eco 'super' system being created is inferred and endorsed by most systems theorists. Yet as cited by Robins, various dangers remain inherent in any new system that is not tied into ecological sustainability - especially when such connections could serve to legitimise, even endorse, regressive ideologies. At the same time, the Borg alien invaders pose an extreme narrative danger because they embody a malevolent vision of radical difference, which disguises a fundamentalist form of regressive sameness. This threatens to exceed the bounds of *Star Trek: The Next Generation's* utopian future, circumscribed as it is by the original nineteenth-century humanist assumptions. Like the original series, *TNG* appears to construct its utopian future by drawing on a modernist faith in rationality, progress, human perfectibility and expanding frontiers.

TNG's continuing vision of a communitarian utopia depends on a particular constellation of concepts -'progress, perfection, and social harmony, that all revolve around essentialist definitions of the self and of human nature' (Harrison et al. 1996: 95). Picard tells Data, 'You are here to learn about the human condition and there is no better way of doing that than by embracing Shakespeare.' This attempts to reclaim the 'humanist imagination from charges of complicity in oppressive practices' (*ibid*.: 97), which remained a pertinent, deep concern of the original series in the light of dissensus over the Vietnam War in particular.

Having eliminated economics and other structuring factors, *TNG*, like its predecessor, builds its utopia on the foundations of nineteenth-century notions of progress, synergy and infinite human potential. Just as Matthew Arnold (1869) had contended that the 'best' self is 'not manifold and vulgar and unstable, and contentious, and even varying, but noble, secure and peaceful - and the same for all mankind' (cited in Harrison et al. 1996: 204), so *TNG* promotes an 'essentialist view of human nature that favours consent and harmony rather than recognising the inevitability of difference' (*ibid*.: 111). As products of late nineteenth-century thinking, most recent so-called utopias remain rooted in a modernist rationalism that confirms mankind's ability to understand and control the world. The utopian myth, including that of the American frontier, focuses on infinite abundance, which validates *TNG's* emphasis on the striving for individual perfection.

Picard tells his futuristic audience, '[A] lot has changed in the past three hundred years. People are no longer obsessed with the accumulation of things. We've eliminated hunger, want, the need for possessions. The challenge is to improve yourself, to enrich yourself' ('The Neutral Zone' episode). More like a scholar than a military leader, Picard is able to make his crew function like a type of 'monastic' community through setting aside their own subjective positions and learning to appreciate *his* nineteenth-century 'liberal' belief systems.

Ultimately, *Star Trek's* 'limited oppositions' template means it does not fully articulate a 'third way' between or beyond the all-consuming totalitarian system of the Borg and the tradition of liberal humanist individualism represented by Picard. Nevertheless, a popular text of this kind can at least help provoke critical, even utopian, thinking by initiating these debates, even if remaining limited by its own predetermined paradigms. The often contradictory ecological messages of 1960s counterculturalism, which have been explored in a previous chapter, are encoded in the original *Star Trek* and rather than remaining on the utopic periphery, are animated more clearly in the later series.

In general, non-human agency seldom achieves popularity (unless it is cute) within an identification-driven Hollywood aesthetic. Consequently, I will argue in the final chapter that for the near future at least, progressive discourses concerning planetary harmony, together with the hope of a radical ecological human agency, remain most successfully codified through the representational other of the female cyborg in Hollywood film.

1970s Eco-Paranoia

While early science fiction films often revert to what's 'out there', (re)creating, so many critics claim, a spurious sense of unity via a common enemy threatening the very survival of 'man',[23] later science fiction plot lines at first appeared

> to turn away from extraterrestrial menaces (what's out there after us?) and towards the enemy within (what's in here with us?). Don't watch the skies - watch the insides . . . In theme and imagery, science fiction traced a movement from nuclear to digital, from fear of extinction to intimations of obsolescence

> *(Doherty in Grant 1996: 182B3).*

Conspiracy texts in particular promote a more critical ecological and ideological agenda as the fit between the 'believability' of events and audience knowledge and credibility narrows. Conspiracy-driven texts became more anchored in 'social-realist' trajectories rather than the more allegorical 1950s science fiction, which often reinforced crude oppositions between human and non-human life forms. Ecological thinking in the 1970s, however, emphatically transcended this simple 'protection of nature' and became more concerned with a conceptual transformation of the environment, together with the philosophical interrelations and conflicts embedded within humanity. A concrete scientific appreciation of the threat to the health of humans and other sentient life forms, resulting from technological developments and increased pollution of all types, validate this form of paranoiac thinking.

Such affirmation of a global eco-conspiracy corresponds with a growing public awareness of scientific experimentation, which was widely believed to upset the ecological balance. Whereas the 1950s fear of the bomb remained prophetic and on the fictional cultural periphery, by the 1970s such expression became more mainstream and believable and not just on the level of analogy or buried within the subtext. Yet Hollywood aliens from the 1970s ônwards were surprisingly kinder and gentler, with notable exceptions such as *Alien* (1979). [24]

While 1950s B-movie texts dramatised the polarising opposition between the forces of benevolent nature and alien otherness, such dramatisation remained somewhat one-dimensional. For example, whereas the 1951 *Body Snatcher* film portrayed the military as heroes and the scientists as villains 'who care more for the thing than their fellow humans' which was consistent with 'post-war, anti-intellectualism and the Eisenhower administration's McCarthy-assisted attack on the "egg-head"; the

1993 version[25] casts the military as persons in whom impassive conformity elicits body snatching' (Trushell 1996: 99). Anderson confidently affirms that during more recent times the growth and consolidation of environmentalism helped 'stimulate radical questions about the ends of personal and social life and in so doing, warns of the crucial problems facing complex societies' (Anderson 1997: 207). At one level the nascent ecological critique of human nature explored in the original *Body Snatcher* became more reflective and critical with the later 1970s paranoiac texts, having first gone through the countercultural and explicit environmental awareness of the 1960s.

Yet, as Michael Sragow suggests, while the equally successful 1970s Body Snatchers version ploughed the same thematic ground as the original version, it produced a lack of humanity and especially emotion. Sometimes 1970s science fiction films thematically reverted back to what's 'out there', (re)creating a spurious sense of unity via a common enemy which threatened the very survival of 'man' and often reaffirming the Cold War consensual polarisation of positions emanating from 1950s science fiction. [26]

Endangered Species

These apparent contradictions can be illustrated by a contemporary film which connects back to the DDT chemical wars first highlighted in 1950s films and illustrates how a surfeit of 'scientific realism' and paranoia permeates the narrative and sets it apart from its ancestors. *Endangered Species*, directed by Alan Rudolph (1982), was reviewed as 'a strangely stylish, bizarrely eclectic conspiracy thriller'. Out in the rural American mid-west, cows are found slaughtered and mutilated, the crimes having been perpetuated by UFO-like flashing lights in the sky. The film was structured around published contemporary 'facts' connected with documented illegal tests conducted into the effectiveness of germ and chemical warfare.

The overtly green agenda of *Endangered Species* dramatises the detrimental effects of pesticides and is framed by a textual introduction using evocative red lettering to affirm that the film is a dramatisation based on available facts and evidence. This informs the reader that in 1969 the US Congress had officially banned any further testing of chemical and germ warfare. The typographic font used and the manner in which the text is typed across the screen help to signify the journalistic process of filing reports and thereby reinforces its legitimacy as a form of scientific documentary evidence. After the resolution of the classic narrative, the cause/effect relationship involving pesticides is concluded by the textual coda that reintroduces a lingering conspiratorial residue, affirming that 'since the 1969 ban there has been 10,000 recorded incidents of cattle mutations in USA'. Such journalistic 'facts' serve to question and even undermine the hegemonic effectiveness of official government policy. As in *Body Snatchers*, individualised human agency remains impotent in the face of corporate/government power.

The Andromeda Strain

Whereas *Endangered Species* focuses on government conspiracies, *The Andromeda Strain* (1970) seeks to expose more universal fault lines within western technology, while connecting most explicitly back to 1950s B-movies and their preoccupation with all-pervasive viruses. Following the mantra inviting ecology activists to 'think globally but act locally', *The Andromeda Strain* connects many important arguments regarding the potential role of technology within a future eco-system.

Conventionally, the primary paranoia of the text is the discovery of the connection between the 'micro-thing' from outer space and a secret bacteriological warfare project (also suggested in *Endangered Species* via an overweening and secretive intelligence agency), together with the pervasive dangers of global scientific research. The American defence forces are attempting to harness the powers of the 'ultimate weapon', namely alien life forces.

Directed by Robert Wise[27] who began his career as an editor on *Citizen Kane*, the film is based on a novel and screenplay by the prolific and often ecologically provocative author Michael Crichton, who went on to write *Jurassic Park*. The narrative begins with an aerial view of a small remote village in New Mexico with everyone appearing dead from a mysterious 'virus'[28] except for a drunken old man and a crying baby. As a scientific and military team becomes metaphorically and physically cleansed in preparation for an investigation of the virus within a secret underground research laboratory, the audience is treated to a technical display of scientific instrumentation and an evocative use of colour and architectural space within a carefully structured *mise-en-scène*, comparable to the clinical delights of Kubrick's *2001*. As the team examine the survivors from within their protective life-suits, and survey the alien life force from behind glass screens and banks of monitors, audiences are forced to confront the unseen 'horror'. All the sophisticated technology mediating the alien's otherness does not provide a language to decode its awesome strangeness. All the investigators are left with are humorous platitudes like 'it's getting bigger', as they attempt to 'test' the molecules with their (un)sophisticated instrumentation.

Unlike life on this planet, which is implicitly understood and apparently fully appreciated, alien life does not conform to (eco)logical patterns, particularly by leaving no waste of any type and surviving within apparently non-nurturing conditions. Like the Borg in *Star Trek*, its indescribable life force cannot be destroyed by 'conventional force' - a fact which greatly upsets the logical, ordered, scientific minds of the investigators who can only comprehend organisms that conform to planetary ecological rules. Consequently, had the president acted on the scientists' logical deductions to wipe out Piedmont (the pre-designed site of the accident) with a nuclear deterrent, the alien life force would have used this negative energy to increase and multiply instead of being destroyed. Classic narrative demands are rewarded, however, when the individualised, jumped-up medical doctor (considered the lowest risk and therefore given the awesome responsibility of controlling the ignition key to nuclear destruction) deduces that the fast breathing of the baby who survived the incident somehow serves the process of avoiding contamination. Finally, the investigators correctly deduce that driving the microbes into the oxygen-rich sea can destroy the enemy. The inbuilt defence-mechanism of the Gaian earth system serves to protect and save human life as opposed to the man-made, destructive power of nuclear fission. Like the human body's immune system, the earth's more potent immune system is fully dramatised, allowing audiences the filmic space and time to deduce its ecological potency.

This is also clearly present in the overtly eco-conspiracy text *Silent Running* (1971), directed by Douglas Trumbull,[29] which is symbolically set in the year 2001 and adrift in space in a 'Garden of Eden' capsule that was intended to refurbish an Earth devastated by nuclear war. Bruce Dern refuses to destroy his private world when ordered to and instead, with the help of his robot drones, tends his garden and finally 'sends it out into deep space to seed a possible second chance for mankind' (Milne 1998: 789).

The historical transformation of the Cold War consensus already discussed can be recognised most clearly through a reading of *Logan's Run*, together with equally popular paranoid texts like *Soylent Green* from the 1970s. In particular, Doherty's final assertion concerning the movement 'from nuclear to digital' and from 'fears of extinction to intimations of obsolescence' (in Grant 1996: 183) becomes fully articulated in these films. The source of ecological corruption remain firmly within the body politic of their respective futuristic environments and the demand given to the heroic agents is to break through the dystopic corrupting environment to a more ecologically harmonious and ethical vision.

Soylent Green

Soylent Green (1973), directed by Richard Fleischer and based on Harry Harrison's novel *Make Room Make Room*, reflects on the contentious issue of population control coupled with food shortages. New York in the year 2022 is depicted as a run-down ghetto teeming with hungry masses and Charlton Heston plays an embittered cop, Detective Robert Thorn, who investigates the activities of the food company 'Soylent Green'.

As in many conspiracy-based narratives, the enemy remains unseen but is closely linked to the malign forces of government and capitalists controlling the masses below. This allows the text to focus on the effects of such blatant manipulation without necessarily having to appreciate the causes or even pinpoint the enemy. In the final sequence our individualised hero performs a provocative final hand signal of defiance in the face of such cover-ups. Asserting a form of voluntarist rebellion, Heston holds up his blood soaked hand and clenched fist, while voicing his anger against the conformist and corrupt system which is guilty of the ultimate taboo of recycling human flesh back into the food chain. The individual must do all in his power to defend the truth and 'protect the innocent' remains the potent message. Nevertheless, these altruistic, American sentiments are couched within 'local' regressive 1970s attitudes and values. In particular, the commodification and objectification of women described as 'furniture', bought and sold within the dominant patriarchal environment, is apparently legitimised by the Charlton Heston character, who remains the moral centre of identification in the film.

There is little evidence of older people within this dystopic habitat except for the aged human experience of Heston's friend Sol Roth, played by Edward G. Robinson, an academic, aesthete type. Roth understands books and the 'finer things of life', like good food and wine, and also remembers the halcyon times before ecological meltdown. Whether due to genetic preconditioning or not, Roth checks into what looks like a transport station for his final 'departure'. Two handmaids minutely question his favourite colour, together with other final wishes, while helping him out of his clothes and placing him on an altar bed. They provide him with a drink that turns out to be an elixir of death. On leaving the enclosed space, which represents a futuristic mausoleum, an audio-visual ritual/spectacle begins.

For the first time in the narrative, bright natural colours are presented, unlike the washed out, muted evocation of an overpopulated dystopic city with no hope or sanctuary. At last Roth has all the visual, even spiritual, space that he requires, which was severely lacking in the diegetic future world view created by the film, in which even conventional sites of sanctuary like churches were adapted primarily as massive refuge sites rather than fulfilling their true function. Finally, he can quietly observe the controlled sublime spectacle accompanied by the growing cacophony of uplifting classical music from the pastoral symphony. Close-ups of flowers dancing in daylight, displaying their natural beauty, fill the giant screen, followed by similar therapeutic stock romantic images of streams and mountains, even flocks of sheep observed from high up in the clouds.

We, as audience, assume that such over-determined stimulus corresponds with the fantasy dream world of the old man, reminding him of the 'purity' of life and nature before the structures of this futuristic environmental society and 'Soylent Green', in particular, corrupted and wiped out all consciousness of the nurturing pleasures of this sublime raw nature. This evocation of nature is emblematic of the transformative power of light producing new life through photosynthesis. On a narrative causal/effect level, however, the potency of such evocative representation of nature is tainted since the price that has to be paid for exposure is extermination, reminiscent of the myth of Medusa and the Sirens where the price of such scopophilic pleasure was equally high.

Normally within Hollywood classic narratives this form of revelation, even epiphany, is reserved for the film's closure. Instead this *mise-en-scène* is positioned early in the narrative and also functions as a piece of exposition, providing a cathartic 'jumping off point' for the main protagonist in his investigation of this corrupt environment while, at the same time, provoking moments of ecological excess outside of the dominant dystopian environment presented in the film.

Detective Thorn, searching for his friend, quickly reaches the site of this voluntary euthanasia and observes the evocative nature-spectacle, which nonetheless remains a simulacrum. The contented expression of his friend's desire to go back to the womb of a harmonious existence, providing deep ecological sustenance for its believers, is not lost on either his protégée or the audience, as the ecological signifiers are dramatically projected and re-mediated through the glass partition. This form of synthetic nature voyeurism reaches its apotheosis with the realisation that the illusion of firsthand sensory experience comes only at the price of human extermination. Though powerful and evocative, such expression of ecological harmony remains hermeneutically sealed within the enclosed space of the mortuary and the aged consciousness of the old man. Like the ancient Egyptian ritual evoking images of life depicted around the burial chamber, here also the dying agent withdraws into the fantasy of the simulacrum and relives the romantic pleasure of a life worth living in and through nature and landscape.[30]

There are few overtly utopian scenes in mainstream cinema which equal the potency of these mediated images, sutured and displayed as a mini-narrative outside of the dystopian world view made explicit throughout the rest of the narrative. In the majority of the texts discussed in this book, evocation of the primary potency of nature is rarely separated from the narrative trajectory of the text and sometimes remains inconclusively expressed through closure. Here such intensive imagery is dramatically foregrounded within a confined space and serves, at least momentarily, to rupture the dystopian narrative while critiquing most directly the anti-ecological environment which dominates the decaying interior and exterior spaces of the filmic future. Such expressive pastoral evocation is validated when Heston, as witness,[31] affirms the nurturing powers of this harmonious ecological world view. This active witnessing and affirmation of a (post)secular spiritualism reaffirms the potency and purity of nature and runs totally counter to a scavenger based environment presented as the antithetical norm in *Soylent Green*.

By accidentally witnessing this private spectacle, Detective Thorn at last begins to appreciate the potency of such symbiotic representation of nature. The baton is finally handed on to a new generation as he listens through headphones to the secret conspiratorial knowledge, which his friend makes public, thereby also making his life fruitful and useful for others. With the aid of these sublime experiences Heston receives the strength to carry out his quest to expose the inherent pollution and cosmic corruption in the body politic.

This reading projects the text beyond a mere localised, ideological interpretation, which crudely exposes a Marxist base/superstructure model of societal control. Here a form of mythic witnessing, through the development of a non ego-driven individualising agency, helps to expose a more universal message involving deep ecological and ethical parameters for harmonious living.

The ecological problem of overpopulation and scarce resources is resolved through an extreme form of genetically modified human food production and rationing. A signal of such corruption and non-ecological contamination is made in the opening sequence when a senior official is killed. He is literally taken away by men in black uniforms with balaclava-type hoods covering most of their faces. While the body is placed in a waste-disposal van, all the investigators are observed taking a financial cut, reminiscent of hyenas after a kill. One character observes in passing how there used to be some form of ritual and ceremony for the deceased but now bodies are merely disposed. Normative ethical eco-values have little currency in this future dystopian environment where nobody can be trusted and the majority of the population is treated no better than inanimate 'furniture' and slaves to the system rather than individualised symbiotic beings.

Not surprisingly, because the issue of human population control is so divisive and emotive, it is less often addressed in ecological texts. Within more recent post-Cold War paranoiac texts, however, issues like this became more explicit, especially within the displaced environs of science fiction future worlds. While 1950s science fiction concentrated on taboo subjects concerning ideological divisions between humans under the continuing threat of nuclear annihilation, 1970s examples began to articulate more problematic discourses, like the effects of social engineering over life and death. *Logan's Run* also addressed the contentious issue of population control but moved beyond class inequality as a means of addressing the problem of scarce resources. In this apparently utopic world all human desires and needs are actualised within a technologically controlled environment.

Logan's Run

Directed by Michael Anderson, *Logan's Run* (1976) is a sentimental yet fascinating pre-sequel to the preoccupations of *Blade Runner* (see final chapter), which also explores a new type of spaceman. The dystopic universe is controlled by a series of computers which enforce human recycling at the age of 30 - an extremely dystopic system of population control. Logan '5' (Michael York) is first introduced observing a baby behind a hermetically sealed environment. A colleague interrupts the expositional discussion which follows to affirm that the child may be his but that he has no idea who the 'seed mother' is. In this hedonistic, post-nuclear family society, sex is freely available but, as in many other utopian societies, there is a large price to pay for such apparent freedom. Logan's job is to hunt the fugitives who refuse to accept their fate within the controlled eco-system of the city. Like Deckard in the seminal *Blade Runner*, initially he is the compliant servant of the system, eliminating, for the good of his society, dissenters who seek selfishly to avoid their fate in the short cycle of life by escaping to an alternative eco-system. Natural cycles of birth and death cannot be allowed in this dystopian system, probably because the master computers would be unable to control such a chaotic environment, as in *Jurassic Park*, which also perpetuates ordered artificial harmony. Logan, like all of his fellow inhabitants, has little consciousness of the outside world, except what is mediated through central computer terminals.

The artificial society is controlled by pleasure and spectacle, with its inhabitants not required to make personal decisions. Time controls their destiny, which is artificially predetermined. Reminiscent of Roman circuses, the lucky survivors (pre-30-year-olds) periodically observe the spectacle of the chosen ones being 'renewed' on the electrified (Disneyesque) carousel. The digital masters assign Logan the ultimate hunter quest to find sanctuary -the place escapees seek to avoid their conformist destiny on the carousel.

But by unfairly reducing Logan's life span, the re-individualised hero becomes a potentially subversive pawn, opposed to the conformist system. The unnatural symbiotic harmony between the inhabitants and the system has been broken, with Logan at last realising the inequality of his artificially modified life span. He can now become a rebel and acquire the contingent attributes of modern paranoia. Finding a suitable accomplice, played by Jenny Agutter, who earlier refused to have sex on demand (unlike all the other girls in the circuit), they escape up into the 'real' natural eco-system after first encountering the liminal/semi-natural, polar environment controlled by the computer. Like similar mythic quests, the heroes have to overcome various obstacles before they can come into the benevolent light of nature.

Outside they experience a sublime moment of ecological co-existence in time and space, through the nurturing powers of sunlight and its natural warmth and energy.

Unlike the controlling artificial light and pleasure of the carousel, which simulated excitement like a fairground ride, the represented natural potency of the sun's rays encourages these newly-constituted eco-human protagonists to dream of seeking out a more harmonious eco-system. Traversing a swamp-like area, they eventually discover Washington DC, which has been overrun by the forces of nature. Observing the majestic stone statue of Lincoln, an iconic manifestation of liberal democracy, obscured by years of wild vegetation, at first they are shocked by his aged feature.

Natural ageing, together with a literary form of experience embodied by Peter Ustinov, the old man they discover living in a disused library (reminiscent of Edward G. Robinson in Soylent Green), provides a missing dimension of life as they have lived it in their hermetically sealed artificial bio-system. But Logan cannot bring himself to selfishly accept what could become an exclusively personal utopia and needs to share his newly found communitarian vision with his people, so that all can enjoy an ecologically balanced nirvana.

But on returning to their artificial environment, they are captured and threatened with extinction if they do not provide the co-ordinates of what is believed to be a dystopian space. Consequently, only by destroying the main computers, the 1970s embodiment of post-Cold War conformity, can the artificiality and inferiority of their 'unnatural' utopia be fully exposed. As the ecologically and (more obviously) ideologically repressed natives escape, almost literally throwing off the chains of their oppression by coming up out of the buried city towards the rejuvenating springs of nature, they discover the old man standing by the water's edge and finally witness the possibility and potentiality of ageing naturally. Only by accepting a truly natural ecological system can they begin to throw off the shackles of their dystopic conformist society.

Such closure is somewhat reminiscent of 1950s conspiracy science fiction, which posited such a coherent, albeit simplistic, utopic resolution to an alien threat, often by reaffirming individualised humanistic values. It is, of course, easier in Hollywood film to deal with effects rather than underlying causes. Nevertheless, the transformation of human agency towards appreciating an ecological harmony outside of a technologically driven dystopic system can be appreciated as potentially progressive. Jonathan Bate interestingly notes Thoreau's quasi-mysticism - 'to live deliberately' is to live with 'thoughtfulness and with care for the earth' - and suggests that

> the myth of a better life is no less important for being a myth. Myths are necessary imaginings, exemplary stories, which help our species to make sense of its place in the world. Myths endure so long as they perform helpful work . . . Myths of the nat-

ural life which expose the ills of our own condition are as old as Eden or Arcadia -
(their) endurance is a sign of their importance

(Bate 1999: 558B9).

Safe

Unlike science fiction from the 1950s, when these mythic oppositions appeared to
'work', by the mid to late 1970s such an opaque closure appears at odds with the
thematic and ideological complexity of the more contemporary Cold War
environment. A final discussion of a more recent eco-conspiracy text, *Safe* (1994),
will help to illustrate how it serves to explicate a total disintegration of a modernist
sensibility, which ostensibly endorses a heroic individualistic expression of
selfhood. It must be emphasised that this film is a clear example of 'independent
production' and therefore outside the aegis of Hollywood. Nevertheless, it is
justified to include the film in this study because of its potent evocation of
ecological issues that help bridge the boundaries between this and the final science
fiction chapter.

The next chapter will focus on so-called postmodernist agency and its implications
for ecological readings of recent science fiction texts. *Safe* tends to straddle the
modernist/postmodernist axis and helps to deconstruct a belief in agency that
serves as an antidote to the heroic 1950s affirmations of Scott in *The Incredible
Shrinking Man*, or to a lesser extent Ellie in Contact. Scott finally appears to
endorse the modernist 'illusion' that successful agents require a selfless and
coherent ethical attitude, which allows them to know their place and achieve their
true potency within a coherent world view. Unfortunately, such a utopic meta-
narrative is no longer effective for contemporary paranoid agents as explored in
Safe. Concurrently, this apparent break-up has serious implications for the holistic
meta-narrative of deep ecology which appears to lose coherence, if not validity,
within a (post)modernist age. However, this almost irresolvable dilemma must be
left for the final chapter.

For Ulrich Beck, environmental hazards can never be eliminated through the use
of technological knowledge, although they can be anticipated. Beck claims that we
now live in a risk society, which continues to find answers to these problems from
the logic of the nineteenth century - like Star Trek's fixation with traditional
modernist literature. As Mark Smith summarises Beck's ideas:

> while the hazards of a technologically driven society in the late twentieth century
> penetrate every region and level of society, human beings remain wedded to the
> responses to environmental degradation which were more appropriate in the nine-
> teenth century. In industrial societies, he suggests, risks were calculable and fault or

blame could be clearly identified . . . However, in the 'risk society', which we presently inhabit, no such guarantees exist. The scale and scope of human impacts upon the environment produce a range of complex and unanticipated consequences which cannot be contained effectively within the earlier guarantees and safety mechanisms. In addition, whereas in industrial societies the lower classes were also likely to experience the worst effects of industrial pollution, in the 'risk society' all social groups are susceptible to the effects of pollution

(Smith 1998: 94).

Safe is directed by a cult art-house filmmaker Todd Haynes, who became preoccupied with all forms of 'modern' disease, from AIDS to anorexia, which in many ways echoes the thematic preoccupations of 1950s B-movies and clearly articulates debates around Beck's risk society. The normal life of an LA housewife, Carol White (Julianne Moore), is shattered when she develops an allergy to the twentieth century: the chemicals that are everywhere in food, fabrics and fragrances lead to breathlessness and nausea. Finding help in a clinic in the desert, she begins to question her western style of living. The environmental illness explored in this film, described as 'multiple chemical sensitivity', can also be read as an AIDS metaphor. However, more significantly, this film taps into debates concerning human effects of pesticides like DDT, which are continually signalled within the films analysed in this chapter and were first exposed as a scientific fact by Rachael Carson in the sixties.

As Jonathan Rosenbaum asserts, the role of this environmental illness is above all dramatic, helping to organise the plot. White's doctor insists that nothing is wrong with her but once the term 'environmental illness' is introduced, the movie and her character alike gain narrative 'direction' (Rosenbaum 1997: 210). The eerie representation of a 'blissed-out' new age, West coast environment remains fixating in its horrific overtones. But this art-house exposé is less preoccupied with the usual horror generic representation of 'bugs' and their effects on humans. Unlike, for instance, the underdeveloped environmental critique in the opening of Altman's *Short-Cuts* (1993), with the spraying of a DDT-like substance to alleviate the growth of bugs, this narrative deals with environmental issues through a more personalised and communal trajectory. The chief protagonist's disease could almost be regarded as the ultimate environmental terror with no cure, and unlike many earlier examples in this chapter, the film's only dilemma is how to handle its unstoppable effects. The canned artificial air/gas which White later carries around with her everywhere is very different from the 'air' artificially pumped into the lungs of the psychopath in *Blue Velvet*, who 'needs' its vapours to help stimulate his libidinal imagination. The proto-typical, even conventional, housewife in *Safe*, on the other hand, needs such pure air to sustain a normal life and maintain 'harmony' within a polluting western environment.

In fact, the director locates the whole film within Carol White's subjectivity. But rather than alienating the audience from her, the measured wide-angle, hyper-real *mise-en-scène* becomes an efficient expression of the alienation she experiences. According to the director, in an interview with Amy Taubin in *Sight and Sound*, the film is above all a critique of a passive society in which people ignore the ecological disaster all around them and wait helplessly for someone else to tell them what to do about it (May 1996: 32).

Haynes suggests that the disease is the best thing that happens to her: 'It's the thing that kicks her out of unconsciousness, out of this unexamined life.' The director also remains very critical of Peter Dunning, a new age guru who has AIDS, who believes he can save White in his clinic away from the pollution of the city. Peter's new age philosophy - 'love yourself more' - comes out of a 1960s ideology, which applies the reflective eastern tradition to the western context. 'It claims to change the world through self-esteem,' says Haynes, 'but I see it as a reiteration of basic conservative arguments about the self, which are closely aligned to masculinity and patriarchy' (*ibid.*: 32). Like Ellie in *Contact*, the protagonist in *Safe* is also predetermined within a dominant patriarchal society, which inaugurates a psychological identity crisis that must be overcome before she can become fully human.[32]

This film is addressed at the often-dispirited 'Left' audience and remains critical of any totalising philosophy. It is also unlike most conventional radical *avant garde* aesthetic approaches that articulate an alternative lifestyle forged from within a post-1960s critical sensibility which apparently had less cultural currency in the late 1990s.

The director creates a 'synthetic' environment which is reminiscent of the clinical *mise-en-scène* of *The Andromeda Strain* discussed earlier.[33] Haynes' (post)modernist critical sensibility helps create a complex investigation of the human self in its impure (both allegorically and physically) western environment. His film also serves as an effective counterpoint to the oeuvre of Ingmar Bergman, the great modernist and humanist director who continually questioned the ultimate spiritual quest yet remained caught up in its controlling power and influence.

For Haynes, as cited in *Sight and Sound,* environmental sickness is, like AIDS, another horrible fact of life. 'What most concerns him is not the mystery of the disease itself', but - like Bergman, whose aesthetic he appears to emulate - 'the perplexing human response to it: the apparent need to assign blame to it, the inability to accept that "dirt", danger, chaos and all its works are an integral part of life' (May 1996: 60).

Safe uses its stylish, often ambiguous, wide-angle shots to force viewers to scan the images for clues towards understanding Carol's psychological predicament. Her attacks begin in earnest when she watches what could be considered a deep ecology video, which proselytises for 'an understanding of the oneness of all life' reminiscent of the utopic closure of *The Incredible Shrinking Man*. Carol takes the video as it was intended -a mildly consoling 'new age' balm. She is positioned at the other end of the spectrum from the Body Snatchers' mindless conformity or the Borg's all consuming totalising system. But at the same time, she is not provided with the keys to a form of proactive agency or witnessing, which would give meaning to her life. Unlike the crew of *Star Trek* or other protagonists discussed in this chapter who learn to appreciate the correct ethical path to follow, she remains directionless and therefore unable to fight her psychological environmental demons.

Yet Peter Dunnings's treatment in the desert retreat remains one of the most forthright deep ecological messages presented in a film that at the same time posits a rejection of any form of human agency. He commands his patients to

> cut yourself off from ills of the world, accentuate the positive in your view of the world . . . and your inner self will be transformed -to healing effect . . . We are the one with the power that created us. We are safe, and all is well in our world.

While he remains 'safe' in his luxury house on the cliff-face overlooking the commune, promoting at least outward inactivity, the final scene produces a logical conclusion to this confusing and strangely counter-productive 'witnessing of self'. Carol is shown preparing for bed in an empty sterile space of a 'clean room' - an igloo-like porcelain-lined dome - which is the ultimate in ecological simplicity. Confronting her own image in the mirror, she tries to start working on her non-existent self-esteem, with her countercultural mantra of self-love.

The director, as cited in a review in *Sight and Sound*, is certainly 'playing with [your] leftist expectations - making you think Wrenwood has got to be the answer - tricking you into thinking it has the answer'. Peter certainly has a whole philosophy (like communitarianism) and is engaging, manipulative and charismatic -all the things you expect from characters in a classic Hollywood narrative. Audiences also want White to be healed. But the closure cited above does not affirm that healing is in fact possible or that ecological pollution can be contained. Ulrich Beck's cautionary meta-discourse of the risk society has reached its critical apotheosis with all the western material benefits of culture turning against the biological harmony of individualised human nature and no resolution in sight.

Yet *Safe* continues to have a strange affinity with *The Incredible Shrinking Man.*

Both protagonists are infected at the start with a range of pollutants, from car fumes to strange infected clouds at sea. Both films produce distancing effects, using formal aesthetic conventions which privilege the use of *mise-en-scène* to visually dramatise the effects on spatially trapped protagonists inside. But whereas Scott learns to accept his transformed diminutive self and ends up asserting his enlarged eco-sensitivity and human dignity achieving a 'true self' by appealing to a form of ecological universal humility, Carol ends up retreating into her egotistical self (reminiscent of Bergman's *Persona*), shielding a mirror in the hope of finding her true inner self, from which she can again face the world. Both films display very intense central performances, which capture the changing historical and contextual potency of human individuals striving against pernicious forms of polluting environments. *Safe*, however, remains much more subjective and alienating in its signifying effects.

Nevertheless, both films are thematically honest, reflecting their respective historical and contextual deep ecological formations. While Scott questions his masculinity and control over his modernist environment, White tries to cope within a (post)feminist, (post)modernist and (post)materialist world, which at worst has no answers and little sense of communal balance, since part of the cosmos which maintains ecological harmony has been lost. Scott remains the more naively optimistic, acquiring faith in the connectivity with the cosmos and positioned in time before the scientific breakthrough of space travel and the revolution of later ecological consciousness-raising. He becomes more attuned to the deep ethical harmonies of nature as he looks up into the sky at the end of the film.[34] Carol, on the other hand, has a longer and less certain 'pilgrimage' ahead of her, reflecting disillusionment with all forms of heuristic knowledge, including sensory perception. She has long lost faith in the elemental ecological harmonies of nature, effectively dramatised by Sol's final departure in *Soylent Green*. She must find ways to accept living within an ecologically high-risk environment and learn to adapt or be destroyed.[35] Human agency is no longer a composite bulwark against environmental and other terrors, as affirmed by Scott in *The Incredible Shrinking Man*, who finally acquired the will to accept his diminutive status and also feel at one with the cosmos. Representational human agency appears no longer capable of such utopic transcendence.

In researching for the film, the director of *Safe* found this 'beautiful' quote from a cancer patient who believed that 'humans would rather accept culpability than chaos'. In many ways the film serves both as an elucidation and a critique of Beck's seminal critique of post-industrial society where new dangers are ever-present[36] and must be faced up to and accommodated in some way if the human species is to survive.

Doherty's cogent observation that science fiction has evolved towards what is 'inside' human nature rather than simply watching the skies, reaches its apotheosis in *Safe* with its extreme form of psychological introspection. In the end, however, because it is framed within an apparently outdated modernist evocation of agency, it signals a nihilistic cul-de-sac. New models of post-human agency are needed to articulate the primary ecological risks of (post)modern society. The final chapter will look at how the postmodern aesthetic and the development of post-human agency have evolved through a range of cyborg agents to create a more progressive expression of ecological utopianism.

Notes

1. Social realist films that exposed the many problems facing America were seen by such agitators as not just unpatriotic but, in many cases, treasonable. It is even argued that it was because of HUAC that social problem films disappeared from the mainstream of the Hollywood production networks. However, at the outset there was no need for HUAC to control politics in movies since such politics were already generally inoffensive. McCarthyism nevertheless signalled the end of the era of overt social idealism which so permeated the depression and post-war years and had given the problem film genre its vitality. From the 1940s onwards, political and social issues of any kind (including ecological ones), if explored at all, generally had to be both buried and excavated from within the subtext of the narrative structure.

2. Sobchack cogently asserts that science's purpose is to overcome 'man's physical inadequacies'. Its cultural function is 'to give empirical evidence to man's optimistic belief in the biological supremacy, his ability to control and affect himself and his environment as no other life form on earth is able to do. In brief, the cultural function of science is to emphasise man's optimism' (Sobchack 1997: 62).

3. Mark Jancovich in particular argues that the ant society is almost the 'ideal image of Fordist rationality and its application to the military . . . Ants act as images of mass reproduction in which standardised drones are turned out which exist simply to do their will. The ants' reproductive methods are used as a metaphor for a social order in which the populace are little more than standardised, conformist and interchangeable subjects who simply exist to fulfil the needs of the state' (Jancovich 1996: 61).

4. Yet, surprisingly, only in Russia were scientific monsters strictly excluded and censored.

5. It can be seen as symptomatic of how far America has 'progressed' from the paranoid Cold War years that a postmodernist science fiction spoof *Mars Attack* (1997) can portray American military attempting to neutralise the alien enemy with a nuclear warhead, only to have it literally 'eaten up' by such potent invaders.

6. Biskind's grand if overly schematic analysis of 50s science fiction in particular maps ideological positions and audience needs within the framework of detailed textual analysis. For what he calls

the (political/ ideological) 'centre', culture was good and nature was generally bad. It was all that threatened to disrupt or destroy culture. 'Not surprisingly the "Other" in "pluralist" films was most often nature . . . Science fiction has always been fascinated with the "Other" (Freudian Id) - everything the "centre" was not'. In the end, Biskind incorrectly concludes that the whole genre was anti-utopian in character. 'Since alternatives to the mainstream (centre) was dystopian -there was nowhere else to go but back to the centre' (*ibid*.:118).

7. There remains, however, as mentioned in Chapter 1, a major ideological dispute between determinists, who believe that 'human behaviour is primarily determined by outside forces, and voluntarists, who believe that humans possess free will and can act as they wish' (Haralambos et al. 1990: 817). In many ways, these conflicting human beliefs are structurally encoded within most Hollywood generic representations of heroic agents.

8. One spaceman looking back at the planet Earth spoke movingly of how Earth, if it is to be 'treasured and nurtured' must be regarded as 'precious . . . if it is to endure' (Gallant 1980: 6).

9. In many ways the advent of the space shuttle programme served, he concludes, to overtly endorse the values of environmentalism with its scientific valorisation of 'reusable, and recyclable' technology.

10. By 1990 'Earth Watch' day, there were over 200 million people worldwide paying homage to an image of the earth as a unifying eco-system. But, as Bryant asserts, the urge to transform our environment began to rest on the individual, not governments or economic systems.

11. Sagan's utopic project sought to dramatically contemplate three questions: Are there aliens out there? If so, how do we deal with them? And what do they tell us about God? Philip Strick writes in the October 1997 issue of *Sight and Sound* how the original film treatment in 1981 went through many changes while being converted into a blockbuster science fiction film to feed the demands of audiences in the 1990s and suggests that the script was all the better for being 'no longer a didactic affirmation of the two astronomer's predictions about life on other worlds'.

12. While Freudian and Jungian analysis remain outside the remit of this study, such methodological tools nevertheless remain highly pertinent for an analysis of science fiction in particular.

13. 'Without a universe full of equals capable of challenging the Federation, the Prime Directive would be just another version of the old idea of the white man's burden, the idea that the Federation should be an invisible and benign power' (Richards 1997: 2).

14. Nevertheless, *Star Trek's* explicit utopian aims (and the surprising conjunction of 'alien' and human) correspond with the audience aspirations analysed by critics like Henry Jenkins who were raised by conservative Republican parents and taught in racially segregated schools. Jenkins later endorsed *Star Trek* 'and its fandom', for offering him a 'utopian vision of a world which accepted a broader range of cultural diversity than he had encountered in his everyday life'

(Tulloch and Jenkins 1995: 21). However, audience research remains outside the scope of this study.

15. As John Hill argues in his essay 'Crossing the water: hybridity and ethics in *The Crying Game*' in *Textual Practice*: '[T]o claim to "understand" another culture and, by extension, another individual (as Levinas asserts) is to deny that otherness, to appropriate it to your sameness in an unwholesome and arrogant colonialism of the mind' (Hill 1998).

16. The original series of *Star Trek* promised so much for so many. (The series became the 'bread and butter' income for the Paramount studio). Promises of a better future include more advanced technology, greater political efficiency and abundant moral and social progress.

17. Eventually, of course, in this overly laboured and didactic narrative exercise, unrest ensues because of a conspiracy headed by two 'prodigal sons' who were thrown out of their idyllic community because of their unwillingness to accept the rules of total secrecy to outsiders. After solving the problem and recreating the status quo, Picard refuses to succumb to the desires of an 'older (beautiful) woman' and her ideal eco-community, calling on the needs of the Federation as his excuse. However, he keeps his options open by suggesting the possibility of returning to this timeless, idyllic community for future shore leave.

18. The communitarian impulse can hardly be claimed as uniquely American. But American society, with its comparative lack of hierarchy, freedom from the weight of tradition and oneness to social innovation, has historically provided a particularly congenial environment in which communal experimentation could flourish. While such a social phenomena enjoyed its greatest efflorescence in the 1820B50 era (with a second wave in the post-1960 years), it has never been absent from the American experience (Pitzer 1997: xi).

19. Some communitarians argue that liberals both misconstrue our capacity for self-determination and neglect the social precondition under which that capacity can be meaningfully exercised (Kymlicka 1995: 199).

20. Communitarians, feminists and postmodernists have:
    1) 'Voiced scepticism towards the claim of a legislating reason to be able to articulate the necessary conditions of a moral point of view.
    2) They have questioned the abstract/distorted/nostalgic ideal of the autonomous male ego, which the universalist tradition privileges.
    3) They have unmasked the inability of such universalist, legislative reason to deal with the indeterminacy and multiplicity of contexts and life situations with which practical reason is always confronted.'
    Communitarian thinking often serves to re-constitute a community under modernity. For example:
    Integrationism, as a form of communitarianism, involves 'grouping and reclaiming an integrative vision of fundamental values and principles - common action, unlike the plurality of the

postmodern vision' (Benhabib in Tallack 1995: 403-9).

21. Lasch affirms that the appeal of the movement lies in its rejection of both the 'market and the welfare state in pursuit of a third way'. He suggests that we need a 'third way of thinking about moral obligations', one that locates moral obligation neither in the state nor in the market but in 'common sense, ordinary emotions, and everyday life' (Lasch 1995: 101).

22. Writers such as Mark Smith proselytise for a revivified form of 'citizenship', which refers to 'the framework of complex interlocking relations which exist between obligations and entitlements in any legal and moral system. In the modern period we have so far witnessed three phases of citizenship: civil citizenship, political citizenship, and social citizenship . . . In each of these forms of citizenship, the distinction between what is private and what is public moves but the distinction itself remains unquestioned. Ecological citizenship, however, questions the efficacy of this distinction, for the relations of entitlement and obligation break through the species barrier and beyond' (Smith 1998: 98B9).

23. Doherty's appraisal of such texts serves to frame Jameson's dismissal of conspiracy texts as 'degraded' attempts, through the figuration of advanced technology, 'to think the impossible totality of the contemporary world system' (cited in Broderick 1995: 80).

24. Joan Dean, in *'Between 2001 and Star Wars'* in the *Journal of Popular Film and Television* (1978), cited by Sobchack, argues that science fiction of the 1970s 'mirror[s] a developing neo-isolationism' as well as a 'diminished fear of nuclear apocalypse' together with a 'growing concern with domestic, terrestrial issues'. The single theme that dominated science fiction between 1970 and 1977 was 'overpopulation and its concomitant problems of food shortage and old age' (cited by Sobchack 1997: 226).

25. The 1993 version called *Body Snatchers*, directed by Abel Ferrara, translates the story to the contemporary period in an American army camp and, according to some critics, transforms the text into an allegory of family and youthful alienation. John Trushell, however, links the new version to a critique of recent illegal uses of chemical weapons in the Gulf War, with the 'pods' closely connected to the evils of military might, thereby transforming the often crude Cold War polemics of the 1950s into an 1990s eco-paranoia tract.

26. This can be appreciated in particular by a study of the changing definitions of radioactive waste by Abri de la Bruheze, who affirms that the issue of radioactive waste only really became a 'social, scientific and political problem' in the early 1970s during the period that the American Atomic Energy Commission (AEG) announced that it would build an underground repository for high-level radioactive waste in an abandoned salt mine near Lyons, Kansas. Up to then the problem was 'depoliticised and bureaucratised', especially since throughout the Cold War, nuclear technology served 'primarily military purposes' and the composition of wastes was a 'closely kept secret' having little to do with non-military society (cited in Bijker et al. 1997: 140-2).

27. He also directed the classic science fiction film *The Day the Earth Stood Still* (1951), which was one of the few films to treat the aliens as benevolent. The film had a strong pacifist message, which tried to get humanity to step back from the brink of nuclear destruction. This pacifist and ecologically framed cult film is dramatised by the alien's ability to stop all artificial power on the planet. The aliens try to teach humans that they must learn to respect 'nature' and stop their 'senseless wars' or face terrible consequences.

28. (Post)modernism often uses the metaphor of viruses and disease to describe the state of anomie. Jameson and Baudrillard describe the postmodernist condition as 'schizophrenic', requiring 'no experience of temporal continuity' (Rushing et al. 1995: 17).

29. Scott Bukatman's essay 'The Artificial Infinite: On Special Effects and the Sublime', which looks at the work of Trumbull, asserts, at the outset, that his use of special effects coupled with the evocation of the sublime is especially 'contemplative' (in Cooke et al. 1995: 271). Trumbull stages 'an extended encounter with the sublime by including the presence of the diegetic spectator'. But, unlike Ellie in *Contact*, Trumbull's characters 'do not mediate the experience through the psychology of characters' being uniformly 'stunned into a profound passivity' (*ibid.*: 272).

30. Christopher Hitt, recalling words from Thoreau's short story 'Ktaadn', explores a similar epiphany focusing on the 'ecological sublime' as he comes down from a mile high mountain having failed to complete the ascent. 'Think of our life in nature - daily to be shown matter, to come in contact with it - rocks, trees, wind on our cheeks! the *solid* earth! the *actual* world! the *common sense*! *contact*! *Contact*! *Who* are we? *Where* are we?' (cited by Hitt 1999: 615). Hitt continues, however, that contrary to Kant: 'Reason can never master nature. There will always be limits to our knowledge and nature will always be, finally impenetrable. An ecological sublime would remind us of this lesson by restoring the wonder, the inaccessibility of wild nature. In an age of exploitation, commodification, and domination, we need awe, envelopment and transcendence. We need, at least occasionally to be confronted with the wild otherness of nature and to be astonished, enchanted, humbled by it. Perhaps it is time - while there is still some wild nature left - that we discover an ecological sublime' (Hitt 1999: 619B20).

31. It should be recognised that Charlton Heston was especially famous for acting in numerous epic and biblical stories, which involved him 'witnessing' and even becoming transformed by the power of Christian spirituality.

32. Taubin concludes that what the film is ultimately about is the infiltration and paradoxes implicit in a new age language, expressed in the Wrenwood commune, with its 'therapeutic notion of purification in a postmodern age of referential doom and metaphysical disease' (cited in Boorman et al. 1996: 213) as against the ideological failure of the Left and its need to look at itself and how it is losing any effective voice politically and culturally.

33. When asked why it was set in 1987, the director replied that he wanted to place it at the height of

Reagan/Bush 1980s. As in Kubrick's *2001*, he continued: 'We should feel we're in a world where nature has been completely overcome by man and there's no trace of it. It should feel like space but it's really LA. It should feel like an airport where you never touch real ground. You're just in this carpeted air-controlled system world where people just glide by.'

34. This is echoed by the great modernist speeches of the leader of the cyborg rebels, Roy Batty, in *Blade Runner* just before he dies, which is discussed in detail in the final chapter.

35. Freud's death wish or 'schoidenfroide' has produced in Safe an ecological signifier which is highly potent.

36. Society, in fact, both sees and critiques itself as a 'risk society', which Beck calls 'reflexive modernisation'.
An engaging summary of *Risk, Environment and Modernity*: Towards a New Ecology, edited by S. Lash et al. (1996) includes the following arguments:
1) 'Instrumentalist social science aids and abets humanity's technological colonisation of nature - hence the legitimating of notions of sustainable development and management of the planet, etc.
2) The individualisation of late modernity produces heightened uncertainty as decisions proliferate and human meanings are replaced by alien ones.
3) The institutionalisation of ecological politics neutralises its original critical impulse -hence allowing alliance in 'truth' between multi-national corporations, etc. in an era of post-environmentalism where ecological discourse has been normalised' (cited by Peet 1997: 477-8).

5 POSTMODERNIST SCIENCE FICTION FILMS AND ECOLOGY

The totalizing incorporation of Nature by industrialized culture, and the commodification of the Unconscious into a visible and marketable 'desire' produced as media spectacle have now expanded capital to its 'purest form', and with that expansion we have seen the emergence of a new cultural logic: 'postmodernism'

(Sobchack 1997: 244).

This apparently new 'cultural logic' is most clearly expressed in the proliferation of science fiction texts in Hollywood. This final chapter addresses the popular representation of spectacle and the use of a form of sublime excess within a range of popular science fiction fantasies. To do this, a selection of close textual analyses will again be used, focusing in particular on the representation of human agency and applying cyborg theory to illustrate how such apparently transgressive postmodernist expressions can be applied to an ecological utopian discourse.

Postmodernism is often identified with an all-consuming late capitalist economy drained of its critical power. However, we need a more flexible analytical model to help detect traces of varying, sometimes contradictory, discourses. Art Berman's methodology of separating 'groups of ideas into two poles and then walk[ing] back and forth between them', especially using textual analysis, so that in the end a 'visible path' is hopefully worn (Berman 1994: viii), is especially useful. To help create this path, conceptual 'myths' such as transgression, excess and, in particular, Donna Haraway's theorisation of the figure of the cyborg will be used. The following discussion highlights how 'nature' and its co-present ecological sensibility can evoke a potentially subversive, even utopian, presence as opposed to the 'cultural logic' of contemporary Hollywood film.

In effect, the science fiction genre affirms that we are only truly human when we are in contact with what is not human. This section serves to articulate contemporary eco-fears as expressed through science fiction films which are usually dismissed as being preoccupied with empty spectacle. The chapter in general also focuses on the transgressive potential of excessive scenography, but more particularly, on new forms of representational agency which attempt to help revitalise, if not create, potentially new ecological metaphors within postmodernist science fiction. Initially at least, the notion of postmodernity is applied as a crude periodising strategy to connect science fiction films made since the 1980s and to frame various attributes concerning pessimistic readings together with positive, even utopian, constructions of what has coalesced into the postmodernist aesthetic.

Metaphorically, the cyborg embraces the fractured identity of the postmodern world. In many ways it also symbolises and articulates the post-gender politics of ecological consciousness, while also serving to promote a powerful humane expression of eco-responsible agency. The dangers, however, of such metaphoric essentialising concerning varying ontological notions embodying 'human' and 'post-human' ecological agency, must remain foregrounded as a cautionary subtext.

Legacy of 1950s Science Fiction

Modernity helped to legitimise the theoretical foundations of the Enlightenment, 'whose outlook, goals and predisposition characterize the modern world' (Berman 1994: viii). It has hitherto been defined by two central, apparently opposing affirmations which contend that nature must be (totally) dominated as a means to human ends and that human ends can be reconciled with each other and nature through a mutual recognition of free and equal subjects. Such a simplistic, even naive, agenda can be seen as incorporating the total control of nature and has augmented a profusion of commodities that attempt to simulate or fulfil human 'desires' without always understanding, much less exploring, human 'needs'. The postmodernist aesthetic often actively seeks to engage with this dilemma, one with which ecology has always been preoccupied.

1950s science fiction films dealt with ecological fears most explicitly by exploring the potential effects of nuclear destruction together with environmental degradation.[1] With the transformation of science fiction films in the 1980s, the mood had changed, many claim, towards the presentation of a much more complex, pessimistic and nihilistic vision of the future. Human nature itself was no longer accepted as consensual, a fixed entity (as in *Body Snatchers*), which had to be defended by right-minded individuals to protect its sacredness. In this new post-nuclear world, good and bad, machine and human, often could no longer be easily distinguished. Brian McHale correctly regards such science fiction with its 'relative openness to intertextual circulation' as the most valuable model for a postmodernist consciousness (McHale 1992: 12). In fact, as E. Ann Kaplan says, it is this 'blurring of opposition between human and machine, self and other, body and world, like the blurring of distinctions between plot and *mise-en-scène*, which is what makes postmodern science fiction texts so fascinating for cultural critics especially' (Kaplan et al. 1990: 100).

This chapter will illustrate how in many of these ostensibly dystopic texts the cyborgs/machines often manifest more effective, even redemptive, attributes than their erstwhile human role models. They also, I suggest, (re)present post-human or newly-defined 'human' values more robustly and convincingly in the struggle against dehumanising totalitarianism, as evidenced through various forms of ecological imbalance.

The invention and reinvention of nature remains the most central area of hope, oppression and contestation for inhabitants of the planet Earth. Science fiction, which can be considered a primary postmodern genre, explicitly represents and problematises notions concerning 'nature' and thereby addresses specific eco-fears and sensibilities, in particular environmental pollution and the potential risk of human extinction.

> While technological advances encourage huge population explosions, they also bring about new risks of sudden population collapse through nuclear war, industrial pollution, etc.[2]

(Leslie 1996: 2).

Fears around technophobia, together with problems of environmental waste, can often be analysed most effectively within postmodern science fiction films. For instance, *Terminator 2* (to be discussed in detail later) with its explicit anti-nuclear message, can be regarded as more 'effective' as a critique, from a textual and ecological (peace-making) perspective, than many of the more overtly serious, well-meaning realistic exposés of the fear of military and nuclear destruction. All this in spite of the formal structure of the film which privileges consumptive and wasteful action, which at first sight appears to efface a green aesthetic as defined and exemplified in Chapter 1. Of course, this corresponds with the inherent contradictions embedded within popular texts which effectively incorporate and disseminate often mutually contradictory discourses. *T2* (1991), for instance, also invites its readers to critique the violence it presents, most explicitly in Sarah's feminist diatribe to the scientist Dyson: 'Men like you built the hydrogen bomb,' she roars. 'Men like you thought it up . . . you don't know what its like to *create* something.'

Postmodernist Breakdown/`Radicalised' Modernism
Many left-wing critics remain pessimistic about the beneficial cultural effects of what they regard as the impotence, or even the inadequacy, of much postmodernist theory and its attempts to legitimise what they continue to regard as vacuous popular culture. As one critic asserts, the 'map of myth is lost to us. At the pivot of the millennium the high energy, information rich nations share a unique epistemic crisis' (Broderick 1995: xi). Such a 'crisis' is transcribed in popular texts through an apparent 'breakdown' in both formal conventions and aesthetics together with characters and performers inside the pro-filmic event who do not maintain or

affirm a controlling meta-discourse. Nevertheless, I will argue that this 'breakdown' affords more effective, if merely symptomatic, exposition of often conflicting representations of ecological debates than a more apparently coherent meta-narrative exposition which tends to close down meaning and internal debate.

Postmodernism, the optimists affirm, has become the new, libertarian, all-encompassing, periodising strategy for addressing life and art. Instead of remaining bogged down within the vortex of modernist opposition between low and high art, with the inevitable divisive ideological consequences for its audiences, postmodernist theory attempts to break free from the chains of such fixed cultural, textual and ideological strategies. Anxieties concerning meta-narratives began with Jean-Francois Lyotard, and while they often served to 'ground and legitimate knowledge', many are no longer regarded as 'credible' (McHale 1992: 5). Such breakdowns, especially between binary oppositions and the apparent loss, according to Lyotard, of 'transcendental foundations' (cited in Tallack 1995: 360) coincidentally afford more space for new and often less ideologically regressive discourses to break through in popular film.

Postmodernism in this guise has in some ways become the controlling discourse and aesthetic because of its exposure of the weakness of modernism. What it discovers (or rather rediscovers) 'is that rationality cannot ground itself, and that therefore modernity cannot be grounded' (Bertens 1995: 241). Modernity is, of course, also 'enigmatic at its core', as Giddens (Giddens 1990: 49) has remarked, in that it sends out contradictory impulses which have come to constitute its two primary modes of thought - 'the one expansionist, transcendent, and omni-representational, the other self-reflexive, inward spiralling, and anti-representational - that in our day and age have come to clash so violently' (cited in Bertens 1995: 242). Hans Bertens correctly characterises Habermas's modernist position as 'defending philosophy against irrationalism' and his central argument as addressing 'the plausibility of a rationality that distinguishes itself from the rationality denounced by poststructuralists' (Bertens 1995: 111).

Without such a unifying rationality, Habermas feared that a dissensus politics would leave the Left fragmented and unable to organise and mobilise. Post-structuralism had successfully attacked empirical rationalism as only one form of knowing but Habermas affirmed that the project of modernity was more than this 'means-end rationalism' and consequently advanced what Bertens describes as a 'post-rationalist modernity' (*ibid.*: 111). Bertens goes so far as to contend that we might choose between the 'postmodern' or a more progressive form of modernism which draws from both paradigms. He calls this the 'radicalised modern' which coincidentally also helps to legitimise an ecological agenda. It is our fate, therefore, he continues, 'to reconcile the demands of rationality and those of "the sublime", to negotiate a permanent crisis in the name of precarious stabilities' (*ibid.*: 248).

Popular film, through the various breakdowns implicit in postmodernism, together with the ever-present modernist residue, continues to create potential universal as well as micro-narrative signifiers from the ashes of an apparent (non) referentiality. Broderick is certainly correct when he exposes the 'breakdown' inside the pro-filmic event as often serving to crack open crude divisions between modernist and postmodernist sensibilities. These breakdowns can also be appropriated to engender counter discourses which draw from both paradigms. Consequently, we do not always have to accept Bertens' stark choice, since the 'radicalised modern' is often implicit in 'excessive' moments embedded in otherwise postmodern filmic texts - especially at the point of closure, as will be illustrated later. But even more explicitly, conventional human agency has become effectively problematised and 'radicalised' especially by new technological innovations which are illustrated in particular by representations of cyborg and other 'non-human' life forms.

Postmodern Eco-space and the Sublime

If modernity involves a burying of contingency through the reification of forms, then postmodernism involves an emergence of contingency through the transcendence of forms. However, the struggle of life in postmodernism implies a refusal to face up to this contingent boundlessness

(Tester 1993: 131).

The study of space (as explored in previous chapters) has in many ways become more pervasive within postmodernist cultural theory across the various disciplines and often seeks to promote new paradigms which remain central to our new cyber-age. Historically, situationism in particular, with its emphasis on lived urban reality, sets the terms for debates by Henri Lefebvre and others. Lefebvre finally condemns the quest for a science of space, rejecting the loose metaphoricity in which everything has become a 'space'. (Foucault is the clear villain in this debate.) He further argues that the fragmentation of space is the product of a mental 'division of labour' that only sustains the subjection to state power. But as discussed elsewhere, the use of such spatial metaphors has often confused rather than clarified explorations around notions of eco-space.

Some critics more recently remain convinced of the utopian possibilities of cyber-space and have gone so far as to dismiss an over-preoccupation with 'real' space as eco-fundamentalism. They are convinced that the digital universe appears to have unlimited prospects, serving to create a new 'road to nowhere' in cyber-space. This digital cyber-space provides the illusion of God-like control, with the player able to control the 'game' through ingenuity and dexterity. However, this 'electronic techno(space)' and its immaculate, uncomplicated Disneyesque nature can also be understood to extend the illusion of a 'single (almost modernist) vision, like the notion of a pristine wilderness' or the idea of a 'limitless fully immersive cyberspace' (Robins 1996: 93). Such spatial analysis falls into the trap of positioning all abstract notions of space into the same dimension of 'cognitive mapping' mentioned previously, thereby demeaning the more concrete ecological appreciation of space as a constituent of interactive organisms, including human. Criticism becomes trapped in an ethereal cyberspace where 'man can play God' but without having to cope with the ethics of responsibility or the chaotic fluidity of our 'natural' spatial eco-system.

The importance of spatial analysis can perhaps best be understood with reference to Kant's concept of the 'sublime' and the 'pleasure' achieved through human communion with the environment. Kant cogently affirms a conventional romantic sensibility when he asserts that while 'beauty' can be regarded as mere 'restful contemplation', the 'sublime' in contrast creates an 'intellectual feeling' and makes us 'feel moved'. Lyotard nevertheless appears to turn Kant's theory upside down, exposing 'its strange non-connectivity to nature'. The sublime, on the whole, gives 'no indication of anything final in nature itself, but only the possible employment of our intuitions of it. It is ignorant of nature . . .' (Lyotard cited in Haber 1994: 139).

Lyotard goes on to associate the sublime with the 'unrepresentable' which is beyond the mastery of naming and which prompts artistic (and by implication intellectual and social) experiment. Lyotard regards the Kantian sublime as being closely bound up with the essence of modernity. The modernist sublime, which has been explored in earlier chapters, following this line of argument, is essentially nostalgic and its form 'continues to offer to the reader or viewer, matter for solace or pleasure' (Lyotard 1984: 340).

Whereas for Lyotard the postmodern (avant-gardist), sublime

> puts forward the unpresentable in presentation itself; that which denies itself the
> solace of good forms, the consensus of a taste which would make it possible to share
> collectively the nostalgia for the unattainable; that which searches for new presenta-
> tions, not in order to enjoy them but in order to impart a stronger sense of the unpre-
> sentable

> *(ibid.)*

Lyotard specifically focuses on what he sees as the postmodernist inability to represent, which, according to Broderick, now 'surpasses our power to represent and pitches us into a sort of Gothic rapture' (Broderick 1995: 104). Bertens usefully suggests, however, that both modern and postmodernist aesthetics remain preoccupied with notions of the sublime and are equally concerned with the unpresentable. He concludes that Lyotard's art of the sublime is thus an art of negation. Like postmodern science, Lyotard's postmodern aesthetic is based on a never-ending critique of representation which should contribute to the preservation of heterogeneity, of optimal dissensus. The sublime, so conceived, does not, however, lead towards a resolution; but instead such 'confrontation with the unrepresentable leads to radical openness' (Bertens 1995: 133).

I continually demonstrate in my reading of various Hollywood closures that there is evidence of a renewed sublime mode which affirms and produces a 'positive' form of ecological expression. Both modernist and postmodernist expressions of the sublime, including Bertens's analysis of Lyotard's use of the term, evoke contradictory feelings which are potentially transgressive. For the purposes of this study, such continued symbolic expression, as codified within often (excessive) filmic moments, can similarly be employed as evidence of the existence of a potent ecological attitude that can be illustrated through a textual analysis of a recent enigmatic futuristic text, Dark City.

Dark City

Many theoretical reflections on the sublime can be exemplified by *Dark City* (1997), directed by Alex Proyas. The film provides a stylised noir exposition using the transgressive potential of 'excessive' scenography and representational agency which often echoes Blade Runner, to be discussed later. A dying alien race is experimenting on humans by constructing alternative memories for them, so that they can 'learn' from their adaptive behaviour - which is apparently regarded as the defining characteristic and strength of humanity as a unique species. To aid them in this manipulation, the aliens physically remodel the city at night, through a form of mass hypnosis (reminiscent of communal prayer to a deity), inducing what they euphemistically call 'tuning'. Consequently, their experiments (like the cinematic apparatus itself) manipulate both interior and exterior co-ordinates and thereby totally transform their human subjects so they are psychologically in 'tune' with their new physical environment.

The excessive use of special effects to demonstrate this architectural tuning often appears swamped and overly circumscribed by layers of complex narrative exposition which continually stumbles over the need to explicate itself. This in turn appears to hold up the narrative flow and often obscures a stylistic purity, which militates against the possibility of representing some form of affirmative sensibility. Also, the intertextual references are so overt and layered (as defined by Hutcheon's exposition of the 'playful' postmodernist aesthetic), that the film consequently appears to lack a sense of coherent engagement with a linear narrative. However, more positively, Lyotard's strong sense of the unpresentable appears to be in evidence and this narrative incoherence and visual excess is, of course, very much part of the unrepresentability and potency of the sublime, cited earlier. This can be appreciated most especially through the use of *mise-en-scène*, which concentrates on the morphing of the environment (technically and metaphorically), thereby endlessly reconfiguring time and space.

Like the 'cinema of attractions' popularised by Tom Gunning with reference to early cinema, the narrative momentum of the film is held up while matter is spectacularly transformed without apparent explanation. In many ways ,the poor visibility, aided by the neo-noir aesthetic, with much of the transformation occurring in shadow and half-light, affords an even more invasive 'spectacle of excess' while also exposing the ultimate metaphoric evocation of the unconscious dream. Such dramatic material transformation (through techniques found in 1990s special effects) serves to signal, if not embody, Lyotard's 'limits of Enlightenment', which he ascribes to the postmodern universe.

The visual and narrative climax of the film exposes an image of deep-space which, like the black hole in astrophysics, is revealed when the main protagonist finally and literally breaks down his nostalgic romanticised image of 'Shell Beach'. This proves to be an empty signifier, a piece of graffiti on a wall. The truly awesome, sublime of the dark abyss is revealed, however, when he knocks down the wall and looks out into empty space, forcing him to realise that he is actually on a giant spaceship. This radically delimits his transcendent wishful fantasy. As Lyotard affirms, the sublime, like the infinite, is not comprehensible as a whole. Looking out into the nothingness of existence (like looking into the majesty of the Grand Canyon - and other less oblique moments of 'incoherent' epiphany) can also serve to reconnect humanity with the holistic cosmos. Screen time is allowed to stand still and the spectacle of frozen, reconstituted future-space affords its protagonists and audience both space and time (the camera point-of-view has moved beyond the diegetic demands of the narrative) to contemplate their existence.[3]

Humanity has become more and more enthralled by such recharged sublime spectacles in the postmodernist universe. Guy Debord formulated this in 1967 as follows:

> The entire existence of societies where modern production relations prevail, presents itself as one huge accretion of spectacles. Everything directly experienced has been consigned to a depiction. [van Toorn continues] . . . Experience makes way for the registering of impressions. A hiatus occurs between the external perception and the internal experience

> *(cited in van Toorn 1997: 2).*

In many ways what can be regarded as the 'intellectual subconscious', as opposed to the 'subconscious', is often characterised by an 'excess of thought' (van Toorn 1997). This interpretation is possibly ironic in light of the enormous growth in psychoanalytical theories which have come to dominate much feminist critical theory. A greater amount of 'excess' and sublime expression can be experienced by the human conscious intellect, aided by the dark, almost subterranean aesthetic of film noir. Such wakeful cinematic experience is in many ways more transgressive than the conventional classic narrative resolution, which often affirms the dream-like state of the experience, thus reducing its authenticity and believability. A wide-awake sublime experience need not necessarily suffer from such reductive closure, even if it plays with it, as often happens in postmodernist texts like *Dark City*.

This mixture of visual excess is effectively counterpointed in this film by the central narrative enigma, focusing on John Murdoch (Rufus Sewell), who suffers from amnesia, is gifted with telekinetic ability and is striving to find an answer to the meaning of (his) existence. In the opening sequences Murdoch wakes up naked (like the Terminators) in a sparsely decorated bathroom with a pervading sense of disorientation. Finding the mutilated body of a girl in another room sends shock signals through his system, which he describes as feeling like 'living out someone else's nightmare'.

Throughout the film he struggles to find his romantic roots through a mythic place called 'Shell Beach', which represents his evocative metaphorical 'primary scene' from his deep (if false) consciousness. The sudden physical revelation that it is only an artificial construction, hiding the reality that the city is a spherical craft floating within the nothingness of endless space, is by all accounts traumatic for our protagonist and allegorically emblematic for the audience, as the ontological search for meaning is effectively exposed. This revelation is as dramatic, for instance, as the Copernican discovery that the earth revolved around the sun and not vice versa, or that the earth is in fact spherical, controlled by the ever-present law of gravity. *Dark City* effectively dramatises the conformist, metaphoric forces which reduce human nature to a cause-effect organism, driven by innate biological urges, framed within a dark, cage-like, future-city environment and a protagonist's faulty attempts to break down such restrictions. On all levels the inhabitants appear to have little control over their lives. The Kafkaesque hero must learn at least how to assume imaginative control of his environment and recreate a more humanised imaginative habitat.

But the mythic urge for 'humanist' centred solutions to the primary ontological questions, via the nostalgic evocation of a romantic, 'cheap', postcard group memory,[4] is finally shown to be hollow. Water, the life-affirming force binding the earth together, can potentially destroy the alien (just as Gaia affirms) and at the same time is capable of protecting the planet with its integrated biosystems. But, of course, on this alien spaceship - the ultimate expression of the artificial mega-metropolis - such natural life forces are sadly not available. Natural ecological balance, as quantified and defined by the four primary elements, has most certainly become perverted.

Nevertheless, as John Milton, one of the first great romantic poets, contends, man has the power to make heaven out of hell and vice versa. Murdoch finally has the imaginative power to reshape his city environment, building a sea around it. The omniscient external point-of-view shot showing the unrepresentability of a giant city space enveloped by a newly-created coating of life-affirming water is strange and awesome. Empty space is finally brought to life for the first time in the film by a 'sublime' sunrise, painting the dystopic non-natural space with a brilliant warm light. Water and sunlight remain primary ecological signifiers of a harmonious eco-system. The greatest evolutionary power of human beings is their ability to (re)create in their own mind, if nowhere else, the capacity to transcend the physical limitations of their constructed environment and achieve a form of ecological nirvana, outside of the noirish waste of everyday meaningless existence.

Consequently, while such idyllic romanticised closure at first sight appears cheap and sentimental, with a picture postcard seascape sunset filling the space of the otherwise dystopian environment, it can also signal the human power to (re)create a benevolent, even symbiotic environment out of the most 'alienating' of future environments. Such ecological harmony, even if only recreated inside the world of the human mind, affords a potent mythic metaphor for the human capacity or the craving for ecological balance.

With the aid of the doctor's experimental injection, Murdoch achieves total control over the alien power to transform all space to whatever specifications he wants. After a conventional superheroic fight with the alien enemy, he can finally use his powers for good, affirming that what differentiates 'our' nature is not the individuality of the human 'mind' but human 'emotions' (as in *Body Snatchers*) and consequently he creates a benevolent eco-space which induces and validates romantic love above all else. Creating a liminal seaside pier, linking the claustrophobic city space and the newly-created seaside, provides such a conventional romantic site of human fulfilment. Opening the door into the emotionally healing bright sunlight, together with the therapeutic sounds of a seascape, transforms the dominant visualisation of space from a noirish evocation of a dystopic anti-ecological environment into a utopic world which dramatises the human emotional urge towards romantic harmony.

Shell Beach can be read as signalling the 'limits to the Enlightenment' and the romantic desire to connect with nature, which no longer remains a crude over-determined signifier of earthly paradise since it opens the door to a new level of consequence, signalling a realisable eco-utopia within a reflexive but finally humanly controlled narrative. While the visual mise-en-scène is continually constructing apparently contradictory representations concerning the possibility or otherwise of environmental harmony, the filmic protagonist and narrative closure seek to reconstitute and reformulate their regressive environment. The excessive transformation of the *mise-en-scène*, through morphing and other special effects, is finally counterpointed by a multi-sensory closure, which helps at least to question the potency of such alien disruption of a symbiotic and nurturing environment. The 'remediation'[5] of otherwise outdated stock romantic images helps to reconstitute the potency of these therapeutic images, especially when framed through closure in this excessively noirish science fiction film.

Tashiro, cited earlier in this book, in a rare study of the visual aesthetic of film, speaks of how nature as a space is 'controlled by human perception, and in the process renders nature as landscape'. Such 'landscape' through editing 'provides multiple perspectives' since 'nature always exceeds the ability of the eye or the lens to perceive'. Consequently 'photography becomes a stylization' and 'emotions generated by a story substitute for the visceral effect of real space' long ago described by Edmund Burke as the 'sublime' (Tashiro 1998: 35).

In the end, however, Murdoch's motives appear to preclude any form of utopian benevolence, unlike, for example, *Body Snatchers* or *Logan's Run*, where the films' 'modernist' heroic agents uphold a more inclusive humanitarian sensibility which further endorses the desire to save their species as well as themselves. This apparent lack of social 'humanity' - while John Murdoch does in fact commence to rebuild the city in his mind's eye - occurs as a consequence of the extremes of the dystopian universe represented and serves almost paradoxically in some ways to reaffirm the desire for some new form of utopian 'public sphere'. Finally, however, Murdoch remains strangely two-dimensional and does not fulfil the prototypical role necessary to signal the fully fleshed out mythic desire for ecological sustainability; a role which the cyborg has begun to embody.

The Cyborg: A New Form of Post-Human Agency

Cyborg is shorthand for 'cybernetic organism', usually described as a human-machine hybrid and sometimes labelled as 'android', 'replicant' or even 'bionic man'. The word 'cybernetics' derives from the Greek term referring to mechanisms of steering, governing or control, as opposed to the 'evil' of chaos or entropy. The concept was first used with reference to 'human engineering' by MIT mathematician Norbert Wiener in the early 1940s.

The term 'cyborg' was first coined in 1960 by Clynes and Kline to refer to the enhanced man who could survive in extra-terrestrial environments. Many regard such a phenomenon as a metaphor for the profound possibilities for the twenty-first century

(Gray 1995: xv).

Cybernetics seeks to monitor, regulate and modify the dynamic loops of feedback governing the world's continuance. However, while inventors often remain wedded to the 'militarized imaginary', Wiener most notably remained an outspoken critic of the militarisation of science. He was not alone in using military references for his new science (Wiener 1961: 177). This is clear in the work of Donna Haraway, who draws attention to the relationship between cybernetics and the military economy of capitalist patriarchy out of which it has evolved. Conceptualising the logic of cybernetics as a powerful 'theoretical fiction which forecloses other ways of making sense of the world', she concludes that 'information is the ultimate mediated ether' (Haraway 1981: 9).

While admitting the militaristic roots in the cultural as well as the physical construction of the cyborg, other critics, including Judith Genova, have nevertheless begun to use the cyborg metaphor to explore the 'reinvention of nature' and the disruption of the nature/culture binary opposition (cited in Hamilton 1997: 111). Haraway, in her seminal 'Manifesto for Cyborgs' (1985), proposed how the notion of the cyborg can serve to overcome regressive gender power dilemmas in 'an effort to contribute to a socialist feminist culture and theory in a postmodernist non-naturalist mode, and in the utopian tradition of imagining a world without gender' (Haraway 1985: 91).

Scott Bukatman concludes that the cyborg is at once a 'delibidinalized body and a sexualized machine . . . Terminal identity negotiates a complex trajectory between the forces of instrumental reason and the abandonment of a sacrificial excess' (Bukatman 1994: 329). Consequently, as an agent of change, the cyborg can serve effectively to critique established gender norms, for example, as well as other paradigms of acceptable behaviour. But notions of 'human' nature and individualisation need to be continually redefined in their hegemonic association with liberal humanist ideology. While modernity in the broad sense has been considered humanist in its agenda, it is nevertheless endlessly problematised, especially by all forms of 'post' modernist critical thinking. For both post-structuralism and even deep ecology, Sueellen Campbell asserts that 'the assumptions underlying humanism have become untenable; we need new ways to understand our place in the world' (Campbell in Glotfelty 1996: 133). As a result, the utopian possibilities for a new form of 'post human' agency has become an important measure for an eco-textual analysis and the cyborg in particular provides a focus for such exposition.

For some cultural critics the cyborg effectively represents the conventional postmodernist expression of a 'rupturing of identity' beyond gender, and even embodies an expression of extreme schizophrenia. Sobchack, however, is much more positive and productive when she argues that the postmodern science fiction film does not 'embrace the alien' in a 'celebration of resemblance' but 'erases alienation' in a 'celebration of similitude'. The 'alien' posited by marginal and postmodern science fiction texts enables the representation of alienation as 'human' and constitutes the 'reversible and non-hierarchical relations of similitude into a myth of homogenized heterogeneity' (cited in Broderick 1995: 114). This process of transformation and (de)alienation promotes an ecological utopian project, which would break down opposition between various agents (human and non-human) in the interests of a greater understanding and acceptance of the total eco-system. The breakdown of these oppositions also serves to promote radical reconceptualisations across ecological boundaries.

As communal human beings, we apparently cannot do without 'foundational myths': shared stories which define the possibilities and limits of an oppositional politics. Haraway's evocation of the cyborg, in spite of her continual evasion of foundational myths, in many ways serves such a function. Her cyborg myth(s) in particular help extend the insights of post-colonial feminism into a 'fusion of outsider identities' (Thornham 1997: 163).[6] Haraway effectively affirms that the cyborg confounds the boundary between human and machine, subverting the dualisms of western colonial culture, in particular male/female, mind/body. In Haraway's original 'liberatory myth of the cyborg', she argued that we (feminist critics in particular) must abandon the 'feminist dream of a common language' because it operated as a 'totalizing and imperialist' force, appropriating, marginalising, or excluding those [black women, lesbian women, 'third world' women] whose identities could not be constructed within it (Haraway 1991: 215).

However, Jenny Wolmark remains unsure as to whether postmodernist and feminist theories can work together. She is convinced, nonetheless, that science fiction should be regarded as the primary genre for such dialogue and recognises how the cyborg and the cyberpunk help problematise notions around the central motif of 'the human', which remains at the core of humanism.[7]

But many feminist critics stubbornly but understandably remain highly critical of such inclusive postmodernist theories, perceiving that acceptance of a multiplicity of discourses and positions serves to displace altogether the primacy of sexual difference as an organising principle. Some contend that Haraway's cyborg in fact denies the realities of women's material existence as 'women'. Other critics remain even more scathing of such liberatory potential, contending that they often re-inscribe and even legitimise class and racist values. Holland best exemplifies the critical feminist fear of cyber-theory when she asserts that such a narrative operates as a 'myth to reassert the mind/body dualism and those of sex and gender that parallel it, where its ideological aims are achieved by first illustrating the materialist position, and then showing it to be inadequate, naive and in some sense "morally wrong"'(Holland in Featherstone et al. 1995: 170).

Nevertheless, many feminists and cultural critics often concur that the cyborg remains the 'new hope' for creating a 'progressive humanity', at least a metaphorical representation of this, which will serve to erode barriers across race and gender and transform even what it means to be human. Such representational agency (in Haraway's terms in particular) has an extremely important role to play, therefore, with regard to the metaphoric expression of a progressive ecological discourse.

Postmodern Transgression of Boundaries

Many cyber-feminists have tended to place primary emphasis on the moment of pleasure, confusion and final destruction within the cyber-agent. 'Transgressed boundaries, in fact, define the cyborg, making it the consummate postmodernist concept' (Robins 1996: 91). At the outset, I must take issue with critics who dismiss the expression of transgression as not corresponding with any coherent form of rebellion or the breakdown of boundaries or limits. Forms of transgression and limits certainly could not exist without one another and, according to Peter Bebergal, each limit is revealed through such transgression. He defines this as a 'movement towards a threshold' - with each interpretive moment uncovering new symbols, new limits, that it must strive to understand (Bebergal 1998: 1).

Schizophrenia has also become a relatively new metaphor to express and embody such transgression and is effectively represented by the cyborg organism that embodies the connectivity between human nature and the patriarchally constructed scientific environment. More radically, the cyborg serves to transform, even subvert both, rather than simply connecting these polar oppositions. By the late twentieth century, Haraway prophetically suggests, 'we are all chimeras, theorised and fabricated hybrids of machine and organism - we are all cyborgs' (Haraway 1991: 149). *Blade Runner*, which is discussed in detail later, attempts most specifically to work through such chimeras, to (re)construct a populist utopian narrative closure which has significant ecological implications.

As already mentioned, conventional representations of human nature find it difficult to represent, much less embody, a coherent form of sublime transgression, especially since this offends the dominant scientific evolutionary sensibility.

However, paradoxically, accompanying the phenomenal development of new technology, especially the proto-human cyborg, such developments have made it easier, symbolically at least, to formulate a potentially pro-active evolutionary human consciousness which can also legitimately appropriate an ecological purpose, particularly with regard to changing the future.

Excessive Technological Determinism?

The Terminator

The 'fly in the ointment' of conventional human fulfilment remains the paradoxical potency embedded in the myth of technological determinacy. For instance, an oppositional/negotiated reading by 'smart readers' (see Trushell 1986: 89B104) might recognise in the evil cybernetic techno-war depicted in *Terminator 2: Judgement Day's* opening post-apocalyptic sequence, an image of the hysterically celebrated recent Gulf War, in which 'our' machines mowed down their human bodies, as the saying goes, 'like fish in a tank'. John Gray is both prophetic and polemical, when he connects such technological developments and ecological issues within a global context in his consideration of such a war with its 'computerised slaughter and ecological terrorism' (Gray 1997: 74).

Instead of endorsing transgressive notions of agency, the original cyborg anti-hero remains 'othered', both as an alien destructive machine and a non-biological outsider who does not adapt to, much less learn from the earth's eco-system. His sole function is destruction. The Schwarzenegger figure in the original film has no redeeming ethical or other human qualities, since he does not feel pain, remorse or fear, being simply a killing machine who 'does not stop until you are dead'. This reductive, conventional machine-like organism remains a thematic preoccupation. The opening narrative exposition written on the blank screen pinpoints how the machines became the enemy, after directly causing nuclear catastrophe, so that they could assert their dominance. Like the paranoid evocation of an alien threat discussed in the previous chapter, the enemy is also not personalised but instead is conceptualised as having a coherent set of non-human values and beliefs. Human nature can therefore avoid any ethical responsibility for future catastrophe.

This form of ethical purity is reasserted in the various flash-forwards to the future, mediated by the human witness Reese, who foretells how such apparently self-motivated machines literally crush all in their path. The future dystopian city space has become totally dehumanised (like the killing fields of twentieth century war) as the ant-like human warriors fight the Goliath-like machines, through sheer determination and the primary biological will to survive. This dystopic primal scene becomes a recurring nightmare for Reese who has come to redeem the future by protecting the leadership lineage of the past.

The final closure of the film isolates Sarah Connor, the chosen one, pregnant with the future hero of the final post-apocalyptic struggle, escaping out into the western desert in her red automobile. Alone, she speaks into a tape machine constructing a new sense of self, which will provide a family history for her unborn son and herself and articulate her newly-found heroic mission. In the far distance, as she drives on 'the road to nowhere', are growing atmospheric signs of a great 'storm' coming, framed within a romanticised desert and mountain landscape. This is the only representation in the film of unmediated pastoral nature. But such storms are also most certainly not a natural phenomenon, signalling the impending apocalypse. Yet she must face her heroic human destiny, predetermined within the narrative framework which endorses a universal mythic agency, unlike the more 'local' gender specific conflicts in *Thelma and Louise*, for example.

Because so much of the narrative trajectory of the film is predetermined using a conventional machine enemy, the narrative seldom rises above a two-dimensional polarised global eco-conflict. Nevertheless the seeds of both (post)human ecological agency together with the transgressive potentialities of cyborgs has at least been sown for the more expansive sequel which cannot function without this mythical framework being developed.

James Cameron, also the director of *T2*, asserted in a publicity interview that there 'was a little bit of the "Terminator" in everybody'. The film, he continues, is a 'dark, cathartic fantasy' and audiences 'want to be him for one moment' (cited in French 1996: 39). This conjunction of filmic cyborg and acceptable human agency serves in some ways to reassert the primacy of individual agency as a site of moral values. Peter Brooks' *Melodramatic Imagination* (1976), pontificates that the only remaining source of moral value resides within the human personality itself. 'From amid the collapse of other principles and criteria the individual ego declares its central and overriding value . . . Personality alone remains the effective vehicle of transindividual messages' (Brooks 1976: 16). The cyborg also serves a dualistic nature which is concurrent with the postmodernist ethos - effectively transmitting both 'transindividualism' together with the potentiality of human disintegration.

Cameron has in fact gone on to show a fascination with the potency of the female as an ultimate dark fantasy from Sigourney Weaver in the *Alien* series to Kate Winslet in *Titanic*, figured as (maternal) heroines who must finally suffer the trauma of losing their men in their struggle for survival. Such representational expression and 'hyperbolic emotions', reminiscent of classic melodramatic performance, also serve to focus attention on the interior moral agency of these protagonists.[8]

Sean French, for example, contends that Fritz Lang (whose seminal *Metropolis* provides so many references for the science fiction genre and *Terminator* in particular) would have approved 'of a film that seems to preach peace while depicting a future of Hobbesian struggle for survival between psychopathic machines and a tribe of Nietzschean human warriors' (French 1996: 11). But taking up Robins's criticism: cyberpunk, surfing, or 'bumper sticker libertarianism', 'is neither progressive nor democratic and despite all the rhetoric of networking, it is hardly communitarian' (Robins 1996: 90). Yet this was the contradictory dream of many from the Easy Rider milieu to 'Trekies' in science fiction. The maxim of cyberpunk is that 'information wants to be free' (Sardor et al. 1996: 89). Cyberspace provides a potentially new anarchic frontier for white colonists, where hackers can be equated with modern rebel frontiers men.

George Bataille pushes Cameron's generalised assertion regarding the ontological needs of human beings to assert that they are, first and foremost, creatures of excess. 'Humans gain pleasure from expenditure, waste, festivities, sacrifice, destruction.' Indeed, for Bataille, these underlying ontological principles, which are manifest in nature as 'universal laws', are (in fact) more fundamental than economies of production and utility (cited in Williams 1998: 66). While such pleasure may help to explain the universal success of both *Titanic* and *T2*, alternatively this form of excess, focusing on bodily pleasures and physical destruction, can also articulate and signify the polar opposite. For example, saving the planet as the Terminator finally does - with an act of supreme self-sacrifice - can simultaneously count as the ultimate (if 'regressive') act of heroic agency for any representative human protagonist. At the same time, we cannot forget that this action takes place within the lived body of a postmodern cyborg agent, which by its nature serves to continually problematise such ontological surety.

This grand anti-narrative trend involving human transformations (or becomings), often packed within a self-reflexive comic format, has become in varying degrees dominant within the new mega-science fiction blockbuster, with often contradictory manifestations of excess being the primary visceral residue. The concluding comic-book fight between the 'good' and 'evil' Terminators, as they tear apart each other's prosthetic bodies, at an overt level articulates conventional generic and narrative resolution. But at the same time this destructive action projects a multi-sensory excessive experience which conflates ethical issues within the leaky boundaries between human and non-human bodies. Such conflicts are less effective, however, when cyborg aliens are reduced to mere two-dimensional machines, as in the original discussed above. Nevertheless, 'high concept' (if necessarily contradictory), action-packed texts continue to be dismissed as simply mindless special-effects vehicles.

The cyborg-driven science fiction film, together with other dystopic future films, can be convincingly read against the grain as serving to critique not only possible futures but also the present. *T2*, in particular, clearly cites contemporary human actions and decisions as heavily responsible for our future, especially for our dystopic visions of the future. Nevertheless, overtly at least, most blockbuster films appear to remain preoccupied with ego-centric heroism and sentimentality which negates the probability of promoting effective universal human agency. Yet the *Terminator* series at least embodies this dichotomy.

Feminist criticism articulates most effectively *T2's* inability to finally become a 'progressive' text. Constance Penley, for example, affirms that while *The Terminator* tries 'to dissipate the fear of the same, to ensure that there is a difference' in gendered terms, it ultimately (re)presents 'a conservative moral lesson about maternity, futuristic or otherwise: mothers will be mothers, and they will always be women' (Penley 1991: 175). Feminist discourse often effectively articulates both the benefits and danger that can result from an attempt to create a new, all- encompassing meta-narrative or some form of micro-narratives which embody human agency and behaviour. But the danger of endorsing some form of totalitarian system which reduces individual expression to systematic homogeneity remains ever present. Looking for hope through an artificial development of holistic systems can be a recipe for disaster. For instance, must ecology privilege the controlling 'system' at the expense of, or in opposition to, the heroic human individual? Hollywood, as has been asserted since the start of this study, finds it impossible not to privilege the latter. This dilemma is skewed and exposed particularly by the way human/cyborg agency effects change through individual protagonists and narrative closure.

Fred Pfeil asserts that such blockbuster texts address a lack of particular political goals and attainable human values which can be traced to:

> the terrible defeats dealt out here throughout the 1980s to every potentially progressive constituency . . . (which serves) to deepen widely held libertarian-individualist suspicions that no structural or institutional transformations for the better are possible, that nothing political can be done . . . What is absent from the present moment of confusion and dejection all along the left, and most necessary for its redemption, is the confidence that individuals can come together in collective action to transform societies structurally and institutionally for the better

(in Copjec 1993: 255).

While such a historically specific political explanation of film may be accurate for many disaffected Left collectives, popular texts often address a much wider all-encompassing, if divergent, constituency so as to reaffirm the primacy of individualism. *T2* and other high concept blockbusters remain essentially humanist, especially through their extension of conventional notions of heroes as agents of utopian change. The resultant praxis encourages a revived sense of individualism, as opposed to new forms of (post-humanist) community expression, to begin again to fight back within a postmodern machine based environment.

In relation to *T2* and the aesthetic potential of other blockbusters, Fred Pfeil dismissively asserts that 'investors are unlikely to invest in a project [*T2* cost $90m] whose meanings, pleasures and rules of editing derive from the principle of the semiotic erosion of narrative conventions and irresolution as an aesthetic way of life'. The overall regime of pleasure in the blockbuster film is, he continues, rather a 'paradigm of late capitalism consumer production'. As proposed by Walser, film-makers 'must keep us constantly (though not continuously) engaged without demanding much attention; knock us out with all the trouble it has gone to, just to give us an instant satisfaction; not only offer us options but also affirm and even flatter us for whatever ones we pick' (in Copjec 1993: 238B9).

These criticisms voice the standard dismissal of the possibilities for oppositional/negotiated readings especially within apparently superficial postmodern popular texts. They are based, however, on a misunderstanding of means and ends within the blockbuster aesthetic. Such texts must *de facto* afford comfortable mass pleasures if they are to succeed commercially and ideologically. But the creation of easy pleasures need not necessarily preclude otherwise unresolved elements being embedded in moments within the *mise-en-scène,* which often includes a surfeit of ecological utopianism.

This study continually addresses how such high concept commercial cinema, which often privileges the visual evocation of sublime moments, together with evocative (post)human agency, can be textually analysed as ecologically potent, even transgressive, by dramatically articulating ecological and ontological tensions within the *mise-en-scène,* embedded particularly within the film's closure. But before this can be fully illustrated, an exploration of specific cyborg manifestations needs to be appreciated.

Modernist/ Postmodernist Agency: Terminators - T800/ T1000

The evolution from hunter to cyborg in American myth is essentially the same as the progress from modernism to postmodernism in western philosophy (Rushing et al. 1995: 11).

While *The Terminator* certainly presents a dystopian future, it apparently does so from a modernist critical perspective which is concerned to 'locate the origins of future catastrophe in decisions about technology, warfare and social behaviour that are being made today' (Penley cited in Jancovich 1992: 3). But Robert Romanyshyn goes much deeper in *Technology as Symptom and Dream* and links the development of technology with a linear perspective embedded in western culture.

He argues that we have historically produced 'a distancing and detached vision' that interprets the body 'as a spectacle' (Romanyshyn 1988: 117). Technology becomes our 'cultural-psychological dream of distance from matter'. It is a dream that ultimately separates us from the world by depicting the self as an 'invented . . . created . . . manufactured' and eventually surplus thing' (*ibid*.: 17). Films such as *Terminator* 'offer us our (own) reflection. They make our "exposed" condition all-too-visible and, by pushing through those surfaces, stake out a future path to recuperating the human' (Telotte 1995: 181).

Whereas for other critics, the original *Terminator* fantasy exposes a 'new' ideological consensus and is nothing less than the logical result of the radical individualism demanded by contemporary capitalism, 'confounded by widespread disillusionment with the proper channels offered for individual success, corrupt Government and a rhetoric of freedom and equity undermined by the obvious systematic maintenance of inequality' (Walser 1993: 164).

Many feminist critics effectively dismiss what they describe as pseudo-transgressive postmodernist theory as masking outmoded male dominated discourse. Some even contend that such postmodernist theory allows male theorists to sidestep the critiques of patriarchy, via guilt if nothing else, by feminist and post-colialist discourse in particular. For example, Barbara Ehrenreich goes so far as to target white males as revolting against what she dubbed 'the breadwinner ethic' and the 'oedipal-nuclear families it produced'. She proposes that white male popular culture in general seems to abandon the breadwinner role without overcoming the sexist attitudes that role perpetuated (cited in Copjec 1993: 257).

However, 'John Connors', who initiated the primary narrative, in fact asserts a libertarian individualist paradigm (which is certainly not post-human) as evidenced by his speech: 'the future is not set'. He tells Kyle Reese, 'There's no fate but what we make for ourselves.'[9] These conventional masculine heroes accept pain and the ultimate responsibility of protecting and redeeming all human nature. As human eco-warriors they have been forced to regress to the level of survivalists like our ancient ancestors. Civilisation and the evolution of new ways of connecting with the eco-system have been abolished to be replaced by the crudest form of Darwinian 'survival of the fittest', in the ever-present war between humans and their machine masters.

For many the sequel is a noir critique of the (post) nuclear family and its values, with Sarah Connor as the 'warrior woman' ready to be reprogrammed from a killing machine to a 'protective' father figure. As Penley affirms, while the original text posits John Connor as 'the child who orchestrates his own primal scene', in T2 'he must be both father to the man and mother to the mom', ensuring he learns not to kill people, as she learns to become domesticated (cited in Copjec 1993: 245).

This is effectively visualised by the original film's closure with mother and son clutching onto each other, both having learned the unique potency of humanity through their display of human empathy as expressed by tears, which is both dramatised and reified by their cyborg friend. The cyborg agent finally helps bring out the nascent nurturing humanity in his newfound 'family', rather than help construct a more radical 'post human' form of group identity. Such rediscovered innate power allows the mother, in particular, to affirm in a final voice-over, her capacity to face the future for the first time with hope. If 'a machine can learn the value of life' so can she and so she acquires the mental strength and nurturing qualities required to help save the planet.

In the sequel *T2*, however, (human) agency affords a more contradictory trajectory. Sean French affirms that *T2* 'humanises the idea of the cyborg; making him civic minded, just as its star, has made himself admired as a public figure above and beyond any of his individual films' (French 1996: 69). The T800 model is replaced by T1000 who is sent back to kill the 13-year-old boy. The humans of the future, presumably still not as technologically advanced as the machines, have reprogrammed a T800 (Schwarzenegger) to return to protect John from the T1000 (Robert Patrick's simulation), which is so sophisticated he truly mimics humanity.

The antagonist T1000 takes on the persona of a white male LA cop, whereas the (modernist) agent T800 embodies the form of the countercultural 'low-life Easy Rider'. While Schwarzenegger (T800) 'learns human values', the more technically proficient prototype (T1000) is completely amoral, being totally in control, yet unable to 'learn' from his environment. Instead it simulates or replicates with the sole object of gaining control, like the Borg enemy in *Star Trek, The Next Generation* discussed elsewhere. Or as Pfeil elegantly puts it, it 'oozes swiftness' via a 'metamorphosis of its liquid shape'. Such transformational ability, like the serpent in Christian mythology, is evil personified and his 'endless semiosis, is the highest form of technocratic death-rationality' (*ibid.*: 247). Sean French is more dismissive of these powers in his reading of Patrick, the cyborg, as both a nerd and symptomatic of the (post-Fordist) company man as opposed to the rugged moral individualism of the technically outdated T800 (French 1996: 30). Consequently, audiences are positioned firmly on the side of human frailty as opposed to the post-human perfection which does not have to consider, much less endorse, the laws of nature.

In contrast, the 'heroic' (Christian) notion of human sacrifice,[10] knowing when and why to commit suicide, is evocatively symbolised by T800's newfound 'socialised humanity'. This is visualised by the excessive *mise-en-scène* focusing on his still beeping red 'heart' at the end of the film and affords us, according to Rushing et al., (trans)modernist hope, even redemption. Such a (white, male American) agent articulates and accepts the need to take on the evolutionary demands of the human race, to maintain its homogeneous ethical purity and ecological purpose. Within this postmodernist text the cyborg other, by becoming the same, can both articulate this essentialist assumption of the biological imperative and also provide the necessary sacrifice to achieve this result.

It is therefore incorrect to postulate that Schwarzenegger is 'a "perfect" icon of the simulated world of postmodernism, whose persona, both body and character, is perpetually constructed and reconstructed by technology' (Rushing et al. 1995: 194). In *T2*, the cyborg hero has apparently become finally (post)human with the assistance of the 'innocent' boy - a prevalent conventional theme in American culture - who instinctively knows the value of life and continues fighting our 'modernist' meta-narrative fight for truth, honour, justice and individualism as well as the 'American way'.

Both 'Terminator' films, therefore, finally serve to endorse to varying degrees almost (pre)modernist humanist notions of agency; recuperating Judaeo-Christian beliefs of heroic martyrdom to negate the corrupting traces of the cyborg organism which embodies the triumph of future militaristic capitalism. In many ways the narrative thrust, especially of *T2*, echoes the patriarchal Christian myth, in which Christ died for the sins of *all* humanity. The Terminator also dies so that humans cannot destroy the planet. His spirit lives on in his 'followers' who, unlike Christ, however, taught him the virtues and values of life.

Whereas *T1* unleashes Schwarzenegger as a most compelling monster, *T2* offers his redemption. This can be seen in the heroic denouement of the Terminator in *T2*, focusing on his 'red' eye and his severely dismembered body. Diegetic time is slowed down and excessively dramatised since he has to use all his cyborg powers to fight his terminal state of disintegration and save his human wards, thereby redeeming his newly-acquired surrogate human nature. This is unlike the original, in which the cyborg is simply motivated by a death rationality and a killing instinct. Such heroic agency effectively cements various otherwise contradictory discourses together, allowing old Promethean myths to become reformulated with renewed potency. The cyborg representational carcass serves to focus varying, often contradictory, discourses, especially this revivified notion of redemption which continues to suffuse populist Hollywood cinema and coincidentally also helps to promote ecological textual signification. Essentially, the cyborg provides new ways of dramatising post-human agency aided by the (self)destructive exegesis of the cyborg consciousness.

These potent moments manifest a universal and benevolent destiny even order of things, as evidenced especially in the fiery furnace of the closure, while eulogising conventional patriarchal (albeit Christian) values. The site of closure is placed in a conventional blue collar patriarchal environment of a steel factory which embodies an extreme example of Fordist rationalisation of energy, where nature is forced to conform to the demands of science and industry. This is all the more symbolic for an individualised fight between postmodernist techno-agents over the very survival of future humanity. It is more than a little ironic that only a vat of liquid steel, framed within such an old-fashioned manufacturing industrial complex, is finally able to exterminate the otherwise invincible future alien nature. Metaphorically at least, this also appears to affirm the otherwise retrogressive potency of earlier capitalist energy in the face of ecological chaos. To solve future problems, human agents must at least symbolically draw strength from the power of older, more discredited forms of capital accumulation. Yet the dominant orthodoxy unconditionally accepts new technology and all its associated attributes. Only hardline Luddites and possibly the original film call for total destruction of such technology. Most appreciate that invention and new technology cannot be simply disinvented, even if superseded and made redundant.

The closure of *T2* serves to endorse the primal power of man-made forms of energy and production as a protective bulwark against these pernicious forms of recent new technology. A Dantesque furnace is finally needed to destroy all traces of this new technology together with the potential for a newly-constituted post-human sensibility. The nature of such mythic and potent signification almost hides this ideological sleight of hand. While conventional epic and mythic exposition have apparently little credence, much less potency, within our postmodern world, nevertheless, such post-human cyborg agents serve to reevaluate the ontological and survival needs for human society. The trick of using heroic redemption (albeit of a cyborg) to obfuscate ecological catastrophe nevertheless 'works' but within the confines of the elastic narrative aesthetic.

Up to now, this study has focused in particular on excessive moments which visually (re)present raw nature in an attempt to freeze and embroider the allure of the narrative drive of such stories. But this final chapter, especially, has also remained preoccupied with transgressive notions of agency which often encourage a form of 'breakdown' and a way out of such otherwise controlling narrative discourses. Nevertheless, in *T2* especially, the evocation of a progressive eco-conscience remains both unresolved and finally terminally incapacitated within its impotent closure. The ideological contents of the text remains trapped within the controlling patriarchal mythic signifiers without fully articulating an equally potent and contradictory range of evolutionary metaphors for audiences to engage with.

The most that can be said with regard to this conventional postmodernist film is that it creates and sustains a Spielbergian effect,[11] where feel-good attitudes and often affirmative values and issues, especially regarding new technology and nuclear destruction, are raised but purposefully left unresolved. Yet at least such an airing deposits a trace of a range of ecological discourses, most especially the need for the West to construct a new, more harmonious composite of human agency, if it is to positively affect the future environment. Ecological changes within these blockbusters tend to occur only if the whole of humanity (which can, in Hollywood terms, be collapsed and serve to disguise the powerful elite who control society) is finally reconstituted and reprogrammed to promote a sustainable future.

New, more radical and transgressive eco-metaphors and allegories are required if such a broadband dialogue is to create fruitful ecological understanding for future generations weaned on the utopian 'illusion' of universal human interactivity, aided by computer technology. While the *Terminator* series remains locked within the grand narrative of human survival on our finite planet, focusing on individual agency and using the Christian myth of self-sacrifice to save the planet, *Blade Runner* and the more recent *Fifth Element* articulate more fully the needs and ways for (future) humans to adapt and learn from ecological norms through the actions of cyber-humans. These rejuvenated representational myths of human agency, together with the potency of the cyborg other, can begin to provide humans with a template for progressive ecological expression among all life forms.

Blade Runner

Blade Runner effectively signals the mythic pre-modern trajectory of man in the role of hunter but at the same time the film also represents a double hunt in which the hunter and the hunted simultaneously stalk each other as prey, instead of merely regressing to a primitive mode of hunting for survival with a common enemy, as in *The Terminator* and *Dark City*. I will explore how both *Blade Runner* and *The Fifth Element* adapt similar trajectories, focusing in particular on their potentially liberatory effects for human agency.

Blade Runner provides a super-example of a cybertext which also serves to address various ecological paradigms. 'Americans, however conservative, however traditional, see the future as a place of equality achieved . . . racism is already understood as an anachronism. *Blade Runner* mirrors the "future of fears" . . . where the anxieties of the present have become the material conditions of an imagined future' (Norton 1993: 19). In spite of this, the scenography of a LA of the future attracts and repels in equal measure. This postmodernist spatial disruption promotes a dystopic vision which counterpoints a wishful fantasy to engage with its sublime alternative. The highly criticised closure of the first version of the film, with the cyborg heroes riding into a utopian nirvana, was dismissed by many as a feel-good Hollywood sell-out and a failure of nerve, within a predominantly nihilistic narrative trajectory. But this could also be seen, at least at the outset, to highlight the human yearning for this mythic utopia.

The use of LA as the quintessential postmodernist space which suffers from various forms of ecological pollution became the norm within Hollywood as it approached the new millennium. This is somewhat ironic, however, especially tracing the geographical movement of the American film industry from New York to the Californian west coast for economic as well as aesthetic reasons. The lucid quality of light enjoyed in California maximised production-time and allowed increased natural visualisation. Consequently, creative film-makers have always been attracted by Hollywood. At first it was the light but, by the end of the millennium, ecological dysfunctioning and dystopic imbalance epitomised this hitherto utopic landscape.

With full appreciation of the geographical fault lines which periodically send tremors through the Californian landscape, together with the air pollution produced as a manifestation of the over-production and serious over-population of the area, LA epitomises subterranean, even terminal ecological difficulties. Possibly the most mediated city in the world, LA simultaneously has become the most ecologically precarious. Consequently, its continual, often noirish representation tends to effectively foreground, if not embody, many contemporary global ecological issues.

The LA of AD 2019 in *Blade Runner* remains perhaps the most dazzling recent cinematic vision of the result of exploitation of the environment for technological progress. 'The city rots with the waste products of its over-technologist, over-commercialised culture . . . The only thing that is recycled is waste, which forms the raw material for architecture, fashion, even transportation . . . the city projects no sense of community' (Rushing et al. 1995: 145). While critics such as Bataille affirm how such 'waste' reflects the essential nature of human excess, evidence of decay and waste, according to Haraway, is both 'exhilarating and mobilizing', with the prospect of disaster feeding 'radiant hope and bottomless despair' (Haraway 1997: 41).

Allegories of the disparate attributes of the built human environment have been extensively used by writers and artists. The city, in particular, has become symbolic of a virulent strand of (late) capitalism in general and has come to evoke apparently contradictory utopian and dystopic spatialities for advanced capitalism. Compared to New York, for example, which surprisingly tends to remain more a site of utopian hope and (ecological) optimism (at least pre-9/11), with its skyscrapers remaining strong modernist icons in the mythic consciousness of Hollywood, LA has become much more problematic with its continued panoptical evocation and representation.

But as many critics and recent events highlight, the representation of a city destroying itself has become a dominant trope in popular culture generally. Mike Davis's *City of Quartz: Excavating the Future in Los Angeles* explores this phenomenon from an insider's perspective (Davis 1992: 225). The use of police helicopters to survey alien life through illumination of the dark recesses, exposing the 'criminal classes' below, has been used extensively, especially within representations of futuristic landscapes. Such a visual, often noir, aesthetic using metaphors of surveillance is in some ways also reminiscent of old-fashioned nature documentaries, which tend to represent their subject protagonists as trapped within an environment which controls their actions.

This exhibitionism permeates the visual aesthetic and is symbolised in particular in *Blade Runner* by the continual representation of 'acid rain', together with gas fire, smoke, hot air and various forms of advertising and artificial light illuminating the murky postmodernist urban setting, as its anonymous, racially-impure inhabitants scurry around. The resultant future-noir aesthetic, like the metaphor of waste, provides a rich but also contradictory range of new sensory and intellectual possibilities. This is most apparent from the opening of the film, which instead of using shadows and darkness to exemplify the paranoiac underbelly of this future ecocidal world, uses muted colours, shapes, signs and repetitive factory-like mass production sounds to dramatise the *mise-en-scène*. The opening camera shot slowly pans through an aerial view of the future urban space with enticing lights marking out the scene and avoiding space vehicles traversing the sky. This evocation of a busy night sky is interspersed with highly incongruous chimneystacks, which appear to orchestrate a series of bellows of fire into the night.

This dystopic vision produces a highly energised visual aesthetic, using the potency of fire, one of the four primary elements. But in this mise-en-scène images of fire are used to represent a pollutant waste product, framed and normalised within the confines of an urban human space which provides an effective anti-ecological vision of a (post)industrial human environment. Only Deckard, the ex-cop and narrative hero, who has been described by his ex-wife as a 'cold fish', is apparently able to withstand such pervasive pollution and even integrate into the dystopic street space. Unlike most of the non-individualised masses who scurry around hiding their bodies under big coats and uniform umbrellas, Deckard has nothing to protect himself from these unnatural elements yet somehow appears impervious to their polluting effects. Like the classic private detective, he has also developed a form of extrasensory perception and consequently can articulate upon the dysfunctionality of this ecocidal environment.

In Philip K. Dick's *Do Androids Dream of Electric Sheep* (1968), the novel on which the film is loosely based, people are urged to relocate from a dying Earth by a massive advertising campaign that even promises personal slaves, or androids, for those choosing to migrate to Mars. The potent link between capitalist exploitation and global ecological pollution pervades the narrative. In the background of the *mise-en-scène* exaggerating human insignificance, huge postmodern gothic buildings scream out excessive advertisements hailing them both to consume and escape the ecocidal decay. The most dominant advertisement appears throughout the film on a dedicated floating airship, like the romantic post card of 'Shell Beach' in *Dark City* discussed earlier. It entices its inhabitants to escape this ecodical corruption and decay for a utopian customised Disneyesque 'off world' holiday. Such advertisements affirm that there is a more harmonious environment for humans to inhabit, even colonise, which in turn serves to over-dramatise the pervasive dystopic noirish *mise-en-scène* of the film for both its trapped inhabitants and, by extension, its audience. This excessively visualised tale of what happens if rampant capitalist consumption continues at its current pace into the future remains a continuous theme running through such films. As Wood puts it:

It is important that the novel's explanation of the state of the world (the nuclear war is withheld from the film) lays the blame on capitalism directly. The society we see is our own writ large, its present excesses carried to their logical extremes: power and money controlled by even fewer, in even larger monopolies; worse poverty, squalor, degradation; racial oppression; a polluted planet, from which those who can, emigrate to other worlds (in Belton et al. 1996: 213).

Ridley Scott presents a world in which humanity (at least those with the power) has committed the ultimate environmental crime, 'ecocide' - the destruction of 'normal' ecological systems. While not explicitly revealed, it is clear that ecocide has resulted from global warfare and the ultra-utilitarianism and exploitation of late capitalist production techniques. Such ecocide, like that foretold by the *Terminator* series, has caused a sense of spiritual loss as well as the more obvious physical manifestations mentioned above. This is embodied in the ex-cop who, like many Cold War, film noir protagonists, begins the narrative waiting for a job to come by and announces in an opening voice over: 'They don't advertise for killers in advertisements.' He later affirms that he quit 'blade-running' because he had a 'bellyful of killing'. Again, like many noir protagonists, he is seeking some more ethical form of employment but is eventually enticed back into his profession by an unscrupulous, even racist police chief. Deckard, however, accepts and justifies his decision to reactivate his terminator role by explaining how he would 'rather kill than be a victim'.

The resulting physical and spiritual vacuum reverberates through the film and the attempt to fill this hole is, according to Tama Leaver, a central tension for Deckard, searching for his own 'golden land of opportunity and adventure, be that escaping, physically and mentally, or searching for ways to fill the ecological and thus spiritual, void' (Leaver 1997).

Animals are also absent from this ecocidal world set in Los Angeles in the year 2019, thereby also severely reducing the human potentiality for symbiotic harmony with nature in all its diversity. Only the rich can afford to recreate them as pets, like the symbolically wise old owl which signals Rachael's grand entrance into Tyrell's office. Tyrell has become the technocratic king of this urban nightmare and is able to escape the squalor, smog and corruption by living high enough in his penthouse apartment. Everything in the spatial environment, from the architecture to the animals and even the human agents, is consciously designed for functionality or pleasure, just like any other commodity endorsed within its (late) capitalist logic. The broader macro environment is also artificial but to a much lesser extent than in *Dark City*. Therefore, in this nightmare of simulation, commodification and artificiality, it comes as no surprise that not only animals but also humans themselves have been artificially replicated.

Although *Blade Runner* is based on Dick's novel, its points of departure from the original text are instructive. In the novel, the presence of empathy is what allows the bounty hunters to distinguish the androids from the humans, with empathy imagined to be the uniquely human trait. The only sure means of distinguishing a replicant from a human in *Blade Runner* is the 'Voigt-Kampf' empathy test, which detects the failure of a replicant pupil to dilate when placed in a hypothetical situation that normally evokes empathy in a human.[12] What in practice exposes the replicants in the film, however, is not the lack of empathy so much as the lack of a past - 'the lack of memories' (Landsberg in Featherstone et al. 1995: 182). The inherent irony of the empathy test is nonetheless clear. Humans can only determine their difference from the species that they have created (replicants) by invoking their nostalgic empathy for the (animal) species that they presumably already destroyed. The first question appears to establish that humanity is affirmed by concern for animal welfare.

Postmodernist science fiction especially serves to (re)read history through the future and thereby help construct ecological models of utopia which serve to symbolically create ethical and philosophical frameworks for the present. Foucault accurately defines history as 'one way in which a society recognises and develops a mass of documentation with which it is inextricably linked' (Foucault 1982: 7). Photographs in this film and many others like *Dark City* serve as a metaphoric shorthand to create such a necessary 'history' and 'visual memory' for humans, who require anchorage with a continuous past. Photographs and the representation of space also provide a spurious historical authenticity for the replicants (Bruno in Kuhn 1990: 191) unlike, for example, Blow-Up (1966), which problematises the relationship between signifier and signified (was there a murder in the park?).

Baudrillard, however, argues that humans continuously live in a world of simulation, a world hopelessly detached from the 'real' (*ibid.*: 178). *Blade Runner* strives to consciously believe in its referents, which are continually problematised but nevertheless endlessly seek resolution using various inflections of identity, identification and history. In the postmodern age, memories are reduced to photographs and we, 'like the replicants, are put in the position of reclaiming a history by means of its reproduction' (*ibid.*: 193).

Critics of the film have tended to focus on the fact of the replicants' lack of a past in order to underscore the lack of 'real history' in postmodernity. David Harvey, for example, argues that 'history for everyone has become reduced to the evidence of a photograph' (Harvey 1992: 313). In Harvey's account, the replicants 'lack of a past' illustrates the lack of depth - and the emphasis on surface - which characterises such a postmodernist aesthetic.

Alison Landsberg effectively counters that the film claims just the opposite. After Deckard has determined that Rachael is a replicant, she shows up at his apartment with photographs, in particular one depicting her and her mother. The photograph she hopes will both 'validate her memory and authenticate her past', as Harvey would assert. But instead of accepting the representation as truth, Deckard begins to recall one of *her* own (implanted) memories: 'You remember the spider that lived in the bush outside your window . . . (all) implants.' The photograph (a conventional signifier within the modernist aesthetic of authenticity and memory) dramatically illustrates the impurity of such history. In this way *Blade Runner* proves it is much more unsure of its sensory and intellectual footing than *Blow-Up*, for example, which initially at least strives to endorse human agency within a pre-defined environment. In fact, part of the pleasure of such contemporary mass popular texts lies in their ability to construct a destabilising milieu, compared to the more problematic but sterile questioning of perception and human agency expressed within *Blow-Up*. The postmodernist aesthetic re-mixing of various forms of space and agency remains in the end a potent cocktail, even if there is a greater risk of it all going sour afterwards.

Landsberg critiques the 'reductive' generalisations of writers such as Jameson, who continually regard postmodernity as the 'waning of our historicity, and of our lived possibility of experiencing history in some active way' (in Featherstone et al. 1995: 21). Jameson further claims that within postmodernity, experience is reduced to nostalgia, which invokes a sense of 'pastness' instead of engaging with 'real history'. Consequently, he finds a fundamental incompatibility between a postmodernist nostalgia with its 'empty spectacle' and 'genuine historicity' (Jameson 1991: 19). This reductive narrow version of cognitive experience avoids the transgressive potential and vision of excessive scenography and agency explored throughout this study.

Eco-Closure

Sobchack pinpoints most precisely where to place *Blade Runner*: poised at the meeting point of high modernism's focus on time and postmodernism's concentration upon space:

> On the one hand its *mise-en-scène* valorizes space for its capacity to accumulate and conserve past experience as a future present of tangible things. On the other, the narrative elegizes temporal memory, its invisible flow, its ephemerality, its lack of tangibility

(Sobchack 1997: 272).

Blade Runner, as a postmodern text, most certainly 'valorises space' and 'elegises temporal memory' as Sobchack suggests. However, the conjunction of time and space, as projected through closure, produces the most explicit site of an ecological agenda aided by a form of remediated excess. Focus on closure has remained a preoccupation with film critics generally. For example, David Lyon argues that omitting the 'return to nature' denouement in the director's cut version of the film 'simply leaves one with increased apocalyptic unease' and pessimistically wonders 'are decay and death the terminal postmodern condition?' (Lyon 1994: 3). The audience must also 'work harder' to appreciate the narrative complexity of this version, having no mediated voice-over explication. Instead, audiences are left with the non-diegetic (remembered) evocative words of an otherwise conventional policeman to articulate the most profound voice-over statement of the film -'Too bad she won't live . . . but then again, who does?' - implying and reinforcing the necessity of mortality and calling into question Deckard's human status.

Essentially this can be read as a paean to human, cyborg and replicant mortality which is counterpointed by the frailty of all creative forces, especially 'human art', as represented by the origami paper figure of the unicorn discarded on the floor by Gaff the policeman. This is also evoked by the mythic dream of the white unicorn (another fantasy hybrid figure), which can be read as symbolic of both imaginative otherness and escape from oppression.

The therapeutic closing moments in the film (re)mediating a form of sublime raw nature is totally at odds with the dominant urban future corrupted by 'acid rain', decaying infrastructure and environmental pollution generally, as expressed through the claustrophobic noirish aesthetic. The use of conventional representations of an idyllic environment helps to construct nature as fulfilling the psychological function of mediator and exemplar for its protagonists, who have finally accepted the ephemeral nature of their existence and the strength to experience such transformation. The excessive dysfunctionalism of the dystopian *mise-en-scène*, which dominates the film, becomes displaced by this sublime evocation of pure nature. The otherwise conventional aerial helicopter long shot, focusing on the rugged beauty of nature, provides the climatic 'space' (literally and metaphorically) to contemplate the importance of the earth's holistic beauty, while also affirming its ethical benevolence.

The protagonists have finally reached a potentially Edenic sanctuary whose formal visualisation is consciously echoed and counterpointed in many of the closures addressed in this book, thus linking nature/disaster movies and road movies to so-called postmodernist science fiction films. Reminiscent of a form of classic Gaian ethics, 'life finds a way'. Such essentially feel-good endings are not necessarily an ideological and aesthetic cop-out but signal a form of affirmation of the duality of human and inanimate nature and their striving for ecological harmony. For example, Deckard can begin to off-load his sometimes paranoid, cynical and cold-fish attitudes and preoccupations outside of the all-pervasive dystopic environment and reaffirm a more holistic notion of symbiotic human agency framed within a newly-formed optimistic vision.

On a formal and aesthetic level, by making audiences aware of the artificiality of closure -'the law of difference', as Haber suggests - it also makes 'politics radically plural, and this can make us more sensitive and tolerant of difference' (Haber 1994: 130). The director's cut version in particular problematises the romantic evocation within the narrative closure of the original film, avoiding the romanticised representation of a rural idyll. But even this aerial escape, ostensibly promoting a more 'authentic' representation of romanticised nature, was possibly ironic (if only for intertextually literate readers), as it re-uses out-takes from Kubrick's horror film *The Shining* (1980). Kaja Silverman's review proposes that this first conclusion works not only to 'problematise further the notion of the "natural" but also to extend *Blade Runner's* critique of referentiality to its own final images, which constitute a literal implant' (Silverman 1991: 130).

One critic, however, is much less positive in his reading of the varying endings:

> [O]ne of Rachael and Deckard descending into the abyss of the dead-eye of power; the other of their fleeing into those spaces that subsist beyond the reach of Los Angeles 2119. Both endings amount to the same: a deep ambivalence with respect to the hypothesis of what it is to be(come) human; and a deep ambivalence towards its others (replicants, schizophrenics, 'little people') . . . Whether swallowed, expelled, on the run, or experimented upon, both Deckard and Rachael are given (borrowed) time, and are thereby obligated to live to the full the life that is credited to them on account of their enslavement to a slow death

(Clarke 1997: 162).

While such a reading may appear convincing, the negative connotation of a 'slow death' in many ways corresponds with the pinnacle of human existence, whose acceptance of inevitable termination allows such organisms to truly experience life in harmony with their inclusive eco-system. This therefore becomes a 'higher' form of mythic heroism than *T2* and this romanticised dream(space) remains as valid and authentic an expression of eco-consciousness as the more concrete real-life experience. These existential positions were often the primary source of pleasure in much (European) art cinema, for example, which became preoccupied with form and in particular the theme of art versus artifice taking precedence over content. *Blade Runner* taps into such debates for a new generation and a mass audience.

The primary if conventional binary opposition of nature versus culture continues to be effectively evoked for new audiences, symbolised by the origami artefact, while at the same time this mythic exposition has, unlike in *Dark City*, become more sophisticated and questioning about such romantic evocation. The postmodernist aesthetic has at times found a way beyond the often crude dualisms of binary oppositions. The apparently controllable and disposable art of origami paper design signals in its own small way the potentially redemptive malleability of such a postmodernist artefact.

Similarly at the level of agency, Rachael, initially serving merely as a love-interest cyborg, becomes 'an important focus of (re)identification, a replicant anima figure' who slowly awakens Deckard's long dormant humanity (Rushing et al. 1995: 159). This can be appreciated by the convincing way she recalls her 'mythic' mother together with her instinct to escape the ecocidal squalor of her postmodern city space and begin the process of reinventing an environmentally centred self as part of a conventional meta-narrative. But this nascent germ of a nurturing female agency remains extremely underdeveloped, with Deckard continually taking the motivational lead, concentrating on blind escape rather than any more noble motivation. The more recent *Fifth Element*, to be discussed presently, can be read as potentially more liberatory, especially with regard to female agency.

Because the director's cut raises the possibility that Deckard himself is a replicant, it therefore takes a giant step towards erasing the normative intelligibility of the distinction between the real and the simulated, the human and the replicant. The ending here suggests that the cop knows about Deckard's memory of a unicorn in the same way that Deckard knows about Rachael's memory of the spider. 'It suggests that his memories too are implants - that they are prosthetic' (Landsberg in Featherstone et al. 1995: 185). This ambiguity concerning humanity serves by default to empower its cyborg protagonists as expansive role models for the demanding and selfless process of human evolution. This inclusive rather than exclusive appreciation of bio-(human) diversity helps to ennoble such cyborg protagonists.

Roy, the leader of the android rebels, entreated by his maker (Tyrell) to 'revel in his time', adapts a conventional revenge pose when he discovers his beloved Pris terminated by Deckard. Taking on the role of a hunter, he covers himself in her blood and cries like a wolf as he hunts his prey. He is the most powerful of the escaped cyborgs and capable of withstanding great pain, even to the point of using a Christ-like stigmata to maintain focus for the final encounter with the killer of his 'species'. But the cyborg agent, who has seen great horrors, is also capable of adapting, even transcending, his acquired (de)humanising impulse. This is dramatised in the final speech by Roy, who now has the power of life and death over his hunter opponent Deckard. His speech articulates the ever-present ontological struggle over self-worth and the need to continually (re)define humanity within a radically changing environment: 'Quite an experience to live in fear, isn't it? That's what it is like to be a slave . . . All these moments will be lost in time, like tears . . . in rain. (Pause) Time to die.' As Peter Brooks astutely concludes with regard to culture in general, 'ethical imperatives in the post-sacred universe have been sentimentalised, have come to be identified with emotional states and psychic relationships, so that the expression of emotional and moral integers is indistinguishable' (Brooks 1976: 42).

Leaver also affirms that Roy's mission as the Christ-like figure is to 'save' Deckard, teaching him empathy and a newfound sense of morality. Roy's sacrificial death releasing the white dove of peace in many ways corresponds with the final closure of T2 discussed earlier. But this is not the final narrative closure of the film. Such exemplary altruistic exposition is necessary for Deckard to learn a 'deep' ethical lesson so that he can go beyond being transfixed by conventional heroic agency and his professionalised lone hunter mentality. The hunter must learn to step out of these unnatural cycles of brutality and discover a more harmonious relationship between selfhood and the rest of the symbiotic community. While unable to fully learn this lesson, at least he learns the value of (post)human relationships. Rather than being simply an artificial, tagged-on reprise to revitalise the feel-good and hopeful denouement, the pastoral closure can alternatively be seen to visually counterbalance and even polarise the explicit critique of the ecocidal universe, which dominates the majority of the film narrative.

Sobchack is correct in her conclusion that whereas postmodernism conflates past, present and future into one, Roy Batty's last speech remains a 'high modernist elegy' in a postmodern *mise-en-scène*, for it 'elegises temporal memory, its invisible flow, its ephemerality, its lack of tangibility' (cited in Rushing et al. 1995: 272-3). The replicants cogently serve to represent the postmodern dilemma for human agency and the universal need both to maintain some sense of unique individuality within an (in)determinate past history, while also asserting control over the present and preserving a recognisable and effective environment which supports such agency. While the philosophical exploration of self, identity and psychological schizophrenia remain dominant, the environment through the *mise-en-scène* serves to radically visualise such imbalance and chaos from a wider ecological perspective. In particular, extreme and excessive visual representation of decay and environmental corruption, as discussed in the film's opening, serves to (re)position the protagonists' response(s) and provide potent objective correlatives of the dangers of ecological chaos.

Zygmunt Bauman articulates an important ethical correlative which can also be applied to such a therapeutic closure. Applying other critics, he contends that 'modernism's attempt to structure our existence leads to nothing less than our imprisonment', whereas a 'postmodern attitude sets us free, not to do as we like, but to behave ethically' (Bauman 1992: xx10). Bauman acknowledges that this involves a paradox, since 'it restores to agents the fullness of moral choice and responsibility while simultaneously depriving them of the comfort of the universal guidance that modern self-confidence once promised . . . Moral responsibility comes with the loneliness of moral choice' (*ibid.*: xx11). The protagonists in *Blade Runner* endure this form of post-existentialism as they begin to face up to the dangers and effects of such (universalised) ethical chaos.

The Fifth Element

Haraway, in a recent (re)view of cyborg theory, remains optimistic when she reasserts that cybertexts can provide 'a fiction mapping [of] our social and bodily reality' which serves to challenge regressive modernist dualisms like 'nature versus culture' or 'man versus woman' in which 'we have explained our bodies and our tools to ourselves' (cited in Hamilton 1997).

Bukatman's worries that the cyborg signals a 'sense of human obsolescence' and is somewhat confused by Haraway's response that:

> The cyborg is the personification of a future untroubled by ambiguity and difference. It reconciles mechanism and organism, culture and nature . . . the cyborg is a living symbol of difference (sexual, ethical and otherwise) that refuses to be resolved or repressed

(cited in Dery 1996: 243).

The 'progressive' evocation of cyborg agency introduced above is more effectively articulated in *The Fifth Element* (1997) with all four primary elements brought together for a primal ecological synthesis. While each of the major agents discussed so far (Murdoch, Terminator and Deckard) use various primary elements, especially fire and water (even tears), in various dramatic ways, they all metaphorically converge in this film.

The Fifth Element's visually sophisticated and humorous European take on the postmodernist science fiction phenomenon can in some ways be used as an antidote to the critical seriousness of the more conventional Blade Runner. These films certainly present two provocative if contrasting versions of similar aesthetic preoccupations. Yet many dismiss *Fifth Element* as a 'poor pastiche' of *Blade Runner* (Hayward 1998: 175). Where *Blade Runner* promotes an often over earnest exposition in its postmodernist aesthetic, The *Fifth Element* is much more tongue-in-cheek and comical in the execution of its dystopian narrative(s).

The comic-book narrative of *Fifth Element* begins with an examination of hieroglyphics in an Egyptian tomb in 1914. Trying to decode the signs, the priest/scientist believes he has made a major discovery. Meanwhile, fearing the coming of war, the Mondoshawan, a benevolent alien race, return to take away the four mystic stones representing the four primary elements which affirm and control life, together with a closed casket containing the fifth element - the 'supreme being'. The following match-cut collapsing three hundred years of time is comparable to the famous ellipsis in 2001, while exhibiting a more ironic postmodernist sensibility. Now, with the threat of evil about to consume the planet, they return with the 'fifth element' to protect life. But short-sighted humanoid infighting, as perpetrated by the dog-like rebels, cause major disruptions to their life-affirming purpose.

The metaphor of evil (anti-matter) hurling like a ball of flame to the planet earth has strong biblical overtones. What is interesting (as also discovered in the *Andromeda Strain* in the previous chapter) is that attempts to destroy its mindless journey with nuclear warheads serve merely to increase its growth and thereby further dramatise the precariousness of our environment. The human face of evil is gloriously portrayed by the flamboyant Zorg (Gary Oldman), described by one critic as a 'multi-racial Fu Manchu' (Bernardi 1998: 89), who breaks a glass to illustrate how 'destruction' serves to keep people in jobs. 'By creating a bit of destruction . . . I am in fact encouraging life,' he pontificates, dressed in an outfit inspired by Nazi iconography with high collars and wide trousers tucked into sleek boots, like many comic book villains. Such visual if frivolous exposition does not lend itself to a serious appreciation of the only piece of philosophising in the film. But then this is part of the playful postmodern aesthetic.

The quintessential Hollywood lone hero Korben Dallas (Bruce Willis), who ostensibly performs the role of an angry taxi driver with only his white cat and stereotypical 'nagging' mother on the phone for company, remains preoccupied with a personal quest for the 'perfect girl'.[13] The woman of his dreams, the fifth element (a post-feminist representational dream?) draws her pedigree and sense of visual spectacle straight out of the classic German film *Metropolis*. Earlier, the 'fifth element' agent who first appears entombed in a casket, embodied a deity who cannot be observed. Three hundred years later, however, she is transformed into a punk female fantasy cyborg called Leeloo (Milla Jovovich), unlike more conventional male varieties.

Reconstituted and transformed into a female humanoid cyborg with a surface manifesting conventional female beauty, she is framed within a mysterious scientific ectoplasm. Such a dualistic embodiment serves to recreate a contemporary non-threatening notion of agency. In many ways she becomes the antithesis of the conventional horror/science fiction 'alien', whom Barbara Creed codifies as the 'monstrous feminine' with its 'archaic maternal power over reproduction, life and death' (cited in Rogin 1998: 60). But the men in white coats are unable to transform themselves, only perceiving a fragile commodified woman, who they cannot explain and need to both objectify and control.

As David Harvey suggests, it has become dangerous to 'confess about being meta about anything' (Harvey 1996: 2) these days. Consequently, both critics and scientists find it almost impossible to take a leap of faith and see beyond the apparent immediate physical evidence, which is necessary if they are to uncover the playful significance and potency of such postmodernist exemplary icons.

In some ways Leeloo's sexualised representation can be compared to the test tube cloning of Ripley (Sigourney Weaver) in *Alien Resurrection* (1997), to be discussed later. While Ripley has been cloned from alien (and human) tissue and presented in a giant test tube, mutating into maturity, she is similarly observed by equally hideous conformist old men in white coats. The 'fifth element' must literally escape the scientists' predatory clutches and potentially intrusive examination (which Ripley was unable to do).

Leeloo escapes from this clinical, patriarchal control into the radical chaotic and excessive vision of twenty-third century New York as drawn from the work of two legendary French comic book artists, Moebius and Jean Claude Mezieres, who have influenced Besson since he was 16 and first had the idea for this picture. Only now, with the assistance of Avid, the digital editing system, is Besson able with his special effects expert Stetson to pre-edit sequences for speed, action and composition and fully suspend audiences' perceptions and transport them to a truly postmodernist time and place in the twenty-third century. The urban set-piece advances the vision of *Metropolis* in its controlled systematic chaos. As Leeloo stands on the ledge of a skyscraper, like Harold Lloyd in the silent films, a renewed visceral sense of spectacle and vertigo is created with a layered, controlled flow of flying vehicles on regulated flight paths weaving their way through the skyscraper elevated streets in this postmodern city of the future.

However, unlike the spectacle of the 'cinema of attractions' experienced in so-called primitive cinema, new expressions of excess allow audiences not only 'to look at, but to look through' (Bolter and Grusin 1999: 156) and experience new forms of selfhood. Such futuristic spectacle rather than being 'mindless and empty', can become an effective trigger for audience engagement. This is most evident, however, to varying degrees in a reading of many of the filmic closures discussed in this chapter and elsewhere.

Korben Dallas, the taxi driver of the future, negotiates buildings and slip-ways as he drives, slotted into controlled vertical airways, through space with other vehicles crowding out his view. Terra firma has little currency in this apparently unnatural chaotic urban space. Down at street level everything is obscured by dense layers of smog and remains a no-go area. The futuristic urban eco-system has extended the normalisation of a physical underworld (as in *Blade Runner*) as a direct consequence of environmental degradation.

The gibberish-speaking waif-like female Leeloo, unaware of her destiny, literally falls into his taxi. Now at last he can acquire a legitimate quest, apparently acting on behalf of the (American) government while maintaining his lone, individual and non-conformist character. Instead of a meaningless (life) journey, he can now begin a pilgrimage to discover his true love and save the world in true comic book fashion. This conjunction begins to articulate the harmonising of the individual with the communal through the ecological trajectory embodied in the fifth element.

In the denouement however, the goddess of punkish beauty and extraterrestrial purity, after studying human history, cannot come to accept the need to save the planet, which contains such 'nasty organisms' who cause so much suffering and evil. (The Terminator, unlike the Blade Runner, never questioned human ethical motives.) How can the human species hope - much less deserve - to survive if it cannot create sustainable communities? This remains the primary 'first directive' of ecological agency. 'I was built to protect, not to love' (like the Gaia consciousness), she confides. Her ethical dilemma reflects the dominant representation of the future planet, lacking any unifying sense of biotic co-equal existence among and between organisms, which becomes the dominant ecological paradigm encoded in the text. Even the priest who recognises her true essence does not know how to converse with her, thereby serving as a cautionary tale on the limitation of even spiritual leaders to understand the purpose, much less the language, of 'true' human nature.

Only when the conventional heroic everyman becomes truly vulnerable and begins to accept the 'transcendent' power of love (as symbolic of his selfless symbiotic heroic nature), can the 'God-head' finally accept her divine destiny and display her 'maternal' unifying power with all the primal life-giving elements of earth, air, fire and water. Only when this fifth element is fully expressed can humans finally become reconciled with their environment and rise above the destructive tendency inherent in the male gaze in particular.

Ideally, a new quasi-heroic nurturing myth is invoked, which can at the same time express the primacy of female potency or alternatively promote a cynical, or at best a kitsch, evocation of the meaningless of it all. By proving his love for her with a conventional classic narrative kiss, Dallas can finally convince Leeloo of the intrinsic value of homo-sapien nature. In the end, the personal self defines and validates a revivified sense of humanist values. This has always been Hollywood's dominant message and Luc Besson, in spite of his extraordinary European style, concurs in this overly (comically) excessive narrative, with Hollywood's prime directive firmly validated through individual agency and identification within the heroic and romantic couple.

The ending is similar to the *mise-en-scène* of a Bond movie, unlike the more conventional therapeutic nature evocations in other texts discussed in this book. The heroes finally satisfy their libidinal natural urges hidden from the audience's gaze yet coyly observed by the repressed scientists, who originally let the genie out of the bottle. Instead of the two protagonists looking out into the newly-resurrected landscape achieving nirvana, the protagonists explore in a more direct and conventionally intimate way their communion of spirits and newly-formed flesh. Their spiritual and physical life-affirming love and reaffirmation of the values of humanity help to remythologise the primary force of nature and love which can, as Gaia asserts, finally protect its inhabitants.

While *Sight and Sound* reviewer Kim Newman is finally unable to decide whether the film is either a 'homage, a parody or a subversion of cited conventions and iconography' - much like the postmodernist aesthetic generally - he does affirm that Besson's 'comic irreverence is welcome in that it downplays the over familiar big alien threat to the universe plot engine in favour of inspired comic goofiness' (Newman 1997). One could go further and assert that the pro-active use of otherwise marginalised punk-female representations as emblematic and personable saviours of the world can at least be recognised and appreciated, if not finally affirmed, as potentially progressive.[14]

It maybe dangerous to claim that a new fifth eco-metaphor has been created which begins to articulate and combine human nature within the powerful holistic context of the primary natural elements but without the need for a controlling discourse. I would assert, however, that a potentially new ecological super-heroic structure is reconstituted and evoked, which uses the recuperative female version of agency, though all the while promoting a playful postmodern aesthetic.

Haraway more recently speaks of new forms of 'witnessing' and the need for a 'new experimental way of life to fulfil the millenarian hope that life will survive on this planet' (Haraway 1997: 270). While she looks to the Internet and gene technology for such 'hope', I would contend that a witnessing of this kind could also be found in varying degrees within mainstream science fiction films. While Samuel Beckett and others drew on the lowest form of comic representation in *Waiting for Godot*, for example, to affirm the complexity, if not the break-up of the modernist sensibility, many science fiction texts are putting the weight of a playful but provocative postmodernist sensibility on the inadequate and often equally insubstantial synthetic shoulders of (post-humanoid) cyborgs. Surprisingly, however, such liminal types afford the greater potency for an expression of changing conditions within the prototypical eco-human species.

Haraway correctly concludes that both 'conventional' feminists and Marxists have 'run aground on Western epistemological imperatives to construct a revolutionary subject from the perspective of a hierarchy of oppression and/or latent position of moral superiority, innocence and greater closeness to nature' (Haraway 1991: 176). This can be appreciated most especially through her vicious critique of conventional feminism and 'victimhood'. The question remains, however, whether such a female cyborg embodies as much feminist and ecological potential as Haraway and others claim for cyborgs as evidenced within popular culture. This question cannot, of course, be fully answered in the affirmative but at least such issues are addressed. The Pandora's box has been opened and such 'metaphoric simulacra' are now becoming available and used within a wider cultural context which can adapt and diffuse progressive ecological sensibilities within a postmodernist mythic framework.

Postmodernist art at its best contests the 'simulacralisation' process of mass culture: not by denying it or lamenting it but by problematising the entire notion of the representation of reality and thereby pointing to the reductionism of Baudrillard's view.

> It is not that truth and referentiality have ceased to exist, as Baudrillard claims; it is that they have ceased to be unproblematic issues. We are not witnessing the degeneration into the hyperreal without origin or reality, but a questioning of what 'real' can mean and how we can know it

(Hutcheon 1988: 223).

Linda Hutcheon is convincing when she argues that postmodernism represents the attempt to re-historicise, not de-historicise, art and theory. 'Parody is the ironic mode of intertextuality that enables such revisitations of the past. Such self-reflexive, parodic interrogations of history have also brought about a questioning of assumptions beneath both modernist aesthetic autonomy and unproblematic realist reference' (Hutcheon 1988: 225). Furthermore, critics affirm that postmodern culture is inherently contradictory and often uses and abuses the very discourses it sets out to challenge.

Postmodern parody, Hutcheon continues, functions 'as repetition with critical distance that allows ironic signalling of difference at the very heart of similarity'. It 'paradoxically enacts both change and cultural continuity', and as it uses the strategies of dominant culture to challenge its discursive processes from within, postmodern parody also reveals its 'love of history by giving new meanings to old forms' (cited in Natoli 1997). The postmodern paradoxes effectively both reveal and positively question prevailing norms, including those which continue to legitimise ecological degradation, and they can do so because they embody both processes. *The Fifth Element* effectively (re)presents, as already expressed, this form of postmodern parody by the way it constructs both its human and post-human agents within an otherwise comic book super-narrative which continually uses various forms of spectacle and excess to foreground its often contradictory messages.

As was affirmed at the outset, the postmodernist paradigm promoting a 'both-and' frame of consciousness which copes with apparently contradictory discourses is taking the place of the less inclusive modernist 'either-or' paradigm. Because of the elastic and inclusive nature of the postmodernist aesthetic, this enriched form tends to draw from all strands within the modernist/ postmodernist divide and could more comfortably be described as 'radical modernism'. This enrichment can be achieved by breaking down heroic male myths, which often endorse ecological regression, towards a more inclusive incorporation with the human hero. This strategy is coalesced through a surfeit of progressive ecological representation using female agency in particular. At least the other has moved on from being either simply exoticised and/or victimised or sacrificed on the altar of conventional notions of human agency.

Emmanuel Levinas's idea of 'radical otherness' is, as John Hill affirms, as good a position as any to start to 'produce a model of postmodern ethics which reflects the possibility of transgression with regards to the other' (Hill 1998: 97). The mythic gender representation of Leeloo is as good an agent as any to start exploring such radical otherness but agency of this kind will need much more fleshing out if it is to become truly potent for the future. *Alien Resurrection* extends this process most effectively.

Epilogue

Alien Resurrection

Alien Resurrection (1997) provides a potent example that helps to clarify many of the issues and concepts discussed in this chapter. On a narrative level, the film's closure (re)presents four assorted life forms (in some ways reminiscent of the runaway replicants in *Blade Runner*) who have succeeded in saving the planet yet also appear to embody a breakdown of conventional human agency. In spite of their assorted roles as stereotypical outsiders, they finally embody an inclusive form of community as they look out upon the sublime majesty of the earth's eco-system. Metaphorically the shell of their battered space carcass, like their damaged bodies, allows them space to be reborn as post-human agents in the benevolent light of the earth's luminosity.

All the surviving protagonists in the film have come from very different 'paths' in the evolutionary (post)human genetic pool. From the ultra right-wing macho male to the childlike, silent, wheelchair-bound scavenger, both men appear very inadequate prototypes for any form of transformed/recuperated human species. The two females, on the other hand, are far more interesting and progressive examples of post-humanity. Framed together in close-up, with their heads held high, looking into the far distance, they embody the heroic magnificence and ethical solidarity often evidenced by classic western heroes but without the conservative and ideological baggage. Instead, they have become truly (post)human icons for a revisioned frontier-planet Earth (not the wild unchartered West) which requires protection and effective stewardship, not ownership and control.

In this science fiction film, human identity becomes much more fractured and transgressive, yet at the same time less indulgently neurotic, not having to privilege subjective individual consciousness. (*Blade Runner* remains symptomatic of this transformation). While Ripley is part alien and part human, she nevertheless transcends the revenge trope endlessly expressed in the dominant male action genre, like *The Searchers*, which incidentally is intertextually referenced when she cuts the 'tongue' out of her conquests. By retaining a residual human gene consciousness, which reaffirms a form of foundational ethics, she instinctively acts on a clear set of priorities for the survival of a human-based eco-system. By the total rejection of her alien genetic make-up with its destructive agenda, she demonstrates her ethical credentials through her shepherding of survivors in her quest to save the planet. Her ethical affirmation of 'natural' evolution is dramatically expressed by the destruction of her own genetic 'mother' but even more effectively by her therapeutic dismantling of the grotesque genetic experimental laboratory which helped create her. The cathartic destruction of these gothic representational organisms corresponds in some ways to the twisted, controlling forces of future genetically controlled society.

The Winona Ryder character, on the other hand, remains a more advanced prototype of cyborg, rather than a carbon-based life form (by which natural life forms are usually defined), yet she aches to be 'human'. When her true nature is discovered, one of the crew quips: 'I should have known . . . no human is *that* humane.' She is programmed to care (just as *T2* is reprogrammed by the young Connor) and almost instinctively appreciates foundational eco-ethics which endorse nurturing and a more pro-active form of 'witnessing' towards the rest of humanity, including other life forms. Both female characters embody various polarities within the broad-based feminist discourse and its attempts to humanise patriarchal culture. The potency of such artificial life forms and their non-questioning quest to affirm the ethical rights of human nature, reveal the radical potential of these agents as progressive prototypes for humanity.

As in *The Fifth Element,* both transgressive forms of female agency almost instinctively resolve to fight the threat to human nature without requiring conventional indulgent motives like revenge. Yet these four 'inadequates' - 'damaged human personhood(s)', as Bell calls them, who are looking for a sense of 'community' (Bell 1995: 100), strive for a new, more inclusive form of community/citizenship. If we are to use a normative measure for ecological post-human nature, these figures become the new hope to save the planet. Looking out into the sublime (utopian) harmony of planet Earth, these four distinct agents resolutely reaffirm the value of the struggle to fight dystopic chaos over and above any personal rationality. Nevertheless, unlike the communion of flesh in *The Fifth Element* or the resignation or possible transformation of the heroes in *Blade Runner*, who finally accept 'human' romantic nirvana, the un-recuperated outsiders in *Alien Resurrection* retain their otherness and their marginality. At the same time, they affirm a range of ecological micro-narratives, especially stewardship and a form of non-heroic humility in the face of a benevolent eco-system.

Looking out through their protected window, they can finally begin to empathise with the therapeutic wholeness and purity of the earth as a unique macro eco-system which (ontologically and ecologically) affirms life. After the traumatic and excessive struggle and experience of their attempts to save the planet, now at last, they have the 'space' (again, literally via screen-space and metaphorically, as in earlier examples) to perceive their newfound ecological coexistence as part of an empathetic ecological system. At last they have found a 'home', which they have never known, to go back to. The translucent blue sphere of the earth is (and becomes again) hyper-significant and has been ever since cameras first filmed the sublime non-fictional beauty of the earth's surface, when it first became the central metaphor and clarion call for ecological harmony and protectionism.

As the camera's point-of-view oscillates between their 'innocent' vision and that of its filmic audience, meaning and cause/effect become collapsed. Tashiro, mentioned earlier, speaks of how nature as a space is 'controlled by human perception and in the process renders 'nature as landscape'. Such 'landscape' through editing 'provides multiple perspectives' since 'nature' always exceeds the ability of the eye or the lens to perceive. Consequently, 'photography becomes a stylization' and 'emotions generated by a story substitute for the visceral effect of real space long ago described by Edmund Burke as the 'sublime' (Tashiro 1998: 35). The sublime beauty of the earth in particular provides the magnetic power (naturally and aesthetically) for the witnessing protagonists. But filmic time and space is also provided above and beyond the narrative requirements which also serve to reconnect the audience with its inclusive eco-system, framed from many miles above the planet. The overpowering pull of this harmonious eco-system, unlike the spectacular excess of preceding scenes, reinvigorates and reaffirms the potency of this science fiction primary eco-metaphor, which endorses the desire in the end to come 'home' to ecological sanctuary.

However, unlike the anti-gravitational environment and inhabitants of *Dark City*, the motley crew of *Alien Resurrection*, who are slowly drawn by the gravity of earth, have not grown to accept such benevolent universal moral agency.[15] Also, they do not embody and most certainly do not emulate the potent meta-religious and spiritual connotations implicit in the film's title. Yet in contrast to the guilty, if contemplative ascent of the survivors in *Jurassic Park*, who escape the ecocidal hell they helped create and finally witness, these eco-warriors deserve their heroic status as they descend to earth.

They adopt a pluralist form of redemption, leaving all four protagonists unsure of their role within the newly visualised earth's eco-system. Their relatively fixed expressions, semiotically at least, hide the deep evocation of feelings, ranging from indifference and incredulity to acceptance of their fate. The reformulated and recuperated radical otherness of such agents, evidenced by the excessive gothic signification of genetic disorder, renewal and rebirth, experienced through the narrative, finally comes to the surface in the closure. Space is allowed for this range of otherwise incongruous life forms to coexist and express a sincere, if not totally coherent, message of hope for the future of 'our' eco-system.

A sense of aperture, instead of classic narrative closure, is especially effected through the two (post) human female protagonists. They do not suffer from or have to react against the baggage of an imperialis, or patriarchal yoke and their newly-formed female 'eco-gaze' at planet earth is not registered through a frontier or colonising vision. Instead, their truly incredulous and innocent looks oscillate with the film's audiences multiple point-of-view. This helps to create the capacity to contemplate this sublime spectacle through their newly-formed eco-vision with a renewed sense of potency, affecting the ultimate 'primal rejuvenated scene' for the human species. They have witnessed, even literally embodied, the extremes of a dystopic future and consequently serve as potent if unrepresentative signifiers of a revivified and deep ecological form of post-human agency.

This ethical and ecological dialogue always involves the need for choice, dramatising the need for core values while allowing space for ambiguity, even multiple dialogical space. Film has finally helped to affirm the potency especially of these dialogical 'moments',[16] allowing audiences to both look at and through these opaque representational diegetic significances. While (over-used) concepts such as 'excess' and 'sublime', even the Joycean narrative device of 'epiphany', often appear to endorse a conservative romantic heroic experience, predicated on closure, I would affirm their liberatory, even residual transcendental powers. By opening out all the senses to the experience of the primary elements of nature through a therapeutic form of aperture, especially after experiencing the breakdown of various dystopic universes, this helps to counterpoint a potentially progressive, if sometimes incoherent, form of ecological exposure, even legitimation.

The affirmative pleasure of the postmodernist critical aesthetic endorses a 'both-and' frame of reference without having to conform to the limiting and controlling straitjacket of an 'either-or' scenario, which continually privileges sometimes restrictive rationalist paradigms. Appreciating these mythic human fantasies need not infer that they have to conform to established norms, such as rationality, logic and compatibility. Consequently, often contradictory mythic tropes can happily overlap and merge into each other without causing unnecessarily disruptive dissonance. Such potentially disruptive fusion - if only evidenced through excessive moments in otherwise conventional narratives - is almost encouraged within the postmodernist aesthetic in its seemingly endless creative expression of new forms of entropy. Many of the films discussed in this book express in varying degrees such contradictory ecological tropes, implying both dissonance and dissent as well as consent.[17]

Notes

1. 'In the post Hiroshima world, S.F. made emotional sense. The fears that S.F. had treated in the past were too real and the genre flourished as a means of simultaneously highlighting and banishing these fears as film after film depicted the awful consequences of the misapplication of technology and man's inability, after much destruction, to regain control of his destiny' (Hardy 1995: xiv).

2. Biodiversity is, according to Leslie, lost as a result of four main causes which can loosely be connected with the various chapters of this study:
   1) Destruction of the wilderness – addressed in Chapter 2.
   2) Pollution – addressed in all chapters, but particularly with regards to science fiction.

3) Modern agricultural methods – addressed in several chapters.

4) Overusing natural resources – explicitly addressed in several chapters (Leslie 1996: 68)

3. This is reminiscent of the 1950s evocation of the transcendental sublime in the closure of *The Incredible Shrinking Man*, discussed earlier.

4. Like nostalgia, 'utopianism is of course commonly associated with escapism; with a distracted, unrealistic gaze towards a perfect future rather than a preferred past' (Brooker 1997: 273).

5. Remediation is defined as 'the formal logic by which new media refashion prior media forms' (Bolter and Grusin 1999: 273).

6. Haraway further readdresses many of the primary essentialist and pedantic feminist debates and asserts how 'monsters have always defined the limits of community in Western imagination' (Haraway 1991: 180). The marginalised other has remained a site of contention within cultural studies, and feminist discourse in particular, since their inception. However, cyborg identity goes beyond the reductive opposition of male/female and represents an 'imaginative resource', says Haraway, in developing an argument for 'pleasure' and 'excess' in the confusion of boundaries and creating a sense of responsibility in their reconstruction (Haraway 1985: 66B7).

7. These notions are addressed in her appreciation of cyberpunk narratives which she describes as: 'focusing explicitly on the destabilising impact of new technology on traditional social and cultural spaces, with the collapse of traditional cultural and critical hierarchies and the erosion of distinction between experience and knowledge, which has provided the decentering and fragmentation of the subject. Cyberpunk explores the interface between human and machine in order to focus on the general question of what it means to be human' (Wolmark 1994: 110).

8. Feminist critics tend to undervalue action heroes (as purely goal-oriented and narrative-driven) compared to melodramatic texts which more faithfully address the 'interior self' of emotions. I would take issue with this generic comparison and affirm that such action genres can effectively connect with the interior self of their protagonists as much as their melodramatic counterparts.

9. In many ways the framing narrative is structured like a classic Greek tragedy which exposes a (Christian) controlling meta-discourse, with oppositional future forces looking down on 'contemporary' humans as they send back proto-agents to fulfil their predetermined destiny. Such a narrative structure privileges a 'conservative' teleological time-shift and frame of reference, unlike more elastic and open-ended postmodernist texts which do not appear, on any level, to privilege any one position. Consequently, the film must remain stunted as a prototype for a progressive form of eco-sensibility.

10. See, for example, George Bataille's cross-cultural study of violence and the sacred analyses of deep-seated psychological motives for such sacrificial devices, which affirms sexual motivation.

Such 'sacrifice' allows for a sense of control over the passing of time. Like the carousel in *Logan's Run* discussed earlier, renewal/death is legitimated as 'natural', even 'spiritual'.

11. Peter Biskind asserts that Spielberg and Lucas et al. have attempted to 'restore traditional narration' but it has had an 'unintended effect - the creation of spectacle that annihilated story. The attempt to escape television by creating outsized spectacle backfired and led to television's presentational aesthetic' (cited in Neale et al. 1998: 171). While I would accept the possibility of such connections with television, such excessive spectacle often serves to reinvigorate 'narrative' instead of annihilate it.

12. The myth of the eyes being the window to the human soul is again used to help define authentic individuality; similarly, the mechanistic red eye in *The Terminator* serves to signal his appropriation into the human body.

13. Daniel Leonard Bernardi, in a convincing thesis on race, affirms that her perfection is due in no small measure to such 'physiognomic characteristics as blue eyes and great (white) skin', which are the apparent result of her 'perfect genes' (Bernardi 1998: 90).
Such inherent racism is read from the statements by Korben Dallas (Bruce Willis), whose idea of perfection is not surprisingly projected from his textual and intertextual persona, which perceives female beauty in very 'conventional' terms. But to deduce that the film simply endorses a racist, even fascist, agenda involves a serious misreading of the 'playful' determination of both race and gender in the film. (Nevertheless, I would agree that the overly mannered black DJ is most certainly represented as a 'perverse queer', which is oddly jarring in the film as a whole.)

14. Also, the back-story of the majestic diva (a motif used in many of Besson's other films) fulfils the ultimate heroic sacrifice by dying Phoenix-like (as in *T2* and other texts discussed earlier) to provide the re-birth of the four elements which are connected inside our heroine's 'body'. Such emotional exposition of an eco-heroic desire remains potent even if the embodiment of agency can finally be read as suspect and even derisory.

15. This can be compared to the inferred transformation of the protagonists as they ascend in a helicopter at the end of *Jurassic Park*, witnessing an ecocidal man-made nightmare.

16. Which can in many ways be regarded as good filmic examples of a form of 'heteroglossia' - which often sets up conflicts between 'official' and 'unofficial' discourse within such texts. Consequently, an ecological discourse can be embedded within a much more 'superficial' or 'materialist' discourse.

17. Just as the eco-mantra affirms 'life finds a way', concurrently productive ecological dialogue also finds a way. Film, in all its forms from still to the more mimetic moving image, can be used like a prism to refract an often nascent eco-discourse with varying degrees of effectiveness. Such an

eco-discourse remains a (re)construction of human representations and values through a variety of cultural artifacts.

Conclusion

Ecology has certainly become a new, all-inclusive, yet often contradictory meta-narrative,[1] which this study has shown to be clearly present within Hollywood film. While Leo Braudy (1998) suggests that this preoccupation with nature is a relatively recent phenomenon, I have demonstrated how such concerns can be read through Hollywood film since the 1950s. Recent popular films such as *Titanic* or *Men in Black* at first appear to have little to do with ecology but even here various metaphors and tropes embedded in the film texts help to signify core ecological beliefs, attitudes and values.

Chapter 2 focused on explicit explorations of nature and ecology, from *The Yearling* in the post-war period to *The Emerald Forest*, which affirm the potency of such issues within the 'public sphere' of contemporary Hollywood. Surprisingly, the didactic evocations of ecological awareness in Boorman's quest appear less 'progressive' compared with other less explicitly ecologically framed films. This is exemplified in the films of Spielberg, who adapts and sometimes transforms a nascent ecological agency of 'innocence' within some of the most successful blockbusters in recent history. The chapter culminates with a study of more synthetic (SFX) [2] nature representations in *Jurassic Park* and its sequel, which serve to dramatically foreground contemporary ecological debates.

The closely related subsequent chapter explores the roots of road movies in the western genre, where human agents became defined and individuated by their relationship with and journey through a landscape. While often remaining preoccupied with a narcissistic form of 'adolescent' agency, the road movie nevertheless helped to dramatise the quest for ontological knowledge and contentment, using a range of ecological issues and preoccupations. Through sublime moments evidenced in the closure of *Grand Canyon*, or even *Thelma and Louise*, space and time are given over to therapeutically promoting the wishful fantasy for deep ecological harmony.[3] In most of the films discussed, audiences are presented with an excess of signification through narrative closure, encouraging a metaphysical engagement with spatial identity, which is posited as co-existing with more conventional psychological and temporal identity. As a coda, *The Straight Story* provides a powerful elegiac evocation of nature and ecology from an old man's perspective.

Nevertheless, it is within science fiction that many of the debates explored in this study become most resonant and engaging for mass audiences. Chapter 4 begins with an exploration of 1950s science fiction B-movies and their preoccupation with a fear of total destruction by 'unnatural' forces like the atom bomb. Such fears are often lost sight of within more conventional ideological readings, privileging their allegorical articulation of Communist fears, which permeated the American body politic at the time. These films also helped to foreground deep ecological questions regarding humans' relationship with their planet. Continuing this form of historical revisionism, it is suggested that there was a profound paradigm shift, when science fiction became actualised for the first time and space travel enabled humans to observe and appreciate the planet as a total unifying eco-system.

Extensive application of universal notions like 'sublime' and popular ones like 'excess' and 'transgression' to make textual analysis more aesthetically understandable and perceptually accurate has remained a feature of this study. The potency of sublime representations of the planet together with identifiable natural features like the Grand Canyon, as excessively represented in a range of film closures, should not be so easily dismissed by critics. Suspect intentions, like those exposed in the so-called Spielbergisation or Disneyfication of popular culture, do not necessarily invalidate or negate the positive and productive utopic potentialities within these dramatic visualisations of nature and landscape, as they continue to frame and reflect on human consciousness.

The broad science fiction genre helped to create new narratives and metaphors for coping with futuristic ecological dystopias. This can be exemplified using paranoia, as in *Soylent Green* or *Logan's Run*, or more recently through the promotion of a 'postmodernist' aesthetic, which helped to 'playfully construct' new ways of looking at life and nature, aided by the creation of revitalising forms of cyborg agency. Parallels can be drawn with the representation of native American Indians for example; who became emblematic within American consciousness of a deep form of ecological agency. Similarly futuristic cyborgs help to produce radical new frames of reference and identification within popular culture. Metaphorically, at least, the cyborg embraces the fractured identity of the postmodern world and symbolises the post-gender articulation of ecological consciousness, while also serving to promote a powerful humane expression of responsible agency.

Central to this preoccupation with representation of self and human agency is the feeling of 'loss and the desire for unity that is born of (such) loss' (Campbell in Glotfelty 1996: 134-5). Ecologists often highlight this experience of lost unity, even separation from the rest of the natural world and a desire to regain it, as central to the core meaning of human nature. Such utopian desire as expressed in various Hollywood films helps promote a form of deep ecological affirmation above and beyond the ideological mapping of human nature predicated on more recognisable parameters of race, class and gender differences.

But the dangers of endorsing utopic fantasies and essentialising around varying ontological notions of human and posthuman ecological agency has remained a cautionary principle throughout the study. The final reading of Chapter 4 questions a number of modernist/postmodernist attitudes and value systems concerning counter-cultural evocations of human identity and fulfilment within a growing ecologically fractured and risk based western society. *Safe* most notably uses the idea of environmental illness to help illustrate the changing agency of human nature in the lead character's unpredictable quest to find some form of harmony with nature.

While outside the scope of this study, the inherent difficulties of promoting a utopic reading of film could be offset by extensive audience research to help underpin and critique Hollywood's mapping of ecological metaphors and their aesthetic articulation in film. Martin Barker, for instance, insists that all film analyses make claims about the audience but seldom make this explicit. While not wanting audience studies to replace textual analysis, few critical theories, he suggests in *From Ants to Titanic: Reinventing Film Analysis* (2000),actually seek evidence to explain audience pleasures, which could underpin an investigation of film. Yet an assumption that empirical audience research would necessarily anchor, much less determine film analysis is, I argue in a review, open to question.[4] Nevertheless, as Kristin Thompson cogently affirms, if there is no connection with actual audiences, film criticism remains a 'barren venture' (in Barker 2000: 41). Barker embraces the strategy that 'all story telling involves "audience responsiveness" because all stories activate us, by the manner of their organisation'. Cued responses by an implied audience include 'guessing ahead', 'taking sides' as well as 'assembling a construct of the "whole film" from which it becomes possible to ask the question: what is this story "about"' (Barker 2000: 48).

The strongest antidote to overcome such dangers in this study is extensive use of close textual analysis using interpretations and readings from a wide range of academics and film reviews. So often essential formal cues are omitted from narrative analysis, even by canonical gurus like David Bordwell. A recent study by Thomas Elsaesser and Warren Buckland (2002) affirms this need for a comprehensive textual analysis approach and further grapples with tensions between 'analysis' and 'interpretation'. From an educational perspective there is need for further research to differentiate and co-ordinate effective strategies for 'bottom up' textual analysis alongside 'top down' theorising. Hopefully, the detailed contextual and critical reading of the films cited in the filmography help to posit a prototypical and potentially progressive expression of ecological debates and issues.

Clarifying and outlining new representational relationships between humans and their environment has been couched within terms like 'radical otherness' (Levinas), 'partnership ethics'[5] (Merchant) and other related deep/shallow theories. The previous chapter illustrates how these concepts and various 'breakdowns' implicit in postmodernism can be used to crack open crude divisions between 'modernist' and 'postmodernist' sensibilities as expressed in popular film. Nevertheless, a critical endorsement of the notion of radical otherness does not escape the possibility of separateness from the often fickle mire of postmodernism. Nor do recent ethical affirmations by Merchant and others necessarily avoid the gendering of nature as a nurturing mother or a goddess, or overcome the eco-centric hierarchic assumptions which displace humans from their central role as ecological agents.

Val Plumwood most recently veers close to this essentialist trap.[6] Yet Plumwood and others are correct when they cite contemporary suspicion and scepticism about the very term 'nature', which continuously needs to be reappropriated to create a critical space for more productive ecological film analysis.

The final reading of *Alien Resurrection* provides a most explicit example of many of these concepts and observations cited above, with its motley crew finally descending onto a pristine planet earth. The film draws on evocative biblical myths, making them resonant for an idyllic new world order, which has begun to put the environment at the centre of meaning. A progressive form of otherness is created through the synthesis of human and non-human agency. This is used in the service of a more holistic, yet sceptical, form of partnership ethics to help reconstitute the primary relationship between humans and their environment. My reading highlights a renewed form of eco-utopic expression that potentially has deep resonance for a wealthy liberal western audience that apparently craves the cultural signification and insight of a renewed form of ecological 'otherness'.

While there remains a lack of conventional ecological literacy[7] with numerous debates locked into complex scientific paradigms, Hollywood fiction transcribes these broad cultural discourses into popular narratives using evocative aesthetic forms. Mainstream films have at least covertly exposed direct links between environmental and human problems with the resonant hope of ecological harmony becoming embedded within the Hollywood dream factory.

As Marcia M. Eaton proclaims, we rarely experience something 'purely aesthetically or purely ethically or purely religiously or purely scientifically'.

> The task for all of us is to develop ways of using the delights that human beings take in flights of imagination, connect it to solid cognitive understanding of what makes for sustainable environments and thus produce the kind of attitudes and preferences that will generate the kind of care we hope for
>
> *(Eaton 1998: 149-56).*

In spite of various reservations, I would suggest that ecological meta-narratives have become the most relevant, exciting and provocative area of study for new generations of students, as they relate directly to the future survival of the human species. For instance, new research into non-fictional ecological risk (from 'mad cow' disease to nuclear and chemical abuse of the environment) affirms that its impact is strongly predicated on how audiences/citizens use such 'stigmas' to produce 'cognitive maps'. Such effects are composed of 'a series of psychological transformations by which individuals acquire, code, store, recall and decode information about the relative locations and attributes of phenomena in their everyday spatial environments' (Flynn et al. 2001: 11). The study of ecological representations in fiction film can certainly learn a lot from such research. The dream factory of Hollywood has and can continue to play its part also by foregrounding the increasing importance of ecological debates within a global cultural consciousness.

To fully articulate the wide range of planetary and local ecological process and issues, close textual analysis of film must become embedded within wider interdisciplinary studies. Literary studies, which has a more advanced research profile, remains the most obvious crossover discipline. As has been frequently demonstrated, some of the most fruitful research in film emanates from outside the core discipline. A good example is Ellen Strain's 1998 essay on E. M. Foster's literary oeuvre, citing a study by James Buzard.

> The role of the spectator is all-important as the act of seeing corrects and completes the landscape. With the discovery of the vantagepoint that provides this balance of foreground and background, a 'sublime synthesis' occurs: [T]he authenticity of effect takes place in the epiphanic moment in which the unified aesthetic essence of the place shines forth

> *(Buzard 1993: 188).*

Such literary reflections closely correspond with this book's exploration of the aesthetic effects embedded within deep ecological readings of film texts. The filmmaker, as 'surrogate witness for the filmgoers', Strain affirms, captures this moment of sublime synthesis in an image that conforms with audience's pre-existing conceptions of the 'real world'.

> Viewing the landscape as picturesque or sublime serves to personify the land. In other words, although a filmmaker's or tourist's perception is required to make the vision come to life, the land with its 'authenticity of effect' becomes a narrative character affecting spectator and diegetic character alike. The spectacular landscape may have a pleasurable effect on the spectator at the same time that the land's mysterious effects are foregrounded by the narrative itself

> *(Strain in Degli-Esposti 1998: 163).*

Strain endorses close connections between looking at 'tourism' and 'cinema' as 'similar visual practices'. As a film theorist, I have been impressed by the importance of tourist studies for the greater appreciation of film analysis, which is seldom acknowledged. Hence, I would finally call for more formal inter-disciplinary connections with 'postmodern' geography in particular, which forcibly reaffirms the central importance of space/place within cultural discourses and where future productive synergies can be made. Ecological representational debates cross over major boundaries of science and humanities and can be used to promote holistic linking of discourses. In turn this would help to keep film studies at the forefront of future interdisciplinary research.

Notes

1. Nature is certainly 'recognised as a contested ideograph in both environmental theory and practice' (DeLuca 1999: 196). Yet many academics affirm its unifying potentiality, which can be somewhat premature, as I argue in a review of *Cultural Ecology: The Changing Dynamics of Communication*, edited by Danielle Cliche in *Convergence*, 3, 3, Autumn 1997: 148-150.

2. The potency of 'special effects' particularly with regards to *Jurassic Park* is well expressed by a recent study: 'However much we may wish to reduce the realism of the digital image to just another cultural *vraisemblance*, we need to take note of these technical advancements and determine their ontological, epistemological, and aesthetic potential. The composite nature of today's filmic image (photographic and digital) has utterly transformed the spectator's relation to the cinema. With the aid of digital technology, film-makers can fabricate a believable photorealistic effect without being limited to the physical imprints left by the profilmic events' (Elsaesser and Buckland 2002: 218).

3. Kant speaks of the 'purposiveness of nature', of which human nature is a part rather than the controller of: 'we view beautiful nature with favour, while we have a quite free (disinterested) satisfaction in its form. For in this mere judgement of taste no consideration is given to the purpose for which these natural beauties exist: whether to excite pleasure in us, or as purposes without any reference to us at all' (Kant 1972: 227).

4. See review of Martin Barker's *From Ants to Titanic: Reinventing Film Analysis* in www.film-philosophy.com, November 2000.

5. For example, Val Plumwood suggests that we need strategies of 'naturalising' in the sense of recognising 'nature's agency', as in providing for the continuation of 'ecosystem services'. Nevertheless, she fully recognises that such a concept 'can be dangerously human-centred if it fails to recognise that such services have a much wider range of beneficiaries than the human and if it supports instrumentalising and servant-like conceptions of the nonhuman sphere' (Plumwood 2001:20).

6. Plumwood asserts how: 'Hegemonic conceptions of human agency are fostered in human-centred cultures; these are linked to denials of dependency, which in turn are linked to the application of inappropriate strategies and forms of rationality that aim to maximise the share of the"isolated" self and neglect the need to promote mutual flourishing' (Plumwood 2001: 9).

7. In a number of research projects it has been discovered that the more strictly 'educational' type of documentary/nature film was found to be frequently unpopular within its intended audience. As one boy said, 'he didn't know nature was so slow' (Mayer 1972: 1). The researcher concluded that such ethical frameworks should always be indirectly provided rather than didactically affirmed, if they are to become successful.

Bibliography

Adair, G. (1997) *Surfing the Zeitgeist*. London: Faber and Faber.

Adorno, T.W. (1997) *Aesthetic Theory*. (Trans. and ed. R. Hullot-Kentor) London:

Athlone.Albrow, M. (1996) *The Global Age State and Society Beyond Morality*. Cambridge: Polity. Allen J. and Hamnett, C. (eds.) (1995) A *Shrinking World? 2 - The Shape of the World - Explorations in Human Geography*. Milton Keynes: Open University Press.

Allen, R. (1995) *Projecting Illusion: Film Spectatorship and Impression of Reality*. Cambridge: Cambridge University Press.

Allen, R. and Smith, M. (eds.) (1997) *Film Theory and Philosophy.* Oxford: Clarendon.

Anderson, A. (1997) *Media, Culture and the Environment*. London: UCL Press.

Anderson, J. (1996) *The Reality of Illusion: An Ecological Approach to Cognitive Film Theory. Carbondale: Southern Illinois University Press.*

Angus, I. and Jhally, S. (eds.) (1989) *Cultural Politics in Contemporary America.* London: Routledge.

Arroyo, J. (1998) 'Massive Attack' in *Sight and Sound*, February: 16-19.

Atkenson, M. (1994) 'Crossing the Frontiers' in *Sight and Sound*, January: 14-17.

Attfield, R. and Belsey, A. (eds.) (1994) *Philosophy and the Natural Environment. Special edition of Journal. Royal Institute Supplement*. Cambridge: Cambridge University Press.

Bahro, R. (1994) *Avoiding Social and Ecological Disaster: The Politics of World Transformation.* Bath: Gateway.

Baird, R. (1998) 'Animalizing Jurassic Park's Dinosaurs: Blockbuster Schemata and Cross-Cultural Cognition in the Threat Scene' in *Cinema Journal.* 37. no. 4: 84-103. Austin: University of Texas Press.

Balsamo, A. (1996) *Technologies of the Gendered Bodies: Reading Cyborg Women.* Durham: Duke University Press.

Barbour, B. (ed.) (1973) *American Transcendentalism: An Anthology of Criticism.* Notre Dame: University of Notre Dame Press.

Barillas, W. (1996) 'Aldo Leopold and Mid Western Pastoralism' in *American Studies*, vol. 37, no.2, Fall edition.

Barker, M. and Austin, T. (2000) *From Ants to Titanic: Reinventing Film Analysis*. London: Pluto.

Barker, M. and Sabin, R. (1995) *The Last of the Mohicans: History of an American Myth*. Jackson: University of Mississippi Press.

Barry, J. (1999) *Environmental and Social Theory*. London: Routledge.

Bate, J. (ed.) (1996) Studies in Romanticism. Special issue: *'Green Romanticism'*, vol. 35, no. 3, Autumn issue. Graduate School Boston University.

Bate, J. (1999) 'Culture and Environment: From Austin to Hardy' in *New Literary History, 'Ecocriticism'*, vol. 30, Summer issue 3: 541-60. Baltimore: Johns Hopkins University.

Bateson, G. (1973) *Steps to an Ecology of Mind*. St. Albans: Paladin.

Baudrillard, J. (1988-91) *America*. (Trans. Chris Turner) London: Verso.

Baudrillard, J. (1993) *The Transparency of Evil: Essays on Extreme Phenomena*. London: Verso.

Bauman, Z. (1991) *Modernity and Ambivalence*. Cambridge: Polity.

Bauman, Z. (1992) *Intimations of Postmodernity*. London: Routledge.

Bauman, Z. (1993) *Postmodern Ethics*. Oxford: Blackwell.

Bebergal, P. (1998) 'A Mediation on Transgression: Foucault, Bataille and the Retrieval of Limit' in *www. Ctheory.com* [Theory, Technology and Culture -ed. Arthur and K. Kroker]

Beck, U. and Giddens, A. and Lash, S. (1994) *Reflexive Modernization: Politics, Tradition and Aesthetics in the Modern Social Order*. Cambridge: Polity.

Bell, E. and Hass, L. and Sells, L. (eds.) (1995) *From Mouse to Mermaid: The Politics of Film, Gender and Culture*. Bloomington: Indiana University Press.

Belton, J. (ed.) (1996) *Movies and Mass Culture*. London: Athlone.

Benko, G and Strohmayer, V. (eds.) (1997) S*pace and Social Theory: Interpreting Modernity and Postmodernity*. Oxford: Blackwell.

Berman, A. (1994) *Preface to Modernism. Champaign*: University of Illinois Press.

Bernardi, D.A. (1998) *StarTrek and History: Race-ing Towards a White Future*. New Jersey: Rutgers University Press.

Berry, T. (1988) *The Dream of the Earth*. San Francisco: Sierra Club Books.

Bertens, H. (1995) *The Idea of the Postmodern: A History*. London: Routledge.

Best, S. and Kellner, D. (1991) *Postmodern Theory. New York*: Guildford.

Bhabha, H.K. (1994) *The Location of Culture*. London: Routledge.

Bijker, W. and Law, J. (eds.) (1997) Shaping Technology: Building Societies -*Studies in Sociotechnical Change*. Cambridge, MA: MIT Press.

Bird, E. S. (ed.) (1998) *Dressing in Feathers: The Construction of the Indian in American Popular Culture*. Colorado: Westview.

Bird, T., Curtis, B., Putnam, T., Robertson, G. and Tickner, L. (1993) *Mapping the Futures: Local Cultures, Global Change*. London: Routledge.

Biskind, P. (1983) *Seeing is Believing: How Hollywood Taught Us to Stop Worrying and Love the Fifties*. London: Pluto.

Blake, M. (1990) *Dances With Wolves*. New York: Newmarket Press.

Bolter, J.D. and Grusin, R. (1999) *Remediation: Understanding New Media.* Cambridge, MA: MIT Press.

Boorman, J. and Donohue, W. (eds.) (1996) *Projections 5: Film-makers on Film-making.* London: Faber and Faber.

Bordwell, D. (1989) *Making Meaning - Inference and Rhetoric in the Interpretation of Cinema*. Cambridge MA: Harvard University Press.

Bordwell, D. and Carroll, N. (eds.) (1996) *Post-Theory: Reconstructing Film Studies*. Madison: University of Wisconsin Press.

Bordwell, D. and Staiger, J. and Thompson, K. (1994, rev. ed.) *The Classic Hollywood Narrative: Film Style and Mode of Production to 1960.* London: Routledge.

Branigan, E. (1992) *Narrative, Comprehension and Film*. London: Routledge.

Braudy, L. (1998) 'The Genre of Nature' in Browne, N. (ed.) (1998) *Reflecting American Film Genres: Theory and History*. Berkeley: University of California Press.

Brereton, P. (1997) *Review of Cultural Ecology: The Changing Dynamics of Communication* (1997) (London International Institute of Communications) in Convergence, vol. 3, no. 3, Autumn issue: 148-50. Luton: University of Luton Press.

Brereton, P. (2000) 'The Audience as reader is seldom caught in the Act'. Review of *From Ants to Titanic: Reinventing Film Analysis*. Barker, M. with Austin, T. London: Pluto. in <www.Film-Philosophy.com' November.

Brereton, P. (2001) *The London: ContinuumGuide to Media Education*. London: Continuum.

Brereton, P. (2001) 'Utopianism and Fascist Aesthetics: An Appreciation of "Nature" in Documentary/Fiction Film' in *Capitalism, Nature, Socialism: A Journal of Socialist Ecology*. December: 33-50. Guilford Publications.

Brereton, P. (2003) 'Ecology and Nature: A case study of Cast Away' in *Film and Film Culture*, vol. 2: 109-111. Waterford: School of Humanities, Waterford Institute of Technology.

Bresnick, A. (1997) 'The Six-Billion Dollar Man, Gifts with Teeth: Steven Spielberg and the Dialectics of Philanthropy; in *Times Literary Supplement*, 18.7.97.

Broderick, D. (1995) *Reading by Starlight: Postmodern Science Fiction*. London: Routledge.

Bronowski, J. (1973) *The Ascent of Man*. London: BBC Publications.

Brooker, P. (1997) 'Slo Mo, Po Mo: Community and Postmodernism in Paul Auster and Wayne Wang's Smoke and Blue in the Face' in *Over Here: A European Journal of American Literature*, vol. 17, Summer 1997: 9-21.

Brooks, P. (1976) *The Melodramatic Imagination. New Haven*: Yale University Press.

Browne, N. (ed.) (1998) *Reflecting American Film Genres: Theory and History*. Berkeley: University of California Press.

Bryant, W. (1995) 'The Re-vision of Planet Earth: Space Flight Environmentalism in Postmodern America' in *Over Here: A European Journal of American Culture*. Nottingham: University of Nottingham.

Buckland, W. (1999) 'Between Science Fact and Science Fiction: Spielberg's Digital Dinosaurs, Possible Worlds and the New Aesthetic Realism' in *Screen*, Summer 1999, vol. 14: 177-92.

Buell, L. (1975) *Literary Transcendentalism: Style and Vision in the American Renaissance*. London: Cornell University Press.

Bukatman, S. (1994) *Terminal Identity: the Virtual Subject in Postmodern Science Fiction*. Durham: Duke University Press.

Bukatman, S. (1995) 'The Artificial Infinite: On Special Effects and the Sublime' in Cooke, L and Wollen, P. (eds.) *Visual Displays: Culture Beyond Appearances*. Seattle: Bay Press.

Bunce, M. (1994) *The Countryside Ideal: Anglo-American Images of Landscape*. London: Routledge.

Burnett, R. (1995) *Cultures of Vision: Images, Media and the Imaginary*. Bloomington: Indiana University Press.

Burnett, R. (ed.) (1991) *Explorations in Film Theory: Selected Essays from 'Cine-Tracts'*. Bloomington: Indiana University Press.

Buscombe, E. and Pearson, R. (eds.) (1998) *Back in the Saddle Again: New Essays on the Western*. London: BFI.

Button, J. (1988) *Dictionary of Green Terms*. London: Routledge.

Button, J. (1991) *The Best of Resurgence: A Selection of the First Twenty Five Years*. Dublin:Lilliput Press

Buzard, J. (1993) *The Beaten Track: European Tourism, Literature and the Ways to Culture 1800-1918*. Oxford: Clarendon Press.

Byars, (1991) *All that Hollywood Allows: Re-reading Gender in 1950s Melodrama*. London: Routledge.

Callinicos, A. (1989) *Against Postmodernism: A Marxist Critique*. Cambridge: Polity.

Capra, F. (1979) *The Tao of Physics*. London: Fontana.

Capra, F. (1983) *The Turning Point: Science, Society and the Rising Culture*. London: Flamingo.

Capra, F. (1996) *The Web of Life*. London: Flamingo.

Carnes, M.C. (ed.) (1996) *Past Imperfect - History According to the Movies*. London: Cassell.

Carroll, D. (1990) *The State of 'Theory': History, Art and Critical Discourse*. Palo Alto, CA: Stanford University Press.

Carroll, N. (1988) *Mystifying Movies - Fads, Fallacies in Contemporary Film Theory*. New York: Columbia University Press.

Carroll, N. (1996) *Theorizing the Moving Image*. Cambridge: Cambridge University Press.

Carter, E. et al. (eds.) (1993) *Space and Time: Theories of Identity and Location*. London: Lawrence and Wishart.

Castells, M. (1997) *The Power of Identity. The Information Age: Economy, Society and Culture*. Oxford: Basil Blackwell.

Chambers, I. (1994) *Migrancy, Culture, Identity*. London: Routledge.

Chambers, I. and Curti, L. (eds.) (1996) *The Post Colonial Reader: Common Skies, Divided Horizons*. London: Routledge.

Chaney, D. (1994) *The Cultural Turn: Scene-setting Essays on Contemporary Social History*. London: Routledge.

Charney, L. and Schwartz, V. (eds.) (1995) *Cinema and the Invention of Modern Life*. Berkeley: University of California Press.

Clark, N. (1997) 'Panic Ecology: Nature in the Age of Superconductivity'. *Theory Culture and Society*, vol. 14, no. 1, February. London: Sage.

Clarke, D. (ed.) (1997) *The Cinematic City*. London: Routledge.

Cliche, D. (ed.) (1997) *Cultural Ecology: The Changing Dynamics of Communication*. London: International Institute of Communication (IIC).

Cloke, P. and Little, J. (eds.) (1997) *Contested, Countryside, Cultures: Otherness, Marginality and Rurality*. London: Routledge.

Coates, P. (1994) *Film at the Intersection of High and Mass Culture*. Cambridge: Cambridge University Press.

Cohan, S. (1997) *Masked Men: Masculinity and the Movies in the Fifties*. Bloomington: Indiana University Press.

Cohan, S. and Hark, I.R. (eds.) (1997) *The Road Movie Book*. London: Routledge.

Cohen, J.J. (ed.) (1996) *Monster Theory: Reading Culture*. Minneapolis: University of Minnesota Press.

Cohen, M.J. (ed.) (2000) *Risks in the Modern Age: Social Theory Science and Environmental Decision Making*. Basingstoke: Macmillan.

Collingwood, R.G. (1976) *The Idea of Nature. Oxford*: Oxford University Press.

Collins, J. (1995) *Architectures of Excess: Cultural Life in the Information Age*. London: Routledge.

Collins, J. and Radner, H. and Collins, A. (eds.) (1993) *Film Theory Goes to the Movies*. London: Routledge.

Cooke, L. and Wollen, P. (eds.) (1995) *Visual Display: Culture Beyond Appearances*. Seattle: Bay Press.

Cooper, D. and Palmer, J. (eds.) (1995) *Just Environments: Intergenerational, International, Interspecies Issues*. London: Routledge.

Copjec, J. (ed.) (1993) *Shades of Noir*. London: Verso.

Costner, K. et al. (1990) *Dances with Wolves: An Illustrated Story*. New York: Newmarket Press.

Coyne, M. (1997) *The Crowded Prairie: American National Identity in the Hollywood Western*. London: I. B. Tauris.

Crang, M. (1998) *Cultural Geography*. London: Routledge.

Crichton, M. (1991) *Jurassic Park*. London: Arrow.

Crichton, M. (1995) *The Lost World*. London: Arrow.

Crogan, P. (2000) 'Things Analog and Digital' (paper delivered at *Special Effects/Special Affects: Technologies of the Screen Symposium* at University of Melbourne, 25 March 2000).

Cronon, W. (1992) 'A Place for Stories: Nature, History and Narrative' in *Journal of American History*, vol. 78, no. 4, March: 1347-76.

Cronon, W. (ed.) (1995) *Uncommon Ground: Towards Reinventing Nature*. New York: W. W. Norton.

Cubitt, S. (1999) 'Introduction . . . The Sublime Time of Special Effects' in *Screen*, Summer: 123-32.

Daly, M. (1991) *Gyn/Ecology*. Boston: Beacon.

Dargis, M. (1991) 'Roads to Freedom' in *Sight and Sound*, July: 15-18.

Davis, E. (1999) *TechGnosis: Myth, Magic + Mysticism in the Age of Information* London: Serpent's Tail.

Davis, M. (1992) *City of Quartz: Excavating the Future in Los Angeles*. London: Vintage.

Degli-Esposti, C. (ed.) (1998) *Postmodernism in the Cinema*. New York: Berghahn Books.

Deleuze, G. (1986) *Cinema 1: The Moment, Image*. (Trans. H. Tomlinson and B. Habberjam) London: Athlone.

DeLuca, K.M. (1999) 'The Possibilities of Nature in a Postmodern Age: The Rhetorical Tactics of Environmental Justice Groups' in *Communication Theory,* vol. 9, no. 2, May: 189-215.

Denzin, N. (1991) I*mages of Postmodern Society*. London: Sage.

Denzin, N. (1991) 'Paris Texas and Baudrillard and America' in *Theory, Culture and Society*, vol. 8, no. 2, May: 121-33.

Denzin, N. (1992) *Symbolic Interactionalism and Cultural Studies: The Politics of Interpretation*. Oxford: Blackwell.

Dery, M. (ed.) (1994) *Flame Wars: The Discourse of Cyberculture*. Durham: Duke University Press.

Dery, M. (1996) *Escape Velocity: Cyberculture at the End of the Century*. London: Hodder and Stoughton.

DiPiero, T. (1992) 'Grand Canyon and White Men Can't Jump?' in *Camera Obscura*, 113-37.

Do-son, A. (ed.) (1990, new ed. 1995) *Green Political Thought*. London: Routledge.

Dulcos, D. (1998) *The Werewolf Complex: America's Fascination with Violence*. Oxford: Berg Press.

Dyer, R. (1981) *Notes on Textual Analysis*. London: BFI.

Dyer, R. (1992) *Only Entertainment*. London: Routledge.

Eaton, M. (1997) 'Born Again' in *Sight and Sound*, December: 6-9.

Eaton, M. M. (1998) 'Fact and Fiction in the Aesthetic Appreciation of Nature' in *The Journal of Aesthetic Art Criticism*, vol. 56, no. 2, Spring: 149-56.

Eckersley, R. (1993) *Environmentalism and Political Theory: Towards an Ecocentric Approach*. London: UCL Press.

Elliot, R. and Gare, A. (eds.) (1983) *Environmental Philosophy*. Buckingham: Open University Press.

Ellis, J. (1992) *Visible Fictions: Cinema, Television*, Video. London: Routledge.

Ellman, S. (1992) *Vinyl Leaves: Walt Disney World and America*. Boulder: West View.

Elsaesser, T. and Buckland, W. (2002) S*tudying Contemporary American Film: A Guide to Movie Analysis*. London: Arnold.

Entrikin, J. N. (1991) *The Betweeness of Place: Towards a Geography of Modernity*. Basingstoke: Macmillan.

Evans, J. (1995) *Feminist Theory Today: An Introduction Second Wave Feminism*. London: Sage.

Eyerman, R. and Lofgren, O. (1995) 'Romancing the Road: Road Movies and Images of Mobility. *Theory Culture and Society*, vol. 12, no. 1, February: 54-67. London: Sage.

Faden, E.S. (1999) 'Assimilating New Technologies: Early Cinema, Sound and Computer Imagery' in *Convergence*, vol. 5, no. 2: 51-79. Luton: University of Luton Press.

Farrell, J. (1997) *The Spirit of the Sixties: The Making of Postwar Radicalism*. London: Routledge.

Featherstone, M. and Burrows, R. (eds.) (1995) *Cyber Space/Bodies/Punk: Cultures of Technological Embodiment*. London: Routledge.

Felpren, L. (1997) Review of Star Trek: Last Contact in *Sight and Sound*, January: 49.

Ferlita, E. and May, J. (1977) *Film as a Search for Meaning*. Dublin: Veritas.

Feuer, J. (1990) *Alien Zone: Cultural Theory and Contemporary Science Fiction Cinema*. London: Unwin Hyman.

Fiske, J. (1989) *Understanding Popular Culture*. London: Unwin Hyman.

Florence, P. and Reynolds, D. (eds.) (1995) *Feminist Subjects, Multi-Media, Cultural Methodologies*. Manchester: Manchester University Press.

Floyd, N. (1997) 'Infinite City' in *Sight and Sound*, June: 6-9.

Flynn, J. and Slovic, P. and Kunreuther, H. (eds.) (2001) *Risk, Media and Stigma: Understanding Public Challenges to Modern Science and Technology*. London: Earthscan.

Foster, H. (ed.) (1993) *Postmodern Culture*. London: Pluto.

Foucault, M. (1982) *The Archaeology of Knowledge*. London: Routledge.

Freer, I. (2001) *The Complete Spielberg*. London: Virgin.

French, S. (1996) *The Terminator*. London: BFI.

Friedberg, A. (1993) *Window Shopping: Cinema and the Postmodern*. Berkeley: University of California Press.

Friedman, M. (ed.) (1994) *Visions of America: Landscape as Metaphor in Late Twentieth Century*. Denver: Denver Art Museum.

Fulton, R. (1995) *TV Encyclopedia of Science Fiction*. London: Boxtree.

Furedi, F. (1997) *Culture of Fear: Risk Taking and the Morality of Low Expectation*. London: Cassell.

Gablik, S. (1991) *The Reenchantment of Art*. New York: Thames and Hudson.

Gablik, S. (1995) *Conversations Before the End of Time.* New York: Thames and Hudson.

Gamson, W. (1992) *Talking Politics. Cambridge*: Cambridge University Press.

Gare, A.E. (1995) *Postmodernism and the Environmental Crisis*. London: Routledge.

Geertz, C. (1973) *The Interpretation of Cultures*. New York: Basic Books.

Geoghegan, V. (1987) *Utopianism and Marxism*. London: Methuen.

Gibson, J.J. (1979) *The Ecological Approach to Visual Perception*. London: Houghton Miffin.

Giddens, A. (1990) *The Consequences of Modernity*. Oxford: Blackwell.

Giroux, H. (1994) *Disturbing Pleasures: Learning Popular Culture*. London: Routledge.

Gitlin, T. (1993) *The Sixties: Years of Hope, Days of Rage*. New York: Bantam.

Gledhill, C. (ed.) (1991) *Stardom: Industry of Desire*. London: Routledge.

Gledhill, C. and Williams, L. (eds.) (2000) *Reinventing Film Studies*. London: Arnold.

Gleick, J. (1987) *Chaos*. London: Abacus.

Glotfelty, C. and Fromm, H. (eds.) (1996) *The Ecocriticism Reader: Landmarks in Literary Ecology*. Athens: University of Georgia Press.

Goldblatt, D. (1996) *Social Theory and the Environment*. Cambridge: Polity.

Gorz, A. (1987) *Ecology as Politics*. London: Pluto.

Gottdiener, M. (1995) *Postmodern Semiotics: Material Culture and the Forms of Postmodern Life*. Oxford: Basil Blackwell.

Goudie, A. (1981) *The Human Impact on Natural Environment*. Oxford: Basil Blackwell.

Grant, B.K. (ed.) (1996) *The Dread of Difference: Gender and the Horror Film*. A Reader. Austin: University of Texas Press.

Gray, C.H. et al. (eds.) (1995) *The Cyborg Handbook*. London: Routledge.

Gray, J. (1997) *EndGames: Questions in Late Modern Political Thought*. Cambridge: Polity.

Grodal, T. (1997) *Moving Pictures: A New Theory of Film Genres*, Feelings and Cognition. Oxford: Clarendon Press.

Gruen, L. and Jamieson, J. (eds.) (1994) *Reflecting on Nature: Readings in Environmental Philosophy* Oxford: Oxford University Press.

Haber, H.F. (1994) *Beyond Postmodern Politics: Lyotard, Rorty, Foucault*. London: Routledge.

Halberstam, J. and Livingston, I. (eds.) (1995) Posthuman Bodies. Bloomington: Indiana University Press.

Halberstam, J. (1995) *Skin Shows: Gothic Horror and the Technology of Monsters*. Durham: Duke University Press.

Hall, D. (1994) A Green Reader: A Reader in Environmental Literature, Philosophy and Politics. London: Routledge.

Hall, S. and Du Gay, P. (eds.) (1996) *Questions of Cultural Identity*. London: Sage.

Hamilton, D. (1973) *Technology, Man and the Environment*. London: Faber and Faber.

Hamilton, S. (1997) 'Cyborg, 11 Years On' in *Convergence*, vol. 3, no. 2, Summer: 104-20. Luton: University of Luton Press.

Haralambos, M. and Holborn, M. (1990, 3rd. ed.) *Sociology: Themes and Perspectives*. London: Unwin Hyman.

Haraway, D. (1981) 'The High Cost of Information in Postwar 2 Evolutionary Biology: Ergonomics, Semiotics and the Sociobiology of Communication Systems' in *The Philosophical Forum*, vol. 13, nos. 2-3, Winter-Spring.

Haraway, D. (1985) 'A Manifesto for Cyborgs; Science, Technology and Social Feminism in the 1980s' in *Socialist Review*, vol. 15, no. 2: 65-108.

Haraway, D. (1991) *Simians, Cyborgs, and Women: The Reinvention of Nature*. London: Free Association Books.

Haraway, D. (1997) *Modest_Witness"Second_Millennium. FemaleMan_Meets_OncoMouce: Feminism and Technoscience*. London: Routledge.

Hardt, H. (1992) *Critical Communication Studies*. London: Routledge.

Hardy, T. (1995) *Introduction to Science Fiction*. London: Aurum.

Harrison, C. and Orton, R. (eds.) (1984) *Modernism, Criticism, Realism.* London: Harper and Row.

Harrison, T. and Projansky, S. and Ono, K. and Helpand, E. (eds.) (1996) *Enterprise Zone: Critical Positions on Star Trek*. Colorado: Westview.

Harvey, D. (1992) *The Condition of Postmodernity.* Oxford: Basil Blackwell.

Harvey, D. (1996) *Justice, Nature and the Geography of Difference*. Oxford: Basil Blackwell.

Hawkins, H. (1994) 'Paradigms Lost: Chaos, Milton and Jurassic Park' in *Textual Practice*, vol. 8, no. 2, Summer: 55-67. London: Routledge.

Hawkins, H. (1995) *Strange Attractions: Literature, Culture and Chaos Theory*. New Jersey: Prentice Hall.

Hawkins, R.Z. (1998) 'Ecofeminism and Nonhumans: Continuity, Difference, Dualism, and Domination' in Hypatia: *A Journal of Feminist Philosophy,* vol. 13, no. 1, Winter: 158-97. Bloomington: Indiana University Press.

Hayles, N.K. (1999) 'The Illusion of Autonomy and the Fact of Recursivity: Virtual Ecologies, Entertainment and the Infinite Jest' in *New Literary History,* vol. 30, no.3, Summer 675-97. Baltimore: Johns Hopkins University Press.

Hayward, S. (1998) *Luc Besson.* Manchester: Manchester University Press.

Hayward, T. (1994) *Ecological Thought: An Introduction.* Cambridge: Polity.

Hedges, I. (1991) *Breaking the Frame: Film Language and the Experience of Limits.* Bloomington: Indiana University Press.

Held, D. and Thompson, J. (1989) S*ocial Theory of Modern Societies: Anthony Giddens and His Critics*. Cambridge: Cambridge University Press.

Henderson, B. and Martin, A. (eds.) (1999) *Film Quarterly: Forty Years - A Selection.* Berkeley: University of California Press.

Heywood, I. and Sandwood. I (eds.) (1999) *Interpreting Visual Culture: Explorations in the Hermeneutics of the Visual.* London: Routledge.

Hill, J. (1998) 'Crossing the Water: Hybridity and Ethics in The Crying Game' in *Textual Practice,* vol. 12, no. 1, Spring: 89-100. London: Routledge.

Hill, J. and Gibson, P.C. (eds.) (2000) F*ilm Studies: Critical Approaches.* Oxford: Oxford Press.

Hill, L. (1996) Easy Rider. London: BFI.

Hitt, C. (1999) 'Towards an Ecological Sublime' in *New Literary History*, vol. 30, no. 3: 603-24. Baltimore: Johns Hopkins University Press.

Hollows, J. and Jancovich, M. (eds.) (1995) *Approaches to Popular Film.* Manchester: University of Manchester Press.

Hooks, B. (1994) *Outlaw Culture: Resisting Representations*. London: Routledge.

Horne, D. (1994) *The Public Culture: An Argument with the Future*. London: Pluto.

Horrocks, R. (1995) *Male Myths and Icons: Masculinity in Popular Culture*. Basingstoke: Macmillan.

Huggett, R.J. (1995) *Geoecology: An Evolutionary Approach*. London: Routledge.

Humm, M. (1997) *Feminism and Film*. Edinburgh: Edinburgh University Press.

Hurley, J.S. (1999) 'David Bordman's Iron Cage of Style' in '*www.Film-Philosophy.com*'.

Hutcheon, L. (1988) *A Poetics of Postmodernism: History, Theory, Fiction*. London: Routledge.

Iaccino, J.F. (1998) *Jungian Reflections within the Cinema: A Psychological Analysis of Sci-Fi and Fantasy Archetypes*. Westport: Praeger.

Icke, D. (1990) *It Doesn't Have to be Like This*. Basingstoke: Green Print.

Jameson, F. (1979) 'Reification and Utopia in Mass Culture' in *Social Text*, vol. 1, Winter: 130-48.

Jameson, F. (1981) *The Political Unconscious: Narratives as a Socially Symbolic Art*. London: Routledge.

Jameson. F. (1982) 'Progress and Utopia or Can We Imagine the Future' in *Science Fiction Studies*, vol. 9, no. 2, July: 147-58. Montreal: SFS Publications.

Jameson, F. (1991) *Postmodernism or the Cultural Logic of Late Capitalism*. London: Verso.

Jameson, F. (1992) *The Geopolitical Aesthetic: Cinema and Space in the World System*. London: BFI and Indiana Press.

Jameson, F. (1994) *The Seeds of Time*. New York: Columbia University Press.

Jameson, R. T. (ed.) (1994) *They Went That Away: Redefining Film Genres*. San Francisco: Mercury House Press.

Jancovich, M. (1992) 'Modernity and Subjectivity in The Terminator' in *The Velvet Light Trap*, Fall: 3-17.

Jancovich, M. (1996) *Rational Fears: American Horror in the 1950s*. Manchester: University of Manchester Press.

Jarvis, B. (1998) *Postmodern Cartographies: The Geographical Imagination in Contemporary American Culture*. London: Pluto.

Jayamanne, L. (ed.) (1995) *Kiss Me Deadly: Feminism and Cinema for the Moment*. Sydney: Power Publications.

Jencks, C. (ed.) (1992) *The Post-Modern Reader*. London: Academy Editions.

Kant, I. (1972) *Critique of Judgement*. New York: Hefner Publishing Company.

Kaplan, E.A. (1997) *Looking for the Other: Feminism Film, and the Imperial Gaze*. London: Routledge.

Kaplan, E.A. et al. (eds.) (1990) *Crosscurrents: Recent Trends in Humanities Research*. London: Verso.

Katz, E. (1982) *The International Film Encyclopedia*. Basingstoke: Macmillan-Papermac.

Kearney, R. (ed.) (1988) *Across the Frontiers: Ireland in the 1990s*. Dublin: Wolfhound Press.

Kellner, D. (1995) *Media Culture*. London: Routledge.

Kelly, K. (1994) *Out of Control: The New Biology of Machines*. London: Fourth Estate.

King, G. (1999) 'Spectacular Narratives: Twister, Independence Day and Frontier Mythology in Contemporary Hollywood' in Journal of American Culture, vol. 22, Spring: 25-39.

King, G. (2000) *Spectacular Narratives: Hollywood in the Age of the Blockbuster*. London: I.B. Tauris.

King, J. and Lopez, A. and Alvarado, M. (eds.) (1993) *Mediating Two Worlds: Cinematic Encounters in the Americas*. London: BFI.

Klevan, A. (2000) *Disclosure of the Everyday: Undramatic Achievement in Narrative Film*. Trowbridge: Flicks.

Kramer, P. (1997) 'Women First: Titanic (1997) Action-Adventure Film and Hollywood's Female Audience' in *Historical Journal of Film, Radio and TV*, vol. 8: 599-619.

Kreider, T. and Content, B. (2000) *Straight Story Film* Quarterly, vol. 54, no. 1, Fall: 26-33.

Kroker, A. and Cook, D. (1991) *The Postmodern Scene: Excremental Culture and Hyper-Aesthetics*. Basingstoke: MacmillanEducation.

Kuhn, A. (ed.) (1990) *Alien Zone: Cultural Theory and Contemporary Science Fiction Cinema*. London: Verso.

Kuhn, A. (ed.) (1999) *Alien Zone* (Two). London: Verso.

Kumar, K. (1991) *Utopianism*. Buckingham: Open University Press.

Kymlicka, W. (1995) *Contemporary Political Philosophy: An Introduction*. Oxford: Clarendon Press.

Landon, B. (1992) *The Aesthetics of Ambivalence: Rethinking Science Fiction Film in the Age of Electronic (re)Production*. Westport: Greenwood Press.

Lasch, C. (1978) *Culture of Narcissism: American Life in the Age of Diminishing Expectations*. New York: Norton Press.

Lasch, C. (1995) *The Revolt of the Elites and the Betrayal of Democracy*. New York: Norton Press.

Lash, S. and Urry, J. (1994) *Economies of Signs and Space*. London: Sage.

Leaver, Tama. (1997) '*Post-Humanism and Ecocide in William Gibson's Neuromancer and Ridley Scott's Blade Runner*'. 'http://kzsu.stanford.edu/uwi/br/off-world.html'

Lefebvre, H. (1991) *The Production of Space*. Oxford: Basil Blackwell.

Leopold, A. (1947) *A Sand Country Almanac*. Oxford: Oxford University Press.

Leslie, J. (1996) *The End of the World: The Science and Ethics of Human Extinction*. London: Routledge.

Levin, D. M. (ed.) (1993) *Modernity and the Hegemony of Vision*. Berkeley: University of California Press.

Levi-Strauss, C. (1966) *The Savage Mind*. Chicago: University of Chicago Press.

Lewis, RWB (1995) *The American Adam: Innocence, Tragedy and Tradition in the Nineteenth Century*. Chicago: University of Chicago Press.

Lipietz, A. (1995) *Green Hopes: The Future of Political Ecology*. Cambridge: Polity.

Lubin, D.A. (1999) *Titanic*. London: BFI.

Lucanio, P. (1987) *Them Or Us: Archetpical Interpretations of 50s Alien Invasion Films*. Bloomington: Indiana University Press.

Lyon, D. (1994) *Postmodernity*. Buckingham: Open University Press.

Lyotard, J.F. (1984) *Postmodern Condition: A Report on Knowledge*. Manchester: Manchester University Press.

MacCabe, C. (1999) *The Eloquence of the Vulgar*. London: BFI.

MacCabe, C. and Petrie, D. (eds.) (1996) *New Scholarship from London*: BFI. Working Papers. London: BFI.

MacCannell, D. (1992) *Empty Meeting Grounds: The Tourist Papers*. London: Routledge.

MacDonald, F. (1985) *Television and the Red Menace -The Video Road to Vietnam*. Westport: Praeger.

Macdonald, M. (1995) *Representing Women: Myths of Feminity in the Popular Media*. London: Arnold.

MacDonald, S. (1993) *Avant-Garde Film: Motion Studies*. Cambridge: Cambridge University Press.

Machor, J. (1987) *Pastoral Cities: Urban Ideals and the Symbolic Landscape of America.* Madison: University of Wisconsin Press.

Mander, J. (1992) *In the Absence of the Sacred: The Failure of Technology and the Survival of the Indian Nations*. San Francisco: Sierra Club Books.

Marc, D. (1992) *Comic Visions*. London: Unwin Hyman.

March, C. and Ortiz, C. (eds.) (1997) *Explorations in Theology and Film*. Oxford: Blackwell.

Marcuse, F. (1972) *One Dimensional Man: Studies in the Ideology of Advanced Industrial Society.* Basingstoke: Macmillan.

Marcuse, F. (1979) *The Aesthetic Dimension: Towards a Critique of Marxist Aesthetic.* Basingstoke: Macmillan.

Marx, L. (1964) *The Machine in the Garden*. Oxford: Oxford University Press.

Massey, D. (1994) *Space, Place and Gender*. Cambridge: Polity.

Matheson, R. (1983) *The Incredible Shrinking Man*. London: Corgi Press.

Mayer, J.P. (1972) *Studies of Film Clubs for Children in UK*. (Studies and Documents, Sociology of Film) New York: Arno Press.

McBride, J. (1997) *Steven Spielberg*. London: Faber and Faber.

McCarthy, C. (1998) *The Uses of Culture: Education and the Limits of Ethnic Affiliation*. London: Routledge.

McDonald, J. (1985) *Who Shot the Sheriff. (Media and Society)* Westport: Praeger.

McDonald, S. (1999) 'From the Sublime to the Vernacular' in *Film Quarterly,* vol. 55, no.1, Fall: 12-25.

McGuigan, J. (1999) *Modernity and Postmodern Culture*. Buckingham: Open University Press.

McGuigan, J. (ed.) (1997) *Cultural Methodologies*. London: Sage.

McHale, B. (1992) *Constructing Postmodernism*. London: Routledge.

McKibben, B. (1990) *The End of Nature*. London: Penguin.

McLuhan, M. (1964) *Understanding Media*. New York: McGraw-Hill.

McRobbie, A. (1994) *Postmodernism and Popular Culture*. London: Routledge.

McRobbie, A. (ed.) (1997) *Back to Reality? Social Experience and Cultural Studies*. Manchester: University of Manchester Press.

Merchant, C. (1992) *Radical Ecology: The Search for a Liveable World*. London: Routledge.

Merchant, C. (1993) *Major Problems in American Environmental History*. Berkeley: University of California Press.

Merchant, C. (1995) *Earthcare: Women and the Environment*. London: Routledge.

Meyer, M. (ed.) (1997) *Educational Television: What Do People Want?* Luton: University of Luton Press.

Miles, S. and Shiva, V. (1993) *Ecofeminism*. London: Zed Books.

Milne, T. (ed.) (1998) *Time-Out Film Guide*. London: Penguin.

Milton, K. (1996) *Environmentalism and Cultural Theory: Exploring the Role of Anthropology in Environmental Discourse*. London: Routledge.

Murray, D. (ed.) (1995) *American Cultural Criticism*. Exeter: University of Exeter Press.

Nadel, A. (1997) *Flatlining on the Field of Dreams: Cultural Narratives in the Films of President Reagan's America*. New Jersey: Rutgers University Press.

Nardi, B.A. and O'Day, V.L. (1999) *Information Ecologies: Using Technology with Heart*. Cambridge, MA: MIT Press.

Nash, R. (1982) *Wilderness and the American Mind.* New Haven: Yale University Press.

Natoli, J. (1997) *A Primer to Postmodernism*. Oxford: Blackwell.

Neale, S. and Smith, M. (eds.) (1998) *Contemporary Hollywood Cinema* London: Continuum.

Newcombe, H. (ed.) (1982) *Television: The Critical View*. Oxford: Oxford University Press.

Newman, K. (1997) Review of Fifth Element in *Sight and Sound*, July: 40.

Nichols, B. (1994) *Blurred Boundaries Questions of Meaning in Contemporary Culture*. Bloomington: Indiana University Press.

Nietschmann, B. (1993) 'Authentic, State and Virtual Geography in Film' in *Wide Angle*, vol. 15, no. 4: 4-12.

Nochimson, M. (2000) 'The Straight Story: Sunlight will out of Darkness Come' in *'www.senseofcinema.com/contents/00/7/straight'*

Norton, A. (1993) *Republic of Signs: Liberal Theory and American Popular Culture*. Chicago: University of Chicago Press.

Norton, B. (1991) *Towards Unity Among Environmentalists*. Oxford: Oxford University Press.

Nye, D. (1994) *American Technological Sublime*. Cambridge, MA: MIT Press.

O'Neill, J. (1995) *The Poverty of Postmodernism*. London: Routledge.

Orr, J. (1993 *Cinema and Modernity.* Cambridge: Polity.

O'Sullivan, C. (1996) Review of Twister in *The Observer*, 14 July 1996.

Pease, D.E. (ed.) (1994) *National Identities and PostAmerican Narratives*. Durham: Duke University Press.

Peck, J. (1996) 'Wild Palm' in *American Studies*, vol. 37, no. 2, Fall.

Peet, R. (1997) Review of Risk, Environment and Modernity: Towards a New Ecology (eds.) Lash S. et al. (1996) in *Journal of Rural Studies*. vol. 13, no. 4, October: 447-78.

Penley, C. and Lyon, E. and Spigel, L. and Bergstrom, J. (eds.) (1991) *Close Encounters: Film, Feminism, and Science Fiction*. Minneapolis: University of Minnesota Press.

Pepper, D. (1993) *Eco-Socialism: From Deep Ecology to Social Justice*. London: Routledge.

Pepper, D. (1996) *Modern Environmentalism: An Introduction*. London: Routledge.

Pile, S. and Keith, M. (eds.) (1997) *Geographies of Resistance*. London: Routledge.

Pile, S. and Thrift, N. (eds.) (1995) *Mapping the Subject: Geographies of Cultural Transformation*. London: Routledge.

Pitzer, D.E. (ed.) (1997) *America's Communal Utopias*. Chapel Hill: University of North Carolina Press.

Plantinga, C. and Smith, G.M. (eds.) (1999) *Passionate Views: Film, Cognition and Emotion*. Baltimore: Johns Hopkins University Press.

Plumwood, V. (1993) *Feminism and the Mastery of Nature*. London: Routledge.

Plumwood, V. (2001) 'Nature as Agency and the Prospects for a Progressive Naturalism' in *Capitalism, Nature, Socialism*, December: 3-32. Guilford Publications.

Porritt, J. (1984) *Seeing Green*. Oxford: Blackwell.

Porritt, J. (2000) *Playing Safe: Science and the Environment*. London: Thames and Hudson.

Porritt, J. and Winner, D. (1988) *The Coming of the Greens*. London: Fontana.

Pribram, E.D. (ed.) (1988) *Female Spectators? Looking at Film and Television*. London: Verso,

Prince, S. (1992) *Visions of Empire: Political Imagery in Contemporary American Film*. Westport: Praeger.

Pym, J. (ed.) (1998) *Time Out Film Guide*. London: Penguin.

Ray, R. (1985) *A Certain Tendency of the Hollywood Cinema (1930-1980)*. Princeton: Princeton University Press.

Reed, T.V. (1992) *Fifteen Jugglers, Five Believers: Literary Politics and American Social Movements*. Berkeley: University of California Press.

Richards, T. (1997) *The Meaning of Star Trek*. New York: Doubleday.

Ritzer, G. (1998) *The McDonaldization Thesis*. London: Sage.

Robertson, G. et al. (eds.) (1996) *Future Natural: Nature/ Science/ Culture*. London: Routledge.

Robins, K. (1996) *Introducing the Image: Culture and Politics in the Field of Vision*. London: Routledge.

Rodaway, P. (1994) *Sensuous Geographies: Body, Sense and Place*. London: Routledge.

Rodowick, D.N. (1994) *The Crisis of Political Modernism: Criticism and Ideology in Contemporary Film Theory*. Berkeley: University of California Press.

Roffman and Purdy (1981) *Hollywood Social Problem Film*. Bloomington: Indiana University Press.

Rogin, M. (1998) *Independence Day*. London: BFI.

Romanyshyn, R. (1988) *Technology as Symptom and Dream*. London: Routledge.

Romney, J. (1998) 'World Without End' in *The Guardian*, 29 May 1998: 24.

Ront, F. T. (1996) *The Third Eye: Race, Cinema and Ethnographic Spectacle*. Durham: Duke University Press.

Rooney, C.J. (1985) *Dreams and Visions: A Study of American Utopias 1865-1917*. Westport: Greenwood Press.

Rose, G. (1993) *Feminism and Geography*. Cambridge: Polity.

Rosenbaum, J. (1997) *Movies as Politics*. Berkeley: University of California Press.

Ross, A. (1996) *Strange Weather: Culture, Science and Technology in the Age of Limits.* London: Verso.

Roszak, T. (1970) *The Making of a Counter Culture: Reflections on the Technocratic Society and Its Youthful Opposition*. London: Faber and Faber.

Rowell, A. (1996) *Green Backlash: Global Subversion of the Environment Movement*. London: Routledge.

Rushing, J. H. and Frentz, T. S. (eds.) (1995) *Projecting the Shadow: The Cyborg Hero in American Film*. Chicago: University of Chicago Press.

Ryan, M. and Kellner, D. (1988) *Camera Politica*. Bloomington: Indiana University Press.

Sagan, C. (1980) *Cosmos*. London: McDonald/Futura Press.

Said, E. (1993) *Culture and Imperialism.* London: Vintage.

Sammon, P.M. (1996) *Future Noir: The Making of Blade Runner*. London: Orion.

Samuel, R and Thompson, P. (eds.) (1990) *The Myths We Live By*. London: Routledge.

Sandel, M. (1984) 'The Procedural Republic and the Unencumbered Self' in *Political Theory,* no. 12: 81-96.

Sardor, Z. and Ravetz, J. (eds.) (1996) *Cyberfutures: Culture and Politics on the Information* Superhighway. London: Pluto.

Sargisson, L. (1994) *Contemporary Feminist Utopianism*. London: Routledge.

Sartelle, J. (1993) 'Jurassic Park, or, Sympathy for the Dinosaur' cited in *Bad Subjects: Political Education for Everyday Life* in 'http://english.www.hss.cmu.edu/-s/06/Sartelle.html'

Schama, S. (1995) *Landscape and Memory*. London: Fontana.

Seed, D. (1999) *American Science Fiction and the Cold War: Literature and Film*. Edinburgh: Edinburgh University Press.

Seidman, S. (1994) *Contested Knowledge: Social Theory in the Postmodern Era*. Oxford: Basil Blackwell.

Seidman, S. and Wagner, D. (eds.) (1992) *Postmodernism and Social Theory*. Oxford: Basil Blackwell.

Sharkey, A. (1993) *Review of Spielberg in The Independent*, 14 August 1993.

Shay and Duncan (eds.) (1992) *The Making of Terminator: Judgement Day*. London: Titan.

Shiva, V. and Ingunn, M. (eds.) (1995) *Biopolitics: A Feminist and Ecological Reader on Biotechnology*. London: Zed Books.

Shohat, E. and Stam, R. (1994-5) *Unthinking Eurocentrism: Multiculturalism and the Media*. London: Routledge.

Sibley, D. (1995) *Geographies of Exclusion: Society and Difference in the West*. London: Routledge.

Silverman, A. (1991) 'Back to the Future' in *Camera Obscura*, vol. 27, September: 108-33.

Simmons, I.G. (1993) *Environmental History: A Concise Introduction*. Oxford: Basil Blackwell.

Sklair, L. (ed.) (1994) *Capitalism and Development*. London: Routledge.

Smith, M.J. (1998) *Ecologism: Towards Ecological Citizenship*. Buckingham: Open University Press.

Smith, M.J. (ed.) (1999) *Thinking through the Environment: A Reader*. Buckingham: Open University Press.

Sobchack, V. (1990) 'A Theory of Everything: Meditations on Total Chaos' in *ArtForum*, November: 148-55.

Sobchack, V. (ed.) (1996) *The Persistence of History: Cinema, Television, and the Modern Event*. London: Routledge.

Sobchack, V. (1997) *Screening Space: The American Science Fiction Film*. New Jersey: Rutgers University Press.

Soja, E.W. (1989) *Postmodern Geographies: The Reassertion of Space in Critical Social Theory*. London: Verso.

Soja, E.W. (1996) *ThirdSpace: Journeys to Los Angeles and Other Real-and-Imagined Places*. Oxford: Blackwell.

Sontag, S. (1966) *Against Interpretation*. New York: Farrar, Straus and Giroux.

Soper, K. (1995) *What is Nature*. Oxford: Basil Blackwell.

Springer, C. (1996) *Electronic Eros: Bodies and Desire in the Post Industrial Age*. London: Athlone.

Staiger, J. (1992) *Interpreting Films: Studies in the Historical Reception of American Cinema*. Princeton: University of Princeton Press.

Stam, R. (1989) *Subversive Pleasures: Bakhtin, Cultural Criticism and Film*. Baltimore: Johns Hopkins University Press.

Stam, R. (ed.) (1992) *New Vocabularies in Film Semiotics*. London: Routledge.

Stavrakakis, Y. (1997) 'Green Ideology: a Discursive Reading' in *Journal of Political Ideologies*, vol. 2, no. 3, October. Cambridge,MA: Carafax Publishers.

Stone, B.P. (1998) 'Religious Faith and Science in Contact' in *Journal of Religion and Film*. Lincoln: University of Nebraska at Omaha, vol. 2, no. 2, October. See 'www.unomaha.edu'

Strinati, (1995) *An Introduction to Theories of Popular Culture*. London: Routledge.

Sturken, M. (2000) *Thelma and Louise*. London: BFI.

Sudan, R. et al. (1997) 'Angels, Dinosaurs, Aliens' in *Camera Obscura*, May: 105-30.

Tabbi, J. (1995) *Postmodern Sublime*. London: Cornell University Press.

Tallack, D. (ed.) (1995) *Critical Theory: A Reader*. Hemel Hempstead: Harvester.

Talshir, G. (1998) 'Modular Ideology: The Implications of Green Theory for a Reconceptualization of Ideology' in *Journal of Political Ideologies*, vol. 2, no. 3, June. Cambridge, MA: Carafax Publishers.

Tam, H. (1998) *Communitarianism: A New Agenda for Politics and Citizenship*. Basingstoke: Macmillan.

Tashiro, C.S. (1998) *Pretty Pictures: Production Design and the History Film*. Austin: University of Texas Press.

Tasker, Y. (1993) *Spectacular Bodies: Gender, Genre and the Action Cinema*. London: Routledge.

Taubin, A. (1996) 'Nowhere to Hide' in *Sight and Sound*, May: 32-4.

Taylor, P. (1986) *Respect for Nature*. Princeton: Princeton University Press.

Telotte, J.P. (1995) *Replications: A Robotic History of Science Fiction Film*. Champaign: University of Illinois Press.

Tester, K. (1993) *The Life and Times of Postmodernism*. London: Routledge.

Thompson, J.B. (1990) *Ideology and Modern Culture: Critical Social Theory in the Era of Mass Communication*. Cambridge: Polity.

Thornham, S. (1997) *Passionate Detachment: An Introduction to Feminist Film Theory*. London: Arnold.

Trushell, J. (1996) 'Body Snatchers: Spectres that Haunt an American Century' in Over Here: *A European Journal of American Culture*, vol. 16, Winter: 89-104. Nottingham: Nottingham Trent University.

Tulloch, J. and Jenkins, H. (1995) *Science Fiction Audiences: Watching Doctor Who and Star Trek*. London: Routledge.

Unwin, T. (1992) *The Place of Geography*. Harlow: Longman.

Urry, J. (1990) *The Tourist Gaze: Leisure and Travel in Contemporary Societies*. London: Sage.

Urry, J. (1995) *Consuming Places*. London: Routledge.

van Loon, J. (1997) 'Of/in the Televisualisation of 1992 Los Angeles Riots' in *Theory Culture and Society*, vol. 14, no. 2: 157-71. London: Sage.

van Toorn, R. (1997) *'Architecture against Architecture: Radical Criticism within Supermodernity'* in 'www: Ctheory@concordia.ca 24 September 1997' (Article 51, Kroker, A. and Kroker, M. eds.)

Von Maltzahn, K. (1994) *Nature as Landscape. Montreal: McGill-Queens* University Press.

Wall, D. (1994) *Green History: A Reader*. London: Routledge.

Walser, R. (1993) *Running with the Devil: Power, Gender and Madness in Heavy Metal Music*. Indiana: Wesleyan University Press.

Warren, K.J. (ed.) (1994) *Ecological Feminism*. London: Routledge.

Waters, M. (1995) *Globalization*. London: Routledge.

Weart, S.R. (1988) *Nuclear Fear: A History of Images*. Cambridge, MA: Harvard University Press.

Webster, D. (1988) *Looka Yonder: The Imaginary America of Populist Culture*. London: Comedia.

Wenders, W. (1989) *Emotion Pictures: Reflections on the Cinema*. London: Faber and Faber.

White, D. and Wang, A. (1998) *'Through the Dark Mirror: UFO's as Postmodern Myth'* in 'www.Ctheory.com' Article 666.

Wiener, N. (1961) *Cybernetics: Or Control and Communication in the Animal and the* Machine. Cambridge, MA: MIT Press.

Wilden, A. (1977) *System and Structure. Essays in Communication and Exchange*. London: Tavistock Publications.

Wilden, A. (1987) *The Rules are No Game. The Strategy of Communication*. London: Routledge.

Williams, L. (ed.) (1995) *Viewing Positions: Ways of Seeing Film*. New Jersey: Rutgers University Press.

Williams, M. (1982) *Road Movies: The Complete Guide to Cinema on Wheels*. New York: Prometheus Books.

Williams, R. (1973) *The Country and the City*. London: Chatto and Windus .

Williams, S.J. (1998) 'Bodily Dys-Order: Desire, Excess and the Transgression of Corporeal Boundaries' in *Body and Society*, vol. 4, no. 2, June: 59-82. London: Sage.

Wilson, E.O. (1992) *The Diversity of Life*. London: Penguin.

Wilson, G. M. (1986) *Narration in Light: Studies in Cinematic Point of View*. Baltimore: Johns Hopkins University Press.

Wissenburg, M.L.J. (1997) 'A Taxonomy of Green Ideas' in *Journal of Political Ideologies*, vol. 2, no. 1, February: 29-50. Cambridge, MA: Carafax Publishers.

Wollen, P. (1982) *Readings and Writings: Semiotic Counter Strategies*. London: Verso.

Wollen, P. (1993) *Raiding the Icebox: Reflections on Twentieth Century Culture*. Bloomington: Indiana University Press.

Wolmark, J. (1994) *Aliens and Others: Science Fiction*, Feminism and Postmodernism. Hemel Hempstead: Harvester/ Wheatsheaf.

Yearley, S. (1996) *Sociology, Environmentalism, Globalism*. London: Sage.

Zimmerman, M. E. (1994) *Contesting Earth's Future: Radical Ecology and Postmodernity*. Berkeley: University of California Press.

Zizek, S. (1992) *The Sublime Object of Ideology.* London: Verso.

Glossary Of Terms

Some framing notions and concepts which are extensively applied to this ecological reading of film:

Anomie: often becomes a symptom of millennial fears, which like dystopian/ecocidal fears, can be used to suggest a counter ecological wishful fantasy.

Agency: cross-fertilising social science theorising alongside fictional appreciation of filmic protagonist's to explore how representational figures can embody an ecological agenda.

Cyborg: applying extensive new media theorising concerning post-human agency, particularly as a means of overcoming regressive male/female oppositions.

Deep ecology: goes beyond the transformation of technology and politics to a transformation of humanity and is continuously contrasted with Light (shallow) ecology.

Discourse analysis: helps to underpin cultural and textual analysis strategies for reading film and ecology generally.

Ecologism: extending the principle of sustainability to all fields of study including film.

Ethics: evaluating a range of attitudes and values with regards to the treatment of nature and its inhabitants, which is a central preoccupation of this study.

Feminism: including the central metaphoric importance of 'mother nature', together with marginalisation debates concerning the 'other', are used to focus on how alternative agencies can be best appropriated for this ecological project. Furthermore, 1970s feminist film analysis, focusing on 'excessive' stylistic expressions within melodrama, for example, to offset the more obvious patriarchal trajectory of such narratives (Screen Theory), is also re-applied to this ecological reading of film.

Gaia thesis: how the biosphere together with its atmospheric environment forms a single entity or natural system. Gaia pushes Darwinian notions to its limit by contending that no matter what humans do to the planet, it will survive.

Nature: is often closely connected with landscape, alongside cultural debates around space/place and becomes the means of visually appropriating our environment, often in the service of promoting a romantic or sublime/deep ecological connection, through the witnessing of human agents.

Other: drawing connections from applications in feminist and post-colonial studies, and extending how 'otherness' can be used through the agency of cyborgs in particular to promote a progressive ecological project.

Postmodernist texts: helps create new ways of conceptualising and stimulating representational debate around the future of humanity. Furthermore this highly contested aesthetic phenomenon can provide a 'third space' for and engagement with ecology outside of rigid Left/Right ideological structures.

Risk: drawing on Beck's notion of how Western society is defined by its inherent problems and risks, especially ecological ones.

Space/place: a defining characteristic and subject for debate within cultural Geography in particular. The area draws on notions like chronotope that allow critics to historicise the use of space and time in film. Privileging film studies in terms of space/place is of central importance for this study.

Spiritualism: helps to valorise a transcendent form of ecological representation and is by all accounts extremely problematic within film analysis. Nevertheless, like other 'myths', moments of 'transcendent epiphany' promote tangible emotions and responses of 'oneness with nature' and with our planet.

Tourism: alongside travel, remains a defining characteristic within Western culture. Traversing landscape involves engaging with nature and ecology in broad terms and ultimately promoting the possibility of witnessing a sublime spectacle. This strategy helps to foreground readings of films like Grand Canyon, which engender a deep ecological awareness in the spectators.

Utopian effect: remains a primary focus of this film study and can be traced from romantic/spiritual/sublime/transcendentalism/communitarian sensibilities, as they evolved in American culture.